RESEARCH IN
COMMUNITY SOCIOLOGY

Volume 7 • 1997

ENVIRONMENT AND
COMMUNITY EMPOWERMENT

International Editorial Advisory Board

RESEARCH IN
COMMUNITY SOCIOLOGY

ENVIRONMENT AND
COMMUNITY EMPOWERMENT

Editor: DAN A. CHEKKI
Department of Sociology
University of Winnipeg

VOLUME 7 • 1997

 JAI PRESS INC.

Greenwich, Connecticut   *London, England*

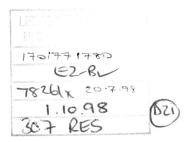

CONTENTS

PART IV.   BUILT ENVIRONMENT AND CITIZEN INITIATIVES

PART V.   PERCEPTIONS OF GLOBAL ENVIRONMENT

LIST OF CONTRIBUTORS

Dean Bavington	Faculty of Environmental Studies York University
Dan A. Chekki	Department of Sociology University of Winnipeg
Stephen R. Couch	Department of Sociology Pennsylvania State University
R. Scott Frey	Department of Sociology Kansas State University
Nick Garside	Faculty of Environmental Studies York University
Richard Hogan	Department of Sociology/ Anthropology Purdue University
Richard S. Krannich	Department of Sociology Utah State University
Steve Kroll-Smith	Department of Sociology University of New Orleans
William Michelson	Centre for Urban and Community Studies University of Toronto
Laurie Miller	Faculty of Environmental Studies York University
Joel Novek	Department of Sociology University of Winnipeg
Pertti Rannikko	Karelian Institute University of Joensuu Finland

Kimberley D. Saliba   Department of Sociology
                                     Indiana University

Scott Swearingen   Department of Sociology
                                     University of Texas at Austin

Jerry Williams   Department of Sociology
                                     Kansas State University

John P. Wilson   Department of Psychology
                                     Cleveland State University

Brett Zollinger   Department of Sociology
                                     Utah State University

STATEMENT OF SCOPE

The *Research in Community Sociology* series aims to publish recent research on various dimensions of communities. The volumes in this series include discussions of theoretical and methodological issues, and empirical research: case studies as well as analyses of micro-macro linkages. Special focus will be on cross-cultural, comparative, interdisciplinary, and critical studies on community structure/change, problems, policy-planning, and related issues. Thematic edited volumes and monographs will form part of this series.

ACKNOWLEDGMENTS

The *Research in Community Sociology* expresses gratitude to the following colleagues for evaluating manuscripts during the 1994-1996 period. Their reviews of manuscripts have been a valuable service to authors and to the discipline.

Mary Ann Allison
Mark Baldassare
Jeffrey C. Bridger
Tom Carter
Karen A. Cerulo
Harvey M. Choldin
Nancy Denton
Leo Driedger
Joe R. Feagin
Parvin Ghorayshi
John Hannigan
Nancy Herman
John P. Hewitt
Will Holton
Craig R. Humphrey
Robert R. Hunt
Glenn Jacobs
Warren Kalbach
Phillip M. Kayal

Tony J. Kuz
Christopher Leo
Andrew Lockery
John Logan
Peter Miller
Tim Miller
Joel Novek
Max Oelschlaeger
Silvia Pedraza
Cecil Pereira
Jacob Peters
John Selwood
Kumiko Shibuya
John Sinclair
Gerald D. Suttles
Charlene Thacker
Gerald Walker
Curtis R. Winkle

The editor acknowledges with thanks the assistance of Laureen Narfason, George Hamilton, Lesley Murphy, and Lou Lépine in preparing this volume.

Dan A. Chekki
Editor

PART I

INTRODUCTION

THE LOCAL-GLOBAL NEXUS OF ENVIRONMENT AND COMMUNITY EMPOWERMENT

Dan A. Chekki

ABSTRACT

The processes of globalization of the economy, advances in technology, actions of multinational corporations, and government policies have tended to damage the local community and global environments. The contemporary local-global milieu has accelerated the need for community empowerment and equitable sustainable development. The complexity of the interplay between environmental problems and the community structure and dynamics, grassroots organizing activities, and community empowerment processes have not been adequately explored. The primary goal of this volume is to advance our sociological understanding of the intricate interactions between the environment and the community. This introductory chapter outlines the major themes reflected in the subsequent chapters. We focus on conceptual and ideological debates, environmental issues

Research in Community Sociology, Volume 7, pages 3-18.
Copyright © 1997 by JAI Press Inc.
All rights of reproduction in any form reserved.
ISBN: 0-7623-0272-0

and movements, the role of technology, community activism, planning, change, and policy implications concerning the environment and the quality of life of communities. The need for more grassroots organizations aimed at achieving the goals of equitable sustainable development and community empowerment are emphasized.

In recent decades, communities around the world, have been exposed to the deterioration of their environmental quality, more than ever before in human history. The magnitude and complexity of the interplay between environmental problems and community life cannot be underestimated. Environmental movements at local and global levels have tended to facilitate a variety of community development projects aimed at sustainable natural resource management and coping with or preventing environmental hazards. As we are at the threshold of a new millennium, it has become evident that human activity has damaged or threatened the natural ecosystems of communities around the world. The local community environment and global environmental issues are obviously intertwined. Needless to say, the interface between local community and global environmental problems needs close examination.

Environmentalists, planners, and researchers have focused their attention on "green cities", "healthy", "livable", and "sustainable" communities. Sustainable development recognizes that communities, through citizen participation, can develop their own solutions to environmental and development problems. The social ecology paradigm incorporating the "ecocommunity" concept refers to human-scale, sustainable settlements based on ecological balance, community self-reliance, and participatory democracy. This model has much to contribute towards achieving the goals of equitable sustainable development. Community-based strategies for "acting locally" seem to have great potential for facilitating increased environmental protection and community empowerment. Eco-development emphasizes participatory planning and grassroots citizen activism, and aims at harmonizing socioeconomic objectives with ecologically sound management.

In recent years, environmental issues have stimulated various grassroots community organizing activities and empowerment (Craig and Mayo 1995). Community involvement in tackling environmental problems, although vital, has become more problematic in the global context. Increasing emphasis has been placed upon the importance of the empowerment of local communities in achieving the goal of equitable sustainable development.

Empowerment enables people to use their capacity to better control resources, gain power over their own lives, and improve their condition (Schuftan 1996). It provides people with choices and the ability to choose and expands the "political space" within which the community development processes of capacity building, advocacy, and social mobilization operate. Recent evidence (Afsah et al. 1996) from Asia, Latin America, and North America suggests that communities that are richer, better educated, and more organized find ways to enforce environmental norms.

Grassroots organizing and community activism, aimed at either protecting the environment or preserving jobs, have manifested confrontation and conflict of different sets of values and priorities (Schnaiberg and Gould 1994). Environmental social movements have tended to play a prominent role in policy decisions, collective identity formation, community empowerment and social change. Furthermore, local activists seem to be at the forefront in the global struggle to end environmental destruction (Durning 1989).

It is increasingly evident that community problems are often the consequence of the process of globalization of the economy, technology, and the ever-increasing power and actions of multinational corporations. Valuable natural resources and ecosystems which sustain many communities are increasingly destroyed for the production of commodities for export. Government policies tend to assist the global corporate economy at the expense of local communities (Pilisuk et al, 1996). Many citizen organizations are holding government officials and corporations accountable for environmental hazards and for the adverse consequences that their communities must face. However, citizen groups rarely have easy access to government or to media. Nevertheless, these grassroots local community groups are oriented toward issues that demand both local and global solutions (Cable and Cable 1995).

Ecofeminists, youth, minority groups and senior citizens, among others, are organizing to confront governments and megacorporations to preserve the environment for future generations. However, workers affected or threatened by the loss of jobs resulting from environmental protection policies are also protesting the efforts of these environmental activists. Environmental activists have formed world-wide coalitions to act simultaneously on environmental problems that are both local and global.

The environmental risk or impact assessment of various economic development projects initiated by big business and industry appear to be ritualistic. More often, recommendations of the environmental impact review boards are either hardly accepted, considerably modified or ignored by governments and corporations. Many environmental groups and community activists experience a sense of frustration when governments implicitly tend to support corporate interests under the pretext of job creation and economic growth. This volume, however, attempts to focus on the interplay between local and global environmental problems and community activism/empowerment.

This chapter delineates some of the major environmental issues that have precipitated community activism. This initial sketch is intended to set the stage for a better understanding of the subsequent detailed analyses of the central themes related to local-global environmental questions and citizen participation. The chapters that follow manifest diversity in content and approach. They do, nevertheless, display some common features characteristic of contemporary debates on the environment and community empowerment.

For a long time, the sociology of community, has focused on the ecological or space-bound concept of the community (Hawley 1950; Hillery 1995). Community sentiment, intimate relations and collectivism (MacIver and Page 1949; Toennies 1963; Durkheim 1966; Etzoni 1993) have been closely linked to the notion of an ideal traditional community. It is only in recent years that non-territorial interest-based communities have been the subject of sociological inquiry (Hughey and Vidich 1993; Chekki 1996). "The end of community" debate in the social sciences has been around for some time (Reitzes and Reitzes 1992; Wellman 1979). Considerable controversy and different nuances in interpretations of the notion of community persist. Those who cling to the ideal community concept have already proclaimed the death of the community. It is not surprising that the community, as a concept, has turned out to be a very complex and difficult social entity to characterize or identify.

Laurie Miller, Dean Bavington, and Nick Garside extend the current postmodern community discourse to a diverse range of academic (science and humanities), professional, political, and social domains. They argue that discussions around the community suffer from a narrow relevance on static *forms*, as exemplified in noble idyllic *images* of the community, and the deconstruction of them. The relevance of the postmodern condition, as it affects the ideas of community, and the connected issues of individuality and empowerment, are examined. If we tend to confine the concept of community to those positive connotations such as a small, closely-knit, interdependent, cooperative realm in which individuals participate in the creation of a symbolic whole, then it is obviously too restrictive a term that is not useful for empirical research.

The earlier ecological theories examined community life within specific spatial boundaries, whereas one variety of modern ecological theory views landscapes as a mere agglomeration of patches which shift allegiance and identity with each successive alteration in the "natural disorder." The authors examine the different forms that the community has taken in recent discourse and address questions such as: "Ought we to maintain community as a valid personal, social, political or ethical ideal?" "In what way might we reconceptualize our understanding of the nature of community?"

Extolling a mystical ideal community, although not uncommon, the traditional ideal images need to be divorced from reality. Theoretical discussions center around the issue of the social construction of (physical) boundaries of any community that include and exclude groups of people. Inclusion and exclusion are always implicit in any community formation. However, today most urban residents live and work in multiple communities. Our perception of the community serves as a means of understanding and organizing experiences where membership in multiple communities may be subject to change.

In advanced industrialized societies, the process of urbanization and the emergence of a growing service-based economy have tended to obliterate community boundaries. It is argued that while the ideal community of citizens no longer exists, the community of capital that involves consumers and clients is widespread. On the one hand, the welfare state services and helping professions have undermined the ability of traditional communities to exist. On the other, the shift from community to the individual consumer (rights and entitlements) facilitates neoconservative governments (and corporations) to reduce or withdraw state social and health services and allows corporations to replace and expand service delivery of their own.

Following Baudrillard, the authors suggest that our current postmodern effort to reclaim the image of the ideal community could only have occurred after communities were destroyed, and they believe that our focus on communities as objects of intervention is occurring at a time when we are no longer embedded in them. Furthermore, they argue that the image of the idyllic community, where citizens interact face to face and are involved in uncommodified relationships, is replaced by notions of community with a collection of individual consumers and clients. It is pointed out that consumers need neither individuality nor community in which to fulfill their roles as consumers or as participants in political processes.

The debate over forms of community as a stable, homogeneous, cooperative unit, and another characterized by difference, disturbance, identity, and individuality, concludes with a future vision of community as having the potential to be both creative and spontaneous. The authors delineate community as art work; citizen as artist, in which community is also artist; and citizen as the work of art. Within such a community, both the artist and the art are expected to be dependent on each other for the common good. This is obviously another idyllic vision of the community. Anyway, these ideas and images provide a basis for further thinking on the concept of community and its environment.

In its need for increasing economic growth and consumption, the dominant values of Western industrial civilization emphasize the role of technology. Few communities pursuing these goals cannot avoid depleting their resources, polluting the environment and upsetting biospheric systems. Leading environmental activists have been struggling to protect the environment in order to maintain a better quality of life for present and future generations. Industry, business, and especially multinational corporations, often in collaboration with governments, are indulged in the exploration of resources and the manufacturing of chemicals, plastics and paper, leading to hazardous pollution of the environment.

It is in this context that Joel Novek frames some of the changing perceptions of technology in the environmental movement. He examines both the optimistic and pessimistic consequences of industrial technology, and explores the implications of our commitment to economic growth and our desire for the conservation of nature and communities. The fundamental contradiction between the need of the capitalist economy and state to expand versus the need of the natural environment for stability has, it appears, paved the way for a search for appropriate or human-scale technologies and renewable sources of energy that are kinder and gentler in their environmental impact.

The notion of "social ecology" refers to those small-scale, decentralized and environment-friendly technologies that empower individuals and communities. These "wholistic" technologies tend to promote local autonomy and control, and favor a transfer of power and wealth from corporate interests and centralized states to local communities. Communities using labor-intensive technologies are presumed to be in a better position to create jobs and protect their environment.

The advanced computer-communication technology and the shift to a post-industrial service-information-based economy have played a major role in the process of the globalization of economy and culture. The new image of the global environment as dynamic, flexible and more open to interchange with communities around the world no doubt has major repercussions for the future of the environmental movement. A split in the environmental movement between the dominant global paradigm and the communitarian perspective needs to be reconciled if the goals of economic development and environmental preservation are to be compromised.

Modern environmental management of global change encourages nation-states, transnational corporations, labor unions and local communities to cooperate in the interests of ecological order. The concept of sustainable development facilitates economic growth with the minimum possible environmental impact. Ecological modernization aims to "anticipate and prevent" strategies instead of the "react and cure" strategies in order to minimize damage to the ecosystems.

Novek, by using two case studies of pulp and paper megaprojects in the Western Canadian boreal forest, demonstrates how environmental impact assessment suffers from the inherent contradiction between the government's role as a promoter of economic development and as an environmental regulator. These case studies expose both the strengths and weaknesses of ecological modernization as a method of resolving competing claims dealing with issues of sustainable development and the concerns of northern aboriginal communities. These megaprojects illustrate a trend toward compromising the goals of economic growth and environmental sustainability by using advanced "green technology." This leads to a new image of a flexible environment which seems to accommodate the demands of resource usage without suffering unsustainable damage. However, it is evident that pressing social concerns were avoided rather than addressed.

Contaminated communities (Edelstein 1988; Freudenberg 1984) are sprinkled over North America. Issues such as the adverse effects of toxins, the difficulties of cleaning up hazardous materials, and the impact of natural disasters on communities have received attention by social scientists. However, it seems that the relationship between toxic contamination, problems with local and extra-local social institutions, and their effects on the individual have not been adequately explored. Stephen Couch, Steve Kroll-Smith, and John Wilson focus on the concept of alienation in order to connect contamination and community disruption to individual distress. They argue that alienation is a means of operationalizing the disillusionment felt by many residents of affected communities.

Victims of toxic exposure in Chernobyl, Bhopal and elsewhere have discovered that governments and other social institutions fail to provide adequate protection, help and compensation. The differing perceptions of the potential risk, the level of danger stemming from the pollution, and the inability or resistance to assume responsibility for the clean-up, and offer fair compensation, are clearly evident patterns characteristic of various polluted communities. Toxic exposure may unleash both divisive and cohesive forces within a contaminated community.

The authors indicate that the discovery of toxic exposure often triggers feelings of doubt and disenchantment with the institutional fabric where issues of power and civil rights are debated in a highly charged political context. It is theorized that the onset of feelings of alienation is part of the personal experience of estrangement from social institutions resulting from toxic contamination. This paper presents the findings of a cross-sectional survey of litigants in a chemically contaminated community (Sunburst) in the United States. This case study supports the hypothesis that alienation is a secondary stressor resulting in amplified levels of psychological distress. On the one hand, the contaminated community experienced increased social activity; and on the other, the formation of a grassroots environmental group, and increasing feelings of social isolation and a sense of powerlessness. This study raises several important questions for further research.

Residents, policymakers, interest groups, and professionals encounter the problem of locally unwanted land-use (LULU) when a parcel of land within or adjacent to a community is selected for locating toxic waste disposal, dumping refuse, mental or correctional institutions, a polluting industry, public housing projects, highways and so forth. William Michelson explores the place of the municipality as a mediating factor and examines the potential impact of a LULU on the quality of life and environment of a metropolitan community in Canada.

Despite the advances in communication technology, which have tended to reduce the need for local support systems, the place of municipalities in peoples' lives and thoughts is relatively unknown. Municipal governments have the responsibility to raise revenues in order to provide a set of services and amenities to those who reside within their boundaries. American and Canadian studies have revealed that municipalities are a long-term meaningful reference point for residents who happen to have a far greater attachment to place than was previously thought. Low geographic mobility and the stigmatization resulting from locally unwanted land-use will reduce real estate values and lead to an adverse impact on the quality of community life. Michelson tests relevant hypotheses by analyzing data gathered from a telephone survey of residents in the municipality of Metropolitan Toronto and two adjacent municipalities. The findings of this study indicate that the overwhelming majority of people in each of the three metropolitan/regional municipalities feel that the municipal place of residence has a major impact upon them. Furthermore, they do feel more of a degree of control over decision making in metropolitan/regional municipalities than in any other level of government.

It is interesting to know that although potential locally unwanted land-use activities within municipal boundaries have a wide-ranging stigmatized impact, residents do not contemplate moving on that account. This research demonstrates the importance of urban municipalities as distinct entities having an impact on daily life, and municipal boundaries tend to frame prospective LULUs as salient to all residents who are not likely to move away in response.

Sociologists and geographers have theorized about the inter-relationship among the urban space, human groups, socio-cultural processes, and symbolic meanings of space that communities create. Scott Swearingen, by focusing on the implicit religious processes of integration, totemism, and sacred space, illustrates a case study (Barton Springs) of Austin, Texas to show how group attachment to space and community may develop. The political economy of urban growth tends to ignore environmental concerns. A grassroots environmental movement, the Save Our Spring (SOS) coalition, encountered real estate developers and city council in preserving an urban space considered sacred by groups of people within a city. Barton Springs thereby served not only as a place of recreation, but also as a symbol of community, becoming both a sacred space and the totem of the environmental group because of its distinctive "natural" qualities. It became a sacred space and totem for residents who opposed the environmental degradation due to urban growth.

Decades of political contest to protect Austin's creeks and springs from growth contributed to a public discourse where environmentalists battled real estate developers. As the sense of community was generated by the use of a specific place, community and space became dialectically related. This study provides a good example of how space becomes sacred and symbolic of environmental groups that challenge urban growth. The alternative meaning of space and quality life promoted by environmental activists are obviously in contradiction to those developers who perceive urban space in terms of quantity of built space and economic growth. This case study shows how certain religious processes act as the mechanisms by which a sense of community is created and sustained.

During the past decade, timber-dependent communities have become more exposed to the environmental movement and environmental protection legislation. The decline of resource industries has led to a loss of jobs and revenues in resource-based communities. The grassroots activism of timber workers and environmentalists, and the ensuing timber debate, has influenced local economics, political institutions and social relations. How do social changes motivate individuals to join environmental movements and counter movements?

Kim Saliba presents a case study of a rural community in Oregon and explores how the loss of timber jobs, losses in services, and decline in revenues motivated community members to organize a counter movement against the environmental movement. This study also looks at the role played by the decline in local government funds in the emergence and maintenance of community counter movement activism. Saliba provides the historical, economic, and cultural background of the region as a prelude to an understanding of the timber debate. When the timber industry was booming, families were living comfortably. What happens when the community and the timber industry are not prepared for the emergence and success of the environmental movement?

The resource dependency, lack of economic alternatives, isolated location, and problems of attracting alternative industries exacerbate the economic strains of the community. The perceived hardships serve as unifying forces for the anti-environmental movement composed of timber workers, citizens concerned about social services and jobs in the public sector, and local government officials who feel that their livelihood is threatened.

The prohibition of logging in the late 1980s contributed to mill closures, the loss of jobs, and financial hardships in timber-dependent communities. Demographic changes were reflected in the decline of school enrolment. Restaurants, grocery stores, and recreational facilities lost business. There was a significant increase in juvenile delinquency and welfare dependency. Timber-dependent communities experienced a higher evidence of alcoholism, drug use, and child and wife abuse. Saliba observes that the combination of a desire to maintain their frontier heritage, the loss of timber jobs, and the resulting community instability served as motivating factors for counter movement mobilization. She describes how the counter movement emerged, who was involved, and what goals they hoped to achieve.

When urban environmentalists challenged their timber lifestyle, heritage, and livelihoods, timber workers' dedication to protect their community provided a ready source of grassroots activists. This counter movement by timber activists focused on how natural resource use contributes to the quality of life in rural communities. But local environmentalists perceived the community's resource exploitation in a negative light and advocated more economic diversification rather than timber dependency. There was a confrontation between ideology and pragmatism. Saliba believes that finding a balance between the two competing interests of environmentalists and timber workers requires finding shared interests and building new alliances in order to restore community stability, concludes that this timber debate is crucial to the very survival of timber-dependent communities, and emphasizes the necessity of balancing the needs of the environment, families, and local economies.

Resource-dependent communities, though not a homogeneous category, continue to comprise a significant segment of the rural socio-economic landscape of North America. It is recognized that resource dependency is a multi-faceted phenomenon. Mining, logging, and ranching communities exhibit a wide range of socio-economic conditions and trends. Some are developing and dynamic, some are exposed to economic cycles, others are in a state of transition or in decline. The socio-cultural fabric of these communities is closely linked with resource-based economic activities. Richard Krannich and Brett Zollringer examine some of the challenges confronting resource-dependent communities and evaluate the prospects for rural community development.

In recent decades, several resource dependent communities have experienced an increase in resource depletion, depopulation, technological change, environmental damage, global economic shifts, changing resource management powers, unemployment, and poverty. This study identifies a series of obstacles, as well as opportunities, in pursuing community development in order to tackle the problems faced by these resource-based communities. In the absence of realistic opportunities to either meet local needs for sustenance and infrastructure, or to alter the regional, national, and global forces, the prospects for the emergence of local, grassroots efforts to improve conditions in resource-based communities are considered to be limited at best. It is suggested that the development efforts of resource-dependent communities should focus on the interactional dimensions of the community for attainment of social well-being and sustainable community development outcomes.

Focusing on the concepts of local community, space, place and region, Pertti Rannikko presents an interesting case study of a small remote forest village in Finland. What significance does the local village community and dwelling place have in people's lives? What happens when the economic base of a local community undergoes change? When the logging process underwent rapid transformation through technological innovation, the village lost its position in the organization of lumbering activity. The local community experienced significant demographic and social changes. Local institutions: schools, and political, economic, and recreational organizations and activities were adversely affected.

With the expansion of the welfare state services, the local community now hardly functions as a network of social relations because of a reverse in mobility and modern communication technology. It is important to recognize, however, that despite the economic and demographic changes, the village has retained its local identity. A strong sense of belonging has preserved and strengthened the symbolic community. The village community's jobs, services, and communal association activities were transplanted in the municipality centre. This case study demonstrates how a major change in the forest industry led to the displacement of a Finnish village's regional role in the spatial division of labor in the forest sector. How the village is transformed from a functional community to a symbolic community is evident in people's consciousness, feelings, and traditions.

The dramatic growth of suburban communities in North America (Baldassare 1994) has significantly changed the built environment. The suburbs have also encountered problems such as population growth, air pollution, traffic congestion, budget deficits, and lack of affordable housing. In various suburban communities, citizens have initiated growth control measures to prevent speculative growth and real estate over-development. The complex interplay between local government, citizens, and real estate developers tends to influence the nature and pace of suburban growth.

Richard Hogan addresses the critical question: Why do suburban communities face growth control initiatives and how do growth control initiatives affect future growth? He makes a distinction between citizen initiated and council/regional or state-initiated growth control which impinge on the planning process aimed at affordable housing. The study of five San Diego suburbs, the most rapidly-growing region of the United States, presents a comparative analysis of the contradictory demands of growth control and affordable housing and the contradictory interests of regional planning authorities, local residents, and developers. It is shown that the speculation in land-use futures followed a pattern of economic boom and bust cycles in Southern California. Furthermore, citizen-initiated growth control was a response to speculative over-building and environmental regulation. Local governments attempted to pre-empt the challenge of citizen-initiated growth control. However, these growth control initiatives did affect subsequent growth because of an anti-developer coalition of environmental and no-growth citizen organizations. The proposals for habitat conservation, open space, hiking trails, and affordable housing made a difference in regard to the type of growth control that was ultimately adopted. These case studies emphasize the role citizens play in controlling the pattern of suburban growth and the community environment.

Environmentalists and advocates of economic growth have been debating about the roles of government, the free market, and grassroots organizations in addressing global environmental problems (Simon et al., 1997). Hazel Henderson (1996) has developed and promoted a new economic paradigm that recognizes quality of life indicators. She also emphasizes "grassroots globalism" as a new force in the world that manifests itself in the emerging civil society.

The objective phenomenon of global warming does not automatically constitute a social problem. The extent of public interest and the amount of media coverage, and the perceived threat of the danger and impact on human communities, may help or hinder the process of social construction of a social problem. Jerry Williams and Scott Frey examine the varied public interest in global warming in terms of a set of factors that have facilitated or prevented its ability to compete in the public arenas of discourse. This study, based on a content analysis of news reports and scientific articles, explores not only the quantity of media coverage but the substantive content of these reports and the factors that have contributed to the ability of global warming to compete in the arenas of public discourse.

How does a situation become identified as a social problem? The realist approach to environmental social problems stresses the role of scientific research in guiding social-political action. The constructionist models view global warming as a social problem constructed in respect to our experience and definition of it. A public arenas model of social problem construction is used to analyze how global warming, as a social problem, has to compete for public attention.

This study shows how global warming was first identified as being like a nuclear winter caused by the depletion of the protective ozone layer by the burning of fossil fuels and other human activities. The competitive factors such as the dramatic potential of global warming, real world events, the complexity of the issue, the viability of a proposed solution, the economic impact of remediation, and existing political realities appear to have led to a distinct developmental trajectory in the process of identifying global warming as a social problem. It is argued that these factors shape the ability of global warming to compete for attention with other social problems in the public arenas of discourse. However, the authors are careful not to draw causal connections between the identified competitive factors and the process of global warming being defined as a social problem. These findings could serve as a basis for further research.

The findings of a recent study (Krogman and Darlington 1996) indicate that mainline sociology journals have paid only limited attention to the environment. This volume, we believe, will enhance our knowledge of the linkages between the environment and community, and stimulate new research. Grassroots citizen organizations have proliferated despite forces that tend to constrict them. In the next millennium, we need more grassroots organizations that strive toward equitable sustainable development and community empowerment. Citizen participation, needless to say, is vital for community empowerment.

The question of why some grassroots organizations involved in environmental issues flourish while others disband, lose momentum, or fail to achieve their goals needs additional research. Undoubtedly, it is necessary to encourage the development and maintenance of grassroots organizations that can enhance the quality of community life. In view of the focus on the local-global environment and its rich diversity, these studies have important implications for grassroots citizen participation and community empowerment.

The devastating effects of hydroelectric projects, gas and oil explorations, mining, manufacturing, deforestation, and industrial toxic and nuclear waste dumping on communities have been documented. However, community activism and empowerment processes, in the context of the local-global environment, are not adequately examined. These recent researches make a significant contribution toward a greater understanding of the nature of environmental issues and the dynamics of community empowerment.

REFERENCES

Afsah, S. et al. 1996. "Controlling Industrial Pollution: A New Paradigm." Policy Research Working Paper 1672, Washington, DC: World Bank Policy Research Department.

Baldassare, M. 1994. "Suburban Communities: Change and Policy Responses." In *Research in Community Sociology*, Vol. 4, edited by D. Chekki. Greenwich, CT: JAI Press.

Cable, S. and C. Cable. 1995. *Environmental Problems: Grassroots Solutions*. New York: St. Martin's Press.

Chekki, D.A. 1996. "The Social Landscape of New Communities in North America."
        In *Research in Community Sociology*, Vol. 6, edited by D.A. Chekki.
        Greenwich, CT: JAI Press.
Craig, G. and M. Mayo (Eds.). 1995. *Community Empowerment*. London: Zed
        Books.
Durkheim, E. 1964. *The Division of Labor in Society*. New York: The Free Press.
Durning, A.B. 1989. *Poverty and the Environment: Reversing the Downward Spiral*.
        (World Watch Paper No. 92). Washington, DC: World Watch Institute.
Edelstein, M. 1988. *Contaminated Communities*. Boulder, CO: Westview Press.
Etzioni, A. 1993. *The Spirit of Community*. New York: Crown Publishers.
Freudenberg, N. 1984. *Not in Our Backyards: Community Action for Health and
        the Environment*. New York: Monthly Review.
Hawley, A.H. 1950. *Human Ecology*. New York: The Ronald Press.
Henderson, H. 1996. *Building A Win-Win World: Life Beyond Global Economic
        Warfare*. San Francisco: Berrett-Koehler.
Hillery, G.A. 1955. "Definitions of Community: Areas of Agreement." *Rural
        Sociology*, 20: 111-123.
Hughey, M.W., and A.J. Vidich. (eds.) 1993. "The Ethnic Quest for Community:
        Searching for Roots in the Lonely Crowd." In *Research in Community
        Sociology*, Vol. 3, edited by D.A. Chekki. Greenwich, CT: JAI Press.
Krogman, N.T., and J.D. Darlington. 1996. "Sociology and the Environment: An
        Analysis of Journal Coverage." *American Sociologist* 27(3): 39-55.
MacIver, R.M., and C.H. Page. 1949. *Society: An Introductory Analysis*. New York:
        Holt, Rinehart and Winston.
Pilisuk, M. et al. 1996. "Coming Together for Action: The Challenge of
        Contemporary Grassroots Community Organizing." *Journal of Social Issues*
        52(1): 15-38.
Reitzes, D.C., and D.C. Reitzes. 1992. "Community Lost: Another Look at Six
        Classical Theorists." *Research in Community Sociology*, Vol. 2, edited by
        D.A. Chekki. Greenwich, CT: JAI Press.
Schnaiberg, A., and K.A. Gould. 1994. *Environment and Society: The Enduring
        Conflict*. New York: St. Martin's Press.
Schuftan, C. 1996. "The Community Development Dilemma: What is Really
        Empowering?" *Community Development Journal* 31(3): 260-264.
Simon, J.L. et al. 1997. "The Global Environment: Megaproblem or Not?" *The
        Futurist* 31: 2.
Tönnies, F. 1963. *Community and Society*, edited by C.P. Loomis. New York:
        Harper and Row.
Wellman, B. 1979. "The Community Question: The Intimate Networks of East
        Yorkers." *American Journal of Sociology* 84: 120-121.

PART II

IMAGES OF THE COMMUNITY:
INTERDISCIPLINARY DIMENSIONS

THE END OF COMMUNITY? FORMS, PROCESS AND PATTERN

The Lumpen Society

ABSTRACT

The idea of community is widely debated and discussed in a diverse range of academic (science, social science, and humanities), professional, political, and social domains. It seems that certain terms offer the opportunity to explore the inter-relationship between science and culture—community appears to be one such idea. In this paper we explore the interdisciplinary dimensions of the idea of community.[1] We attempt to describe the current community discourse and argue that most discussions around community suffer from a narrow reliance on static *forms* as exemplified by noble idyllic *images* of community or on the deconstruction of these same images. We discuss how this narrow debate is present across descriptions of both human and non-human communities. As well, the ways in which the current debate over development, and the creation of needs in place of community, can change our perception, description and potential creation of an ideal(s) are also discussed. In an attempt to

Research in Community Sociology, Volume 7, pages 21-59.
Copyright © 1997 by JAI Press Inc.
All rights of reproduction in any form reserved.
ISBN: 0-7623-0272-0

escape the static logic of community as image or form, we propose
a reconception of community as a dialectical process between citizen
and community, art and artist.

community 1. a group of people living in a particular area **2.** a group of people
living near one another, with distinct societal relationships **3.** a group of people
sharing a common faith, culture, profession, life-style **4.** in ecology, a general
term applied to any naturally occurring group of different organisms
occupying a common environment, interacting with each other, particularly
through food relationships, but relatively independent of other groups. The
size may vary and the larger communities may contain smaller ones. *Concise
Oxford English Dictionary.*

THE OMNIPRESENCE OF AN IDEA

Community is everywhere. We hear about community development,
community health, community resources, community politics,
community ethics, community associations and community
planning—across diverse media, and from diverse proponents. We
discuss the idea of community control over resources in community
coffee shops and engage in academic debates over the issue of who
is included or excluded by any given definition of community.

This discussion appears to include some referent to a place (village)
where "everyone knows your name"; where community is conceived
as being a small, static, closely-knit, interdependent group of average
folk. This version of community is thus implicated in discussions of
idyllic rural life, where things are simpler, quieter and more "down
home" somehow. Or such descriptions may take the form of attempts
to identify the interactions among some distant-imagined group of
aboriginal people, still living close to the land. Projections of this idea
of community are placed over the patterns of current existence: within
urban areas, neighborhoods are often reconstructed as the locus of
the good feeling, while rural areas adopt a protectionist stance of
inclusion by longevity. It is of particular note that many of those
positive connotations which may be attached to certain notions of
community (in the human realm) are reflected in the body of
ecological theory which posits the existence of "mature" communities
in the "natural" realm. Such communities might be characterized as
static, ahistorical (cyclical) and enduring; they develop or unfold, like

organisms themselves, along predictable lines. Such associations are entities in their own right—an interdependent, co-operative realm in which individuals participate in the creation of a symbiotic whole. Everywhere, the idea of community is valorized.

Within newer strains of ecological theory, disturbance and stress are in vogue. Ecosystem and community as unifying concepts are no more, instead *Landscape* is the latest *bon mot*. Landscapes are seen as a mere agglomeration of patches which shift allegiance and identity with each successive alteration in the "natural disorder"; there are no coevolved, (inter)dependent communities of plants and animals. Instead, stochastic change, continual disturbance and endlessly shifting patterns of species adaptation and extirpation are played out against a backdrop of never-ending variance in the broader landscape. Once again, we may note that this newer theoretical persuasion finds a sympathetic echo within certain realms of social science or humanistic discourse where the idea of community is viewed with suspicion. The implicit denotation of a "we" who have some fundamental experiences in common is seen as an erasure of difference, a derogation of the voices of those who are marginalized under the closed, parochial, regimented structure of "community" life. The arrogance of claiming to establish a boundary, or of attempting to decide who is included and who is excluded, is noted and widely scorned. The constructed nature of such boundaries, the conditionality of the ways in which the (meta)physical borders are drawn is elaborated in tandem with discussions of the ways in which identity is constructed in part as a consequence of membership in numerous "communities." Just as (some) ecologists would maintain that communities (as coevolved, interdependent associations of plants and animals) are not to be found in "reality" so to do some theorists in the human realm maintain that there is no longer a static, iconoclastic notion of a community in which "we" can be said to participate. Everywhere, the idea of community is pilloried.

These two main strands in the debate over community (harmonious idyll vs. disturbed difference) can be traced simultaneously through the literature of science (ecology) as well as in the positions and arguments of theorists in the humanities and social sciences (as well as in discussions among many "practitioners" and so-called "common-folk").[2] The acrimony with which this divergent characterization is pursued, and the largely unconscious way in which community is utilized within the public sphere of

planning and resource decision making (among others) inspires us
to ask: What is the relationship between the dissolution of community
within ecological theory and the rejection of static unitary, human
commonalities by many who might be called social scientists? This
theme is addressed in section one (*Forms: Idyll, Counterfeit,
Disturbance*) of this paper. Within our second section we focus on
a number of words or processes which can be seen to affect any
characterization of community (whether idyllic or deconstructed)—
to paraphrase Poerksen: words which are not just themselves, but
which are also agents. Following the implications of this thought,
an examination of the forces exerted by conceptions of urbanization,
need, and the masses forms the body of section two (*The Madness
of General Concepts*). The ways in which such general concepts might
themselves be reclaimed or redeemed is also addressed. Such
considerations of the forms and processes which constitute the idea
of community have lead us, in our final section (*Forms, Process and
Pattern*), to address the question: ought we to maintain community
as a valid personal, social, political or ethical ideal? To this end: in
what way might we reconceptualize our understanding of the nature
of community?

FORMS: IDYLL, COUNTERFEIT, DISTURBANCE

Community Building: Historic Idyll

Community empowerment is the prerequisite to all other changes. The existing
pattern of resource over-exploitation has evolved and been maintained
because local communities have had virtually no control over their local
resource base (M'Gonigle, in Taylor and Wilson 1994, p. 97).

...local citizens can do a better job of promoting economic and environmental
health than corporate and state decision makers located far from the resources
they are managing (Taylor and Wilson 1994, p. 95).

In popular parlance, *community* is bandied about as an expression
which indicates some group of individuals which is supposedly closer,
more integrated than the broader society of which they are
presumably part. Communities, especially with reference to resource
use, are assumed to be incapable of deliberately choosing options
which would be harmful to their members, since, under a definition
of community which is tied to place, communities are supposed to

consist of people who must live with the results of their actions. This scenario is placed in opposition to the spectre of centralized control in which decision makers presumably pass judgment on place, resources and people without the possibility of literally having to *reside* with the effects.[3] Implicit in this use of the term community in the above sense, is the presumption that the character of such existence is constituted in a certain ideal way. Small populations, lack of anonymity, closely connected social relations, a codified set of methods for dealing with offenses, community self-sufficiency, self-reliance, identifiable physical and social boundaries, and attachment to place are all possible connotations or assumptions which are called upon by this invocation of community.[4] Of particular note is the widely exhibited belief that our current society contains such entities (as evidenced by the numerous calls for "community control" or "community participation" and "community building" in decision making). When attached to such unstated inherent "goods," community as a metaphor carries automatic connotations of the *verum, bonum* and *pulchrum* of reality. The ideal of community is taken as something identifiable, constant, *natural* or proper, and apparent to the casual observer. Definitions of who is included or excluded in locating *particular* communities, or the question of the scale at which such entities naturally exist, or the effect that change (in terms of material factors, increasing globalization of culture and simple population mobility) has on the notion of community, is seldom addressed in the forums in which the term is used to signal a connotative Good. Or, if proponents are to admit that community may not exist in quite this form at this time, then they might maintain that as an ideal, it had *once* existed. And if such entities *are* no longer to be found, or are exceedingly scarce, it is due to their destruction by the progression of organizational bureaucracy and the continued threat of the advancing logic of global capital. This *form* of community is held up as an ideal—one which is assumed to exist or one which we ought to be seeking to create.

Deconstructing Community: Counterfeits and Hegemonies

Again, men have no pleasure, but on the contrary a great deal of grief, in *keeping company*.
—Hobbes, *Leviathan*.

Not all assessments of the previous description of community result in its characterization as an ideal. Within recent trends in what might be called critical theory, poststructuralism, or some strands of feminist theory, such supposedly Arcadian idylls or Romantic notions are reconstrued as thinly disguised representations of elite experiences. Community as it is constituted above (self-contained, self-supporting, *noble*) is received as an indication of the suppression or marginalization of the multiplicity of voices within the imposed boundary. This fracturing of the perceived idyll represents a parallel to the increasingly popular notion of fractured identities. In other words, this is a reconceptualization both of the self, and of the way in which such fractured selves can be said to participate in the social or the possibility of unified communities.[5]

In this sense, to speak of "community building" is to describe the process by which certain privileged groups impose their experiences on others. To speak of the "wishes or needs of the community" is to posit the existence of a "we" who have in *common* some of the elements previously described. Yet, it is *precisely* those elements of the ideal, or their assumed connotations, which are to be deconstructed and "revealed" as hegemonic impositions of a particular group.[6] Such theorists might claim that community seems "right" and "proper" to us only through a process of political "normalization" of certain practices and restrictions.[7]

Such theorists might address the question of community thusly: Self-sufficiency? Achieved through appropriation of women's labor. Codified relations to ensure coherence? A mechanism for controlling and eradicating difference. Attachment to place? Blood myths tied to land, husbandry and the feminization of the earth—more oppression. It is supposed that community as it has been described elsewhere (the ideal) is no more than an ideological mirage, a counterfeit, which exists only through a concerted erasure or ignorance of the experiences of marginalized others. It is central to our thesis that these seemingly opposite beliefs surrounding the nature of community are in fact implicated, each in the other, through their reliance on a simple assumption: *that the entity they are either valorizing or deconstructing actually exist.*

There are no Quakers in Quaker Village

[P]ostmodernity, the age of contingency *fur sich* of self-conscious contingency, is for the thinking person also the age of community: of the lust for community, search for community, invention of community, imagining of community (Bauman 1992, p. 134).

During the preparation of this essay, we encountered an advertisement in the *Toronto Star* which seems to us to illustrate a perfect "representation" of the ideal *community*; the same image which deconstructionist critiques utilize in their analyses of that ideal (see Figure 1).

Quaker Village is apparently small enough that everyone will "know you by name." The image we are presented with is one in which a little blond-haired girl stands on a waiting stool to select candies from a jovial 1920s-retro general store clerk (complete with armband and apron) across an "antique" cash register. The man smiles at the little girl with patience and affection, half teasing, as though they just shared some long-standing joke. The implication and connotations we are meant to derive are presumably something like those we outlined under *Community Building*. Namely, here is a community which is small, static, closely-knit and composed of an interdependent group of *average folk*. We are meant to assume that these two people know each other, that the little girl was born here and will die here. That she will shop at the General Store her entire life, her children playing with the storekeeper's grandchildren in the street outside.

If we were to take a deconstructionist view of the same photograph the resulting illumination would be quite different. What is not shown in this picture, we would say, is the sign outside the door which says "no dogs or Jews allowed," or the punishment meted out to the little girl in her Sunday School whites (for getting candy stains on her frills and bows, dirt on the hem of her frock from climbing a tree on the way home—nice girls don't play like boys!). We do not see the store clerk's membership in a right-wing political party, a group devoted to "keeping our community white." We do not see the little girl, grown-up at 18 but not able to leave the smallness of her community behind, taking a waitress job at the soda counter next door instead of leaving home for university, the theater or travel. *We do not see any Quakers.* We might say that this idyllic picture of community

Figure 1. "They Know You By Name At Quaker Village"
(reprinted by permission from Wycliffe Homes).

is playing on white, North American nostalgia for the clean, safe, suburban 1950s, and that those *communities* were not quite the places we like to imagine.[8]

All of this critique might very well be true, but there is another layer to this particular portrayal of community. Prospective purchasers should note that the picture at the bottom of the ad of the "model home" (for only $229,900) is not the home which is actually for sale. "Consumers" will look at the model, and pay money for an as yet undeveloped piece of dirt (former farmland?). Once they own a Quaker Village home, people are most likely to drive home through a village center (a mall, with 'General Store' written in olde English above the promenade) to their 60' lot, use their automatic garage door opener to enter their Quaker-esque model-home and stay immersed in TV-land until the next day, whence they leave (in separate vehicles) for their jobs in the city (a 2 hour commute). That model home, with its faux-gingerbread trim, manicured lawn and double garage is synonymous with all the isolated, isolating suburban developments of the past 30 years. In such a community, people will more likely learn the names and faces of "America's Most Wanted" than those of their neighbors.

The truly disturbing result of all the rhetorical excess generated by this sort of advertisement is the realization that arguments over just what is represented by this image of community amount to no more than that—disagreements over an image. Jean Baudrillard has made a spectacle of himself with just this sort of analysis—one which is as potentially debilitating as it is a powerful means of reconceptualizing the level on which this debate (as well as others) is occurring within our supposedly postmodern context. Briefly, Baudrillard has outlined a progression whereby images, (representations) become divorced from "the real" resulting inevitably in a simulacrum in which referents become impossible to locate amidst the welter of self-referential simulations and simulacra. According to Baudrillard (1983a), the following would be the successive phases of the image.

- it is the reflection of a basic reality
- it masks and perverts a basic reality
- it masks the *absence* of a basic reality
- it bears no relation to any reality whatever: it is its own pure simulacrum (p. 11).

The image of Quaker Village is not a representation of anything which is "out there," it is a *simulation*—a sign cut loose from its referent which now points backwards to itself only. We would maintain that the Quaker Village ad is an example of Baudrillard's third phase of the sign: that is, it masks the *absence* of a basic reality. Thus, the idyllic Quaker Village *image* is not fundamentally challenged by our previous deconstruction since such a critique still maintains that the image is referring to a *real territory*. Yet the image in the ad is not a photograph, there is nothing to indicate that this is archival historical material—it seems quite likely that the little girl and the clerk are actors, the general store an arc of text painted in with a desktop publishing program, the candy counter a prop borrowed from the movie set next door. Those who seek to deconstruct the *image* as being exclusionary of the experiences of others, or of not telling the "real" story of such communities are *deluded in the same way* as those who might romanticize such an image, or those who would be inspired to purchase a Quaker Village home based on the connotations it invokes. This is an image which does not relate to any *real* community past or present. There never were any Quakers, nor a village, nor a General Store. The argument is not properly over what is represented by this image (small, stable, normal vs. homogeneous, exclusionary, erasing) but rather that the discussion of the image *itself* is a mask which covers the *absence of anything solid beneath the discussion.* There is no community in the sense in which this image attempts to prompt us either toward constitution or deconstruction. It is a debate which engages solely with the *form* of community rather than attempting any articulation of community as a *process*. By arguing for a *return* to community under the aegis of some Arcadian idyll or by attempting to *resist* this return we engage in the language of images and signs cut loose from any recognizable context. *In fact, by engaging with the image, any resistance or deconstruction can be said to reinforce the image itself.*

We contend that it is this image of community (Quaker Village) that is being bandied about by many of those who advocate community control, community participation or community health. It is the same image that the theorists, feminists, post-structuralists *et alia*, are attempting to deconstruct or reconstitute, only with the experiences and voices of the margins made *visible*. But what we have been discussing is only a simulation, an image. Our collective gaze is focused on the image, the simulation; we are caught in an endless debate over the definition of something phantasmagoric. We obsessively deconstruct simulations (who is included or excluded by the image) rather than confronting the *absence* that it is masking. In essence, the implicit proclamation that the counterfeit is all there ever was simultaneously forces us to proclaim the *death of community.*[9]

History as Disturbance

> As an organism the formation arises, grows, matures, and dies...Furthermore, each climax formation is able to reproduce itself, repeating with essential fidelity the stages of its development. The life-history of a formation is a complex but definite process, comparable in its chief features with the life-history of an individual plant (Clements 1916, *Plant Succession*).

Evelyn Fox Keller and Elizabeth Lloyd (1992) have argued that, because of the large degree of overlap between ways of thinking about the natural world and ways of thinking about human social relations, certain terms offer a welcome vantage point for viewing the complex interactions which point to the coupled evolution of science and culture. Or, as Jan Sapp (1994) has noted: "To compare the structure of natural forms to the structure of human groups...has remained imaginatively powerful" (p. 95). In just this way, such debates and idylls as exist within social discussions of community can be seen as both *reflected in and reflecting* the discussions within scientific disciplines (whose practitioners, presumably, are also members of human "communities"). This co-determining trend between culture and the study of ecology is particularly evident in many of the theories and precepts relating to the so-called "individualistic vs. community" debate in ecological science. The development of theoretical ecological ideas around *community* is addressed below.

Based on turn of the century observations of the great plains grasslands, Frederic Clements proposed a unifying theory of ecology as constituting the study of the stately progression (development) of natural communities through the process of natural succession. According to Clements (in Worster 1994) "Nature's course...[was] not aimless wandering to and fro but a steady flow toward stability that [could] be exactly plotted by scientists" (p. 210). This is a process which tends, inevitably, towards the establishment of a stable, climax community in which the composite of plants and animals are actually *dependent* on each other for their development and in most cases could not live the one without the other. Clements saw ecological communities as analogous to individual organisms, or as parallels of the human form: communities *developed* from early successional stages to a Climax community in just the same way as a organism develops from zygote to adult. Individual species of plants and animals were thus understood as being incapable of existing independently of the whole. Communities were clear, identifiable, stable, and resilient (not unlike the form of human community presented by Quaker Village) and, in the case of Clements' views, at their best when kept in isolation from the contamination and disturbance of human activity. This stable climax state represented the *normal* condition of nature; disturbance, if it did occur, was likely to be both human-caused and catastrophic. The grand image of the pristine, stable, climax community which was nevertheless susceptible to human perturbation took hold of popular imagination. Ralph and Mildred Buchsbaum, writing in an introductory ecology textbook of 1957 stated it this way:

> Though the communities themselves... have not yet been completely pinned down, the community concept is clear enough. And it is one of the most significant of all ecological concepts, occupying with the ecosystem concept, the same central and unifying role in ecology as does the concept of organic evolution in the whole of biology. It brings together into a meaningful story the myriads of detail about plant and animal structure, distribution and habits that have been accumulated through the centuries... (p. 61).

Not only was the community concept an obvious one, *natural* you might say, but the Buchsbaums placed it in rough relation to the theory of evolution by natural selection in terms of its importance to ecology. On the whole, it was assumed that the obviousness of the "wholeness of the ecosystem" and the interdependence of the members of the community were simple ideas once they were "pointed out." Yet, say the Buchsbaums, they were not clearly apparent even to the most careful scholars before the "necessary facts" became known (Buchsbaum and Buchsbaum 1957).

Nor were the facts even that clear to other ecologists. In 1926, about the same time as Clements' ideas were gaining broad prominence, Henry Gleason published a treatise on the *Individualistic Concept of Plant Association.* According to Gleason's interpretation, plant communities did not exist in the Clementsian sense of an easily identifiable climax, complete with a dominant species. Instead, Gleason reported observations of individual species distributions according to environmental gradients based on life-cycle requirements—not as coevolved interdependent parts of an organismic ecological community. He argued that "plants do form associations... but that these are mere accidental groupings, each the result of the unique circumstances and too loosely related to be likened to an organizing being" (Worster 1994, p. 239).[10] This hypothesis has been corroborated by the workings of statistical ecologists of a later generation, who attempted to demonstrate the appearance and disappearance of plant species according to a series of latitudinal, edaphic, climatic or other environmental gradients. Such understandings of ecology have been popularized by writers such as Paul Colinvaux (1978) who offers the following dismissal of Clementsian ideas:

> Is there some mystic organization beyond the species level that fits communities together? Or could everything Clements saw be explained *more simply* by an hypothesis that *lets* each species in the plant community act selfishly in the pursuit of its own Darwinian fitness?... [this idea] is not so emotionally pleasing as the Clementsian dream of species cooperating for the good of the community, *but it is simpler* (p. 123, emphasis added).

Ockham's razor has thus cut through many debates in ecology—where there was slender or contentious empirical evidence to support either side in the debate over selfishness vs. cooperation, the rule of "simplest" was invoked.[11] Thus, distributions of species were recast as based on "simpler" theories of selfish competition; any perceived association of plants were a mere deceit or illusion of human sensory faculties and emotional yearnings, something the power of statistical analysis was able to dispel.

Despite Gleason's continued opposition to Clementsian ideas throughout his life, the model of stable climax communities held wide sway for most of this century until the seminal work of Drury and Nisbet in 1973. They set out to prove that the process of ecological succession did not lead anywhere—not to a climax state, and not even predictably to a community of similar composition and character. Their challenge to the ideas of succession, climax and

stability were part of a general questioning of established notions
which began to take the form of a new emphasis on "disturbance."
As Donald Worster (1994) has noted, this was a fundamentally new
interest on the part of ecologists. Disturbance, connoting extreme
exogenous change, was not a common subject in the time of Clements
(or indeed of any of the "founding fathers" of ecology) and it rarely
appeared in combination with the adjective "natural" (Worster 1994).
Scientists now appeared to be almost actively looking for signs of
disturbance, especially those which might be demonstrably non-
anthropogenic (Worster 1994). Disturbance was indeed everywhere—fire, wind, water, all were reconstituted as agents of continual
change at a variety of scales. Even Clements' stable prairie grasslands
were reconstituted as a regularly disturbed environment.[12]

From an emphasis on progression, development, homogeneity,
interdependence and stability, ecology's new conception of nature
now featured a continually shifting ground without direction,
consisting of heterogeneity, individualistic distributions, and
ceaseless disturbance. As Worster (1994) illustrates:

> Gleason's "individualistic" view of nature suggested that the climax
> [community] was a haphazard, imperfect, and shifting organization—one that
> man need not worry overly much about *disturbing* (p. 239, emphasis added).

Ecologists in this new "tradition" proclaimed proudly that the *climax
notion was dead*. Human disturbance in the landscape might now be
reconstructed as *natural*. And though some ecologists might still admit
that communities existed as a useful unit of analysis—as chance
associations of individuals with similar environmental requirements
and with a continually changing composition—*community* as an
entity with interdependent, emergent principles was *dead*.[13] The
ecosystem concept itself has faded into a vague and undefinable
discomfort. We look for organized wholes in Nature and find only
loose atoms and fragments (Worster 1994). What has in large measure
replaced these "grand, unifying theories" is the notion of a patchwork
landscape of plants and animals continually shifting in time and space
without any sense of a deep vegetative history rooted in place.

By this point, an emerging parallel between the course of this
debate in ecology and the disagreements over the nature of
community in the human realm should be becoming apparent. The
Nature (or rather, *n*ature) of which the disturbance ecologist writes

is remarkably similar to the human community (or rather, communities) that theorists from many social/cultural studies departments have begun to debate. *Patches, the physical expression of disturbed heterogeneity, are increasingly evident in the metaphorical landscape of human society.*

Renewed nationalism is evident across the globe, and yet many of these nationalist tendencies can be broken down into a mosaic of racial, ethnic and gender differences. Any pretense of characterizing these "nations" as stable entities appears foolish, since their physical boundaries are continually open to question.[14]

The existence of a "normal" state, towards which all societies should *develop* is increasingly in question as an ethical imperative, and is long since disputed as a viable mode of historical analysis. At a different scale, this dissolution of community has been made painfully apparent in recent exposures of sexual abuse involving Catholic priests, residential schools and other "pillars of the community." It seems that even the most stereotypically stable human communities (small, religious, tightly-knit, *noble*) are being revealed as deeply and inherently *disturbed* behind the veil of their *image*. As Worster (1995) has continually noted "Disturbance *is* history. And a disturbed nature is a nature that has a history very similar to the history that humans make" (p. 74).[15]

Borders and Boundaries

It is language that tells us about the nature of a thing, provided that we respect language's own nature. In the meantime, to be sure, there rages round the earth an unbridled yet clever talking, writing and broadcasting of spoken words. Man acts as though *he* were the shaper and master of language, while in fact *language* remains the master of man. Perhaps it is before all else man's subversion of *this* relation of dominance that drives his nature into alienation (Heidegger 1971, p. 146, emphasis in the original).

As we have shown, community as a concept has turned out to be extremely difficult to characterize or identify indirectly. But we have not yet attempted a concrete definition: is it possible to locate such entities more concretely, to denote them on a map? Are maps, whether metaphorical or actual, possible or even desirable? The etymological connotations of the word itself give some clue as to the nature of such an effort. One possible etymology (for there are

doubtless several) can be constructed which shows a derivation from
the Latin *communitas* meaning "community fellowship" itself
derived from the Latin *communis* meaning "shared, common,
general, universal, public." But the "double-m" is hint of a
transliteration. In Latin, many "comm-" words are constructions of
"con+m". *Con* of course, means "with": *munis* is derived from
munio, munire the Latin verb "to surround with a wall." Literally
then, community means "that which is surrounded by the walls"
(con+munis) (Miller 1995).[16] Defining community in this way would
seem to be contingent on the (common) articulation or location of
fairly precise borders or boundaries between what (or who) is within
any given community and that which is to be excluded. With what
possible rigour can such boundaries be said to exist? *If no certain
border is discernible, what can be said for the existence of an entity
whose very definition is seemingly predicated on the presence of
walls?* This is what is at issue when theorists argue over the nature
of community.[17] It is also fundamental to the conflicting claims of
various ecologists about the empirical (or rather, quantifiable)
existence of plant and animal communities.

Social theorists are quick to point out the inevitability of difference
within any supposedly cohesive "community." Although on a broad
level a community may be apparent (a self-identified group) close
interrogation would reveal differences in how each member
constructed the borders of that community (who is included/
excluded, the physical borders, *what* exactly is held in common).
Such theorists would point out that we are not characterized so much
by our commonalities (created by living within a defined place, within
city "walls" say) but by our differences, by the ways in which each
individual constructs her or his identity (or is constructed by societal
categories). Inclusion and exclusion are implicit in community
formation, but in physical, social and emotional terms, the result for
each individual is the construction of multiple communities rather
than ascribing to the edicts of a singular community.[18] It has been
pointed out that any attempt to recreate a singular sense of
"community" thus ignores the complex politics of identity which are
at play in any grouping of individuals.

Attempts to quantifiably identify, categorize and map the
boundaries of plant and animal associations by ecologists have
encountered similar difficulties. This difficulty may be illuminated
through the use of a brief example. If we were to stand on the opposite

side of a valley from a mountain in any hemisphere, we would most likely be able to identify (by variations in color and vegetation height) distinct changes in the distribution of plant species: clear bands of color, relatively homogenous within and distinctly differentiated from each other, are visible with changes in altitude. Quantitative ecologists have argued that examination of such distributions through the lens of statistics reveals that differences *between* such associations or communities are much greater than the similarities *within* such "communities"—changes in species distribution are found to correlate much more closely to underlying edaphic or environmental gradients, rather than with any consociation of species.[19] The visual identification of such communities is thus an *illusion* of human perception.

What these cases illustrate is that the examination of any identified community at smaller and smaller scales results in the dissolution of the image. Like glass chips in a wall mural, the pattern disappears upon closer inspection: no association of colors is discernible. The concept of *color* itself is an apt illustration of this point. The refraction of light presents us with a *continuum* in which we perceive colors. An argument may be made that the colors which members of different cultures identify is a result of the acceptance of certain imposed or shared categories. What is recognized as being part of the category "blue" in one group might be associated with "green" to another. The number of colors, the way in which they are distinguished, and the degree of individual variation in their identification is often noted as a classic example of cultural and individual interpretation. Most importantly for our purposes however, is the understanding that distinct colors as such can be said, empirically, *not* to exist; refracted light is a *continuous* phenomena without concrete delineations. Although as a perceiving subject, one can identify colors (albeit subject to cultural and personal conditioning), a closer (or reductionist) examination would show that "color" itself does not exist as a property of the world.[20] Colors are categories that we impose onto continuous phenomena. Examining the phenomena at levels beneath the scale of unaided human perception again results in the dissolution of the image. This does not mean that we do not see something, nor that the existence of color as a physical property (the defraction of light) is under question, merely that it is an observational phenomena which disintegrates under too finite an inspection.

Walls, whether physical or metaphysical, are constructed in order to bound the ways in which we will extend our concern and to frame and categorize the world. Community, like color, is yet one more concept which we use to place a discrete ordering over the ambiguous continuity of experience and association. We interrelate with one another to different degrees, share goals or aspirations but in different contexts, and live in *relative* distance each one from the other. From this morass of difference, we seek to construct order, distinguishing entities called communities (both human and non-human) in which we participate. We perceive the existence of community as a means of understanding and organizing experience. Thus, membership in multiple communities may be fluid and subject to change, but the borders and boundaries themselves are a construct implicit in our present understanding of the nature of community: such "illusions" are seemingly necessary to our understandings of experience itself.

THE MADNESS OF GENERAL CONCEPTS

Despite the scientists' intentions to invent technical terms that are untainted by the vagaries of ordinary language and cultural contexts, historians, philosophers and sociologists of science have come to recognize that such ideal language devoid of multiple meanings is, in fact, remote in practice (Keller and Lloyd 1992).

Man is no longer recognizable in language. He can no longer give a true representation of himself... language has everywhere become a power unto itself, which now grabs people with ghostly arms and forces them into places where they don't even want to go. As soon as they try to understand one another, and to come to an agreement about some work, they are seized by the *madness of general concepts*. The very sounds of the words enchant them... So to all its other sufferings humanity must add this new suffering: that words lead to actions which no longer correspond with feelings (Nietzsche, *Untimely Meditations,* pp. IV, 5).

In 1995, the translation of linguist Uwe Poerksen's "Plastic Words" became available in North America. Poerksen addresses the way in which certain concepts are present everywhere seemingly at once, and yet no-one is able to trace the particularity of their meanings. Plastic words are those concepts which have many connotations but which do not have corresponding denotations; that is, they do not point to anything "real." These words pave the way for the actualization of their connotations. They display the structure of a particular worldview more clearly than a full ideological treatise might. As Poerksen (1995) notes: "the words do not just make this structure visible; they are also *agents*" (p. 6, emphasis added). As countless ideas get tangled in one plastic concept, the concept itself claims a certain independence—one comes to confuse the name with a thing-in-itself.

Poerksen (1995) identifies a number of words which he feels deserve the epithet "plastic." In particular, he questions the concreteness of terms such as "basic need," "care," "modernization (urbanization)," "development," and "information" in addition to many others (pp. 25-26). It should be noted that we are of the opinion that *community* could well be added to this list of plastic words. With this in mind, we now set out to explore several concepts (plastic words) which we feel are *agents* in the death of community.

Looking for Community within Plastic Urbanization

...like any marketplace, the modern city (community) is the hectic centre of a largely privatized interaction between anonymous buyers and sellers who are more involved in exchanging their wares than in forming socially and ethically meaningful associations. Cities (Communities) today are typically measured more by their success as business enterprises than cultural foci. The ability of an urban entity to "balance its budget," to operate "efficiently," to "maximize" its service with minimal costs, all of these are regarded as the hallmark of municipal success. Corporate models form the ideal examples of urban models, and civic leaders take greater pride in their managerial skills than in their intellectual abilities (Bookchin 1987, p. 8).

The city or town has traditionally been the first place where one can operate as a public being and as a participating, contributing member of society/community. We believe that it is possible to see the idea or concept of urbanization, occurring under the guise of capitalism and its grow-or-die ethic, as being responsible for development which proceeds at the *cost of* cities not, as it is usually viewed, as the actual development *of* cities. The confusion around the plasticity of the term urbanization has led to these two terms (urbanization & the city) being regarded by many as synonymous. Thus the deservedly negative connotations which accompany urbanization may be understood as necessarily devolving *from* the idea of the city. The consistent wrath of urbanization's effect on both

city and country is a process of continual physical attack on both
their form and the dialectical processes by which they mutually
constitute each other.

> [It is] a siege that threatens humanity's very place in the natural
> environment...Urbanization is engulfing not only the country side; it is
> engulfing the city. It is devouring not only town and village life based on the
> values, culture, and institutions nourished by agrarian relationships. It is
> devouring city life based on values cultures and institutions nourished by civic
> relationships (Bookchin 1987, p. 3).

Continuing along this path, Bookchin (1987) argues that
urbanization (rooted as it is in the system which has created the
prevailing plight), has become a *malignant perversion of citification*
that threatens to engulf both town and country, and render their
historic dialectic unintelligible. Urbanization, thus holds full
responsibility for rendering obsolete one of societies most heated
debates and dynamic arenas of resistance, the struggle between the
antagonistic city and country. A struggle which help both city and
rural to mutually define each other and themselves. Without this
adversarial relationship, what was once an individual city or
community simply becomes part of a mass of *borderless* urban
sprawl.

What we are suggesting is that once there is no *other* to relate
to (and differentiate from), there can also be no difference, no
boundaries or borders which separate one community from
another. The result is a relationship to the physical community
which is little more than a pragmatic supplier of material
requirements: "[w]e expect our persons and property to be
protected, our roads to be repaired, our environment to be
physically and socially tidy—which is to say spared from the
invasion of 'undesirable elements'" (Bookchin 1987, p. 7). And the
way we judge the success of these cities is how well they operate
as businesses and what level of economic management is manifested
by their political leaders. In this way, urbanization has gradually
and subtly taken all civic aspects of the city and reduced the once
catalytic city/country dialectic to the silence of an urban belt "with
its smothering traits of anonymity, homogenization, and
institutional gigantism" (Bookchin 1987, p. 3).

The *Need* for Need and the Destruction of Communities

> Just as General Motors needs steel, a service economy *needs* "deficiency,"
> "human problems," and "needs" if it is to grow... This economic *need* for
> need creates a demand for redefining conditions as deficiencies (McKnight
> 1995, p. 29).

John McKnight, in his book, *The Careless Society: Community and Its Counterfeits* argues that communities are destroyed by service intervention. He suggests that "helping" and "caring" professions use the offer of their services to produce clients out of citizens. Flowing from arguments put forward by Ivan Illich (1973, 1977), McKnight argues that "helping" and "caring" professions are in fact a form of *disabling* help that undermines the very processes (active citizens) that sustain healthy communities. Institutions and market interests promote clienthood and dependency, McKnight believes, and this leads to the devaluing of citizen action in favor of passive, expert, service delivery. What is produced is a system which *needs* expanding needs to be discovered in increasingly dependent consumer-clients. McKnight illustrates how the typical enemies that we have waged countless losing wars against—poverty, sickness, disease, and drugs—are not the real enemies but rather the real enemies are "*a set of interests that need dependency masked by service*" (McKnight 1995, p. 99). In other words, the more likely peril to a community's health is a health care system reliant on illness; social service providers whose existence depends on impoverished communities; a criminal justice system which subsists on communities with a "drug problem." In fact, prisons are a particularly obvious example of such "needs mining." The penal institutions, law enforcement professionals, corrections counsellors, prison architects and construction companies (in essence the justice system as industry) now rely on the commodification of both criminals and crime.

This needs mining is also evident in the general population. The *need* for need, in order to feed growing service based economies, emerges as a response to the discovery of disturbance in human communities. Accompanying discoveries of continuous change, turbulence, disturbance and deficiencies, in human and non-human communites, come calls for interventions to optimize, control and fix these processes. If a priest has sexually abused young boys then psychological counseling is in order, for both the boys and the priest.

If fire once "naturally" disturbed temperate forest ecosystems (communities) then controlled burning or clearcutting is required in order to maintain the "natural" condition by mimicking "natural" disturbance. If a tragedy occurs in a school, trauma counselors are immediately needed for all those deemed affected. With all of these approaches service providers are needed in the form of managers, professionals, and experts.

A recent article describing the premeditated murder of an entire extended family that occurred in Vernon, British Columbia, Canada describes the typical service response to a "community" in crisis; it also illustrates how service intervention in communities tends to expand to include all spheres:

> Richard Wilford, program coordinator for the North Okanagan victim-assistant program, pulled together plenty of expert help: psychologists, social workers, registered counselors, mental-health workers, youth and family workers, government social-service workers and 28 volunteers with training in trauma counseling and crisis intervention. The teams first job was to identify those who might be affected. They drew up a lengthy list that included members of the immediate family; neighbors who saw the shooting; family friends; professionals such as police, ambulance drivers and hospital workers, who dealt with the bodies; members of the Vernon's Sikh community; the slain children's schoolmates; the adult victims' co-workers; *the entire city of Vernon*; and local reporters who usually cover much tamer stories...[When asked if this drastic action was creating victims Richard Wilford said,] We are not [creating victims]...If these people do not talk it out, then it remains stuffed in and the next time they'll have two things to deal with. It's a public health issue... *We can not predict who will suffer, so we inoculate everyone* (*Globe & Mail* 1996, p. 5, emphasis added).

The extent to which service provision, aimed at individual clients, has been visited upon communities is astounding. What is seemingly forgotten is that, not unlike all drug therapies, these interventions are not neutral, they have potential side effects.[21] It is conceivable that such service provision could, in fact, undermine communities by framing them as collections of needy *individual clients*. John McKnight has called the unexpected and often paradoxical results of certain forms of intervention *iatrogenic effects*—usually inflicted by "helping" service professionals on Communities.[22]

It is important to understand that community as it is constituted in the ideal (as a Quaker Village) no longer exists, if indeed it ever existed. It is from within this framework (if without this realization) that we now hear calls *for* community based services, programs and interventions to deal with numerous "needs." Community, in the older sense of a social group of citizens, increasingly resembles a mere collection of *clients and consumers* who are little threat to centralist states or multinational corporations. In fact, contrary to being a threat, collections of clients and consumers are necessary *resources* for the expansion of goods and service production and consumption. The only community which is left thriving is the "community of capital" in which consumers and clients are the primary resources (Rogers 1996).

The servicing of communities removes the emphasis from the capacities of collective groups of citizens and places it on an increasing number of deficiencies in dependent individuals. *Therefore "community based" programs and services are actually aimed at individuals not communities.* This shift in emphasis from the group to the individual mimics the disturbance and deconstructionist ideas of community that have occurred in the science of quantitative ecology and in debates within social theory. In both of these interrogations of the idea of community (both human and non-human) our gaze is reduced to the individual level, community disappears and disturbance is seen to be everywhere and in need of servicing. In much the same way as the "disturbance" of Clements' stable grassland, the Vernon example illustrates that when we look closely enough we find that everyone (and every place) is potentially disturbed.

The emphasis on individuals is strengthened and maintained by using rights language in discussions around community services. Arguments around rights are fundamentally tied to individuals and it is important to note that a focus on the individual forms the basis of the deconstructionist arguments against idyllic images of community. This emphasis on rights means that in current debates around community what we hear most often are formerly independent citizens, chanting now as reliant clients and arguing for their universal rights to disabling services. In effect we have students demanding their right to stupefying education, patients demanding their right to iatrogenic health care, advocates of all stripes arguing for their clients right to access "help," and a whole host of other client-based services.

We believe that the shift in emphasis in discussions around the idea of community from the collective citizenry to the individual consumer-client explains why neoconservative governments and corporations are now so willing to target services to the "community" level. Deficit-slashing governments can claim to be closing centralized institutions such as hospitals because they want to encourage "community health care" (and save money at the same time). This is a politically inert move in at least one sense, since community health care now means individualized consumer-client-units purchasing the commodity called "health" from the increasingly global market. This *form* of community plays into corporate interests which are hoping to expand their "community of capital" by replacing government service delivery with their own. If McKnight's critique is to be taken seriously, communities can only be recreated through clients reclaiming their status as citizens. This effectively means reinstating the social by reaffirming the belief that communities are social *places* involved in dynamic social *processes* not economic market *spaces* envisioned as static advertising *images* (see Figure 1).

Why Community Control Now?

> When the real is no longer what it used to be, nostalgia assumes its full meaning...And there is a panic-stricken production of the real and the referential, above and parallel to the panic of material production (Baudrillard 1983a, p. 12).

The current postmodern clamor to desperately seek out, re-discover, restore, and reclaim the image of community as idyll can be seen as another symptom of its loss. Baudrillard (1983a) has discussed how the "reality principle" of an image is desperately maintained through frantically seeking out the real at the very moment when it has vanished (Baudrillard 1983a). According to this view, our current fetish for discussing and addressing the ideal community image could only have occurred after communities were destroyed. A recent discussion with the grandmother of one of the authors reveals this point clearly. When asked what Bethene Bavington remembered about her childhood community she responded: "We never talked about community when I was growing up. I never heard the word until very recently...I guess I lived in a community, but we never called it that" (Bavington 1996).[23] If people are embedded in community, they necessarily lack an outside from which to critique its form.

As we have discussed, community is now being "discovered" at an alarming rate. We maintain that its *disappearance* has been engineered in part through some of the processes we have discussed to this point, leaving us with a debate over mere *forms* of community. This has resulted in the odd situation where the dominant voices calling for a transfer of services to "communities" are most likely to be neoconservative governments and transnational corporations. The traditional "Left" are more likely to be fighting a rear-guard battle to protect "essential" services, delivered by centralized institutions of the welfare state they once denounced as oppressive! The community is now being heralded by the "new" right as *the* effective and efficient place to deliver services. This now provides a justification for the dismantling of centralized welfare states which we are told now cost too much to administer and deliver. Of course economism[24] is the soil from which these arguments are growing and the community rhetoric of such governments plays into the hands of multinational corporations who are ecstatic at the prospect of administering goods and services, to those *individuals* who can pay. Timothy Luke (1991) succinctly describes the current problem with community: "Composed of clients and consumers, communities today are not much more than an aggregation of atomized individuals organized into discrete geographic-legal units" (p. 72). As Luke's comment suggests, the current emphasis on community services differs from that of communitarian movements because it focuses on the individual rather than the collective. This emphasis on the individual is shared by deconstructionist arguments against the notion of community as ideal. It may seem oxymoronic that *community* rhetoric should focus on *individuals* but this apparent contradiction fades when we examine what community now means. As we have argued earlier, *community* no longer refers to groups of citizens involved in working together on a face-to-face basis in public life to create and interact in uncommodified relationships; increasingly, community of this type no longer exists in the West. It has been replaced by a collection of dependent clients and consumers whose activities most often support the "community of global capital" rather than other citizens and their communities.

In this way, we conceive (at its worst) modern social communities as a collection of individual consumer preferences as measured through the market mechanism, not citizenry involved in democratic processes.[25] Legitimacy and community definition has shifted from the *collective citizenry* to the *individual consumer*.

The Masses

For the purposes of this paper we intend to restrict our examination of the postmodern condition to the ways in which its manifestations affect the idea of community, and the necessarily connected issues of individuality and empowerment. In particular we examine the condition of *the masses* as articulated by Baudrillard (1983b) in his work: *In the Shadow of the Silent Majorities,* and the relation of these ideas to politics and community. *The masses,* according to Baudrillard, have become the hypersimulation of the social. No longer a form for social explosion or negativity, *the masses* has become a place of implosion absorbing all which once stimulated the social realm of life and community:

> It is with Marxist thought, in its successive developments, that the end of the political and of its particular energy was inaugurated. Here began the absolute hegemony of the social and the economic, and the compulsion on the part of the political, to become the legislative, institutional, executive mirror of the social. The autonomy of the political was inversely proportional to the growing hegemony of the social...The social won. But, at this point of generalization, of saturation, where it is no more than the zero degree of the political, at this point of absolute reference, of omnipresence and diffraction in all the interstices of physical and mental space, what becomes of the social itself? *It is the sign of its end:* the energy of the social is reversed, its specificity is lost, its historical quality and its ideality vanish in favour of a configuration where not only the political becomes volatilized, but where the social itself no longer has any name. Anonymous. THE MASS. THE MASSES (Baudrillard 1983b, p. 19, emphasis added).

This aspect of *the masses* being "a black hole which engulfs the social" (1983b, p. 4) representing a silent majority which neither is, nor isn't real, represents a sincere threat to the possibility of community. Community as a place populated by active citizens with a personal interest in the betterment of their collective home is not an option within the condition of *the masses*. Rather *the masses* are simply "that spongy referent, that opaque but equally translucent reality...[which] absorbs all the electricity of the social and political and neutralize[s] it forever" (1983b:1) and furthermore are products of their own constructed image. The result is that any appeal to *the masses* is perpetually unanswered—they absorb all which flows through them and reflect nothing back which can be represented or politicized.

But more than simply masking the stimulus for individuality, community and the political, the condition of *the masses* moves the discourse to an entirely new space. A space where even the traditional battle between the liberal autonomous self and the communitarian collective self is made null as there is no longer differentiation or antagonism to create alternative subjectivities and thus political issues. Otherness and differentiation, necessary for both community and individuality to be created, are destroyed through the internalizing of the logic of freedom constructed by capitalism and the state. Thus we achieve the freedom to be *free*-wheeling investors within our community of consumers but lose the potential for developing relationships based on community.

If we agree with Baudrillard and assume that the creation of *the masses* is the result of the unfolding of the latent potentialities within capitalism, his conclusion should come as no surprise, that "today it is necessary to produce consumers, to produce demand" (Baudrillard 1983b, p. 27) in addition to the creation and production of goods. Consumers need neither individuality nor community in which to fulfill their roles as consumers. Nor do they need space within which to practice the political. On the contrary, it is easier for "the constant solicitation, the information, to which it [*the masses*] is submitted," which Baudrillard suggests is "equivalent to the experimental torture on laboratory animals," to succeed if the masses *are* a mass "without conscience and without unconscious" (1983b, p. 29). Above all such a mass erases space where the option to be conscious might exist, namely the realm of politics and the space of the political.

Politics *in* and *of* Community

The Political: The political has to do with the dimension of antagonism which is present in social relations, with the ever-present possibility of an 'us-them' relation to be constructed in terms of 'friend-enemy'...This is why a democratic approach needs to come to terms with the ineradicable character of antagonism. One of the main tasks is to envisage how it is possible to diffuse the tendencies to exclusion which are present in all construction of collective identities (Mouffe 1995, p. 262).

Politics: The ensemble of practices, discourses, and institutions which seek to establish a certain order and to organize human coexistence in conditions which are always potentially conflictual because they are affected by the dimension of 'the political' (Mouffe 1995, pp. 262-263).

Taken in the context of our current discussion around community, a distinction between the political and politics is crucial. Most importantly, it highlights the importance of the community as a place where citizens can engage in the political. That is, it creates a space where differences can be identified, temporarily fixed and affirmed within the pretext of a common desire for equality and liberty and the continued desire for community membership.

What such communities can strive for is a realm of politics which sees "the other" not as "an enemy," but as an adversary whose ideas are struggled with but whose right to defend those ideas is not questioned as it is understood that their otherness is necessary for the existence of individuality. Community politics ideally makes room for the expression of conflicting interests and subjectivities where the political can derive its energy from numerous sources and emerge out of many differing forms of social relations not yet absorbed by the masses.

What this condition suggests is that if we wish to reclaim community we require the development of an alternative form of politics which does not attempt to appeal to *the masses* or other predetermined subjects, but rather speaks to some lingering, not yet destroyed sense of citizenship, individuality or community membership which is denied by the image of *the masses*. That is, a form of politics which both acknowledges that "there is no longer any social signified to give force to a political signifier" (Baudrillard 1983b, p. 19) and seeks to move beyond this conundrum. Or better yet, a form of politics, like the radical democracy espoused by Laclau and Mouffe (1985), which is based on the presupposition that "the hegemonic arrangement cannot claim any source of validity other than the power basis on which it is grounded" (Mouffe 1995, p. 261), as power is responsible for creating the identities themselves.

Understood in this way significance is never given to a signifier in the first place as it is power and differentiation which create nonfixed subjectivities within the political sphere—not prefixed subjects who vie for representation and power within the political sphere.[26] Once we accept the nonessentialist nature of all subject positions and realize they are constituted in antagonistic and therefore political relationships, we not only free them from their fixed identities but we also open up the possibility of freeing many more potentially emancipatory terms from their all too frequent grounding in capitalist discourse. As with the earlier examples of urbanization and the servicing of needs, development is yet another example of a seemingly hegemonic term which has gained its validity and significance from whence it is grounded, and is thus implicated in the death of community.

Reclaiming Development

> The lighthouse of development was erected right after the second world war. Following the breakdown of the European colonial powers, the United States found an opportunity to give worldwide dimensions to the mission their founding fathers had bequeathed to them: to be the "beacon on the hill." They launched the idea of development with a call to every nation to follow in their footsteps.... Today, the lighthouse shows cracks and is starting to crumble. The idea of development stands like a ruin in the intellectual landscape. Delusion and disappointment, failures and crimes have been the steady companions of development and they tell a common story: it did not work. Moreover, the historical conditions which catapulted the idea into prominence have vanished: development has become outdated. But above all, the hopes and desires which made the idea fly, are now exhausted: development has grown obsolete (Sachs 1992, p. 1).

> Development is, from this moment on (more than a century ago), the magic word with which we will solve all the mysteries that surround us or, at least, that which will guide us toward their solution (Haeckel in Sachs 1992, p. 10).

While agreeing with Wolfgang Sachs (1992) that "[t]he idea of development stands today like a ruin in the intellectual landscape," and that *current* development models should be firmly rejected, we suggest that the term development has been so warped and distorted that many practical and theoretical thinkers and actors have, understandably yet haplessly, abandoned it. This abandonment also rejects its potential as a guiding principle which might lead us toward a radically new *vernacular* and *non-essentialist* form of both community and political development. However, unlike these anti-development thinkers and in light of our previous discussion, we suggest that in order to embrace or actualize a utopian vision— something which we believe should be held and unabashedly articulated—we must *reclaim and revolutionize the idea of development within the realm of politics and community building.* In particular we argue that the form of development which has taken place since the industrial revolution is one essentialist *form* which definitely no longer suits our time, and arguably never suited any time.

As Jean Baudrillard (1994) so aptly explains in *Maleficent Ecology*:

> waste is today produced as such. We build huge office spaces which are intended to remain eternally empty (the spaces, like the people, are "laid off"). We put up buildings that are still-born, remnants (our age no longer produces ruins or relics, only wastes and residues)(p. 79).

Similarly as the previous discussion implied, we are laying off words like development, community, growth, progress, rather than reclaiming them and taking advantage of the potential of their process while still denying their normalized, degraded form. We are abandoning terms and concepts at an alarming rate, words which could be essential to the realization of community. What is now occurring is development for the sake of development in the same way that we continue to create profit for the sake of profit and arguably community for the sake of community (again, see Figure 1), all of which are idealized and promoted in advertising and which are without referent or direction. All that seems to be increased by this form of unconscious development is *the masses*. That is, more commodities for the capitalist machine, the reduction of the organic into the inorganic and the reduction of vernacular subjectivity into plastic commodity (what Baudrillard (1994a) calls the *production of man as waste-product*). What *we* might note as the production of community as a dump for this waste-product.

As *the masses* increase, and waste continues to be created for its own sake, community as a viable concepthas a harder time resisting its momentum, gradually becoming merely the place to house, or be populated by, human resources who know little or nothing of meeting their own *needs*, or of consciously developing a sensibility based on sharing and cooperation or responding to ecological imperatives. The dire need to take advantage of the potential *process* rather than *imposed forms* of development in order to create both a sensibility and a place where this sensibility can be harnessed is the reason we are unwilling to abandon such terms.

Ideally what might be attempted is the grounding of development within a political discourse of equality and liberty. To attempt this would necessitate that the *fixity* and *essentialist* baggage acquired through its affiliations with hegemonic capitalist discourse be separated from the concept itself. In differentiating these two aspects of the modern understanding of development we make, at a minimum, one essential and normative claim, that:

> ...for too long the left has ceded all of the important concerns to the right because it thought there was something *essentially* wrong about certain ideas if they were used by its opponents. But the strategy against their hegemony is to occupy terrain, to redefine the terms, to redefine the question of democracy, redefine the question of pluralism, redefine the question of liberalism...the left has not come to terms with the fact that liberal democracy is something worth fighting for—but only in the context of reformulating pluralism in a way that *of course* is different (Mouffe 1992, p. 39).

This statement makes one vital point among others that we can ill afford to cede potentially emancipatory terms to their current essentialized forms. Mouffe (1992) is correct when she says the most fruitful strategy against the neoconservative hegemony is to occupy terrain and reclaim the, (too numerous to name) terms which have been reduced, essentialized and fixed within the destructive discourse of capitalism. For far too long, development, much like pluralist democracy, has been identified with capitalism. The result has been that as an "environmentalist" *you cannot defend development,* and as a leftist *you cannot defend liberalism or pluralism,* and as a leftist environmentalist, heaven forbid, *you cannot defend anything that can help you achieve your goals or vision.*

FORMS, PROCESS AND PATTERN

> Misconstruing the dynamics of language they [postmodernists] are the final spokesmen of a world of *forms* as opposed to *process,* for whom existence is a mix of an infinite number of possible variations making up the linguistic elements of a text (Shepard 1995, p. 20, emphasis added).

> If we are only truly alive when dreaming, the point is not to maximize sleep, but to learn to dream while awake (J. Clark 1993, p. 34).

There is, in Western society, an increasing "primacy of the *neo*" (Lefebvre in Jameson 1991, p. 61). What we might, in fact, call *neophilia.* That is, there is an ever-increasing, rapacious consummation of perpetual novelties—things with gravity, weight, *history,* are erased or reconstituted as new forms. As we lose our sense of the historical, what was formerly held in common, cultural memory if you will, is reconstituted in the autoreferentiallity of the times (Jameson 1991, p. 82). The truly historical is combined with images of the cultural past to create ever newer images.

The postmodern condition results in the random cannibalization of all the styles of the past in a ceaseless play of stylistic allusion. Our inhabitation of the moment is increasingly synchronic; as Jameson (1991) has argued, our cultural languages and psychic experiences are increasingly dominated by categories of *space* rather than categories of *time* (p. 66). Thus we are faced with a society which observes the *forms* of creativity, without itself being creative; poeticizing instead of poetry; mysticalese instead of mysticism; jargon instead of philosophy; Disney instead of community and environment instead of nature/world. As Jean Baudrillard (1983a) has commented:

> Disneyland is there to conceal the fact that it is the "real" country, all of "real" America, which *is* Disneyland (just as the prisons are there to conceal the fact that it is the social in its entirety, with its banal omnipresence, which is carceral). Disneyland is presented as imaginary in order to make us believe that the rest is real, when in fact all of Los Angeles and the America surrounding it are no longer real, but of the order of the hyperreal and simulation (p. 25).

The (meta)physical landscape created by this new sensibility is one of flatness, shallowness—involving great distance but without tremendous divergence in form. We have, in effect, a unidimensional landscape; a homogeneity of heterogeneity. Stability, depth, a sense of time, memory, are replaced (through deconstruction, unbelief, the madness of general concepts, and an accepting embrace of simulations) with a landscape in which, and about which, we no longer feel or know passionately, deeply. Life becomes surficial and safe; deepness as a quality is erased. The distinctions which make things what they have been are disturbed, eroded, discarded. Indeed, we are faced with such an absurd vision that Camus' (1955) dismal prescription becomes certainty: "in a universe divested of illusions (e.g., borders and boundaries)...man feels alien, a stranger. His exile is without remedy, since he is deprived of the memory of a lost home or the hope of a promised land" (p. 5).

What reclamation or accommodation might be reached from what is (to our way of thinking) a decidedly dismal prophecy? It is our supposition that the recovery of a vernacular, the support of the intimate particularity possible between people and between people and physical places, may afford some *hope*. A reclamation of the diachronic sense of history—of evolution or co-evolution of people *in* places—might counter the world-eating, place—less trend of globalization, plasticity, urbanization, need creation and simulations. The reattachment of people to places, in concert with their reattachment to their neighbours may be one way out of our self-referentiality. This may only be true so long as we resist the ossification or imposition of a stasicity of *forms* over processes. The promulgation of some ideal *image* of the *verum, bonum* and *pulcrum* of community living is the ice which freezes and ultimately kills the possibility of genuine relationship.

Thus, what we have discussed so far amounts to a debate over *forms*. Is community a stable, homogeneous, co-operative consociation? Or is it more characterized by difference, disturbance, identity, and individuality? Which form *ought* we to be seeking? In the realm of both human and non-human, the debate over "community" has one thing in common: this endless refraction of forms serves to mask the ways in which the social is being continuously undermined. Our suggested focus on process— history—*requires* development. It is only through development or change that we may still attain the future (as opposed to the stasicity of the present which is posited by theorists such as Baudrillard 1994, 1983a, 1983b). A future which replaces the "dictatorship of reason" with a diversity of human qualities, a community of inter-reliant citizens rather than dependent clients; a community in which history, evolution and memory are balanced by development, a shared sense of the importance of the political and recognition of the necessity of a future vision.

Epilogue: Citizen as Artist/Community as Art, Citizen as Art/Community as Artist

The ideas that follow represent what we feel to be *a* utopian description of community. It is not what we think all Communities should become, nor is it the only community which each citizen will be a member of if we understand community as a place where nonfixed subjectivities are created and elaborated. It will, however, be a community unlike any other.

The concurrent and dialectical nature of this potential future community is fundamentally based on a conception of the potential for community to be both creative and spontaneous (that is, not based on forms, but on processes). For this reason, the best metaphor we are able to employ to describe our personal vision of the "good society" is one in which community is seen as artwork, citizen as artist—but in which community is also artist, and citizen the work of art. The codetermining, conditional, and essentially relational nature of the process by which we forsee future community/citizens coming into being is fundamentally opposed to a world of imposed and rigid forms, whether idealized or deconstructed. Within such a community, both artist and art are continuously dependent on each other. The common good is the desire for the creation of the masterpiece, the common bond is the knowledge that it can never be done. From the living dialectic of possibilities, through the relations of citizens to each other, through the common bond of creation (development), what is created will be an ever-changing but deeply impassioned expression of community. As Antoine de Saint-Exupery has noted: "Man is but a network of relationships, and these alone matter to him" (p. 176). It is the ways in which we relate to one another within context which ultimately offers us the means to conscious participation in the full range of historical, present and future, living expressions of community.

ACKNOWLEDGMENT

The Lumpen Society membership consists of the following individuals (in no particular order): L.B. Miller, N. Garside and D.L.Y. Bavington. It should be noted that this paper was conceived, debated, and written as a communal effort and as such, no first authorship should be taken as implied by the mere physical ordering of the authors' names.

NOTES

1.   In particular, our backgrounds include biology, ecology, geography and political science. One anonymous reviewer commented "this reader wonders to what audience specifically the paper is directed: sociologists? environmental sociologists?

resource managers? ecologists? community activists?" While we must thank this reviewer for their assistance in contributing many insightful and helpful comments on the body of this work, we take the comment regarding the apparently amorphous content of our intended audience as a measure of some success.

2. For example, this debate might be recognized in political discourse as the liberal vs. communitarian distinction. The number of disparate realms in which this debate arises would seem to indicate a broader social (versus merely disciplinary) trend which will be explored later in this essay.

3. This debate is often characterized as the well known "Tragedy of the Commons" as framed by Garret Hardin (1968). This has also been described as an argument over the political, economic and social differences between private and public property. Hardin's neo-Hobbesian argument and its assumptions have formed the foundation of resource management policies dealing with fisheries, forests and wildlife—often with unexpected, unsustainable and frequently disastrous results.

,4. This may be seen as a variation of the Noble Savage argument—community is represented as pure, ecological, rural, and inherently good in much the same way that aboriginal peoples have been historically described as noble (but quaint) savages.

5. Ironically, this cataloging of endless identities in human groups can be seen to flow both from modernist assumptions and positivist practices. Such deconstructions take apart the whole (community) to discover its essence (various identities) in much the same way Newtonian physicists aimed to describe the fundamental units of the atom first by identifying electrons, protons and neutrons as the fundamental units and underlying essence of the whole atom, and then continuing to interrogate and fracture the whole to discover quarks, neutrinos, quirks, and others in what now seems an endless refraction and differentiation to increasingly smaller scales.

6. Who are able to force their experience and perspective onto the broader society by virtue of their assumed authority to construct the "ideal."

7. In this way, the deconstructionist view of community exists in fundamental opposition to the romantic idyll previously described. As such, this view of community defines its position through an oppositional dialectic referring to and relying on the idyllic image as the base for all its interrogations.

8. The cost of these houses (from $189,900 and up!) certainly indicates that membership in this particular community comes through the homogenizing force of a price filter.

9. This can be seen as but part of the never-ending extension of the "inverted millenarianism" (the end of ideology, the individual (subject), history, art, class, social democracy, Nature) noted by Jameson (1991) in *Postmodernism: The Cultural Logic of Late Capitalism.*

10. Note here the difference between this conception of "community" (or rather, its lack) as individualistic/disordered and the elements of the romantic, idyllic notion of community in the human realm (stable, self-reliant).

11. This principle of frugality is attributed to the fourteenth century philosopher William of Ockham: "neither more, nor more onerous, causes are to be assumed than are necessary to account for the phenomena" (Pearson 1937). Yet reaching consensus about which theory is "simplest" in ecology is never so straightforward as Colinvaux would have us believe.

12.   Grassland disturbances apparently include mole tunnels and worm burrows. Once considered among the most stable environments, grasslands have been recast as disturbance ridden by some ecologists. This rationale is best described in Pickett and White (1985, pp. 154-155).

13.   As any modern student of ecology could likewise tell you, today much of Clements' theory is denigrated as being "sound for its time, but fundamentally mistaken." Clements, like Lamarck, is relegated to the ignoble fate of subtle ridicule.

14.   The unity of Canada is apparently in question, and any commonality within the fragmented former Soviet satellites has proved insufficient to prevent continued conflict based on further fragmentation (ethnic categories).

15.   Or alternately, in his 1994 review of ecological history Worster notes: "Humans had become a profoundly disturbing element in the natural environment, and in reaction, *ecologists* began to find the environment itself a disturbing thing" (p. 389, emphasis added).

16.   We gratefully acknowledge the assistance of Lee Herrin in the construction of this particular etymology.

17.   As Etzioni (1996) has pointed out, the mere inability to precisely define a term does not negate its usefulness as a concept (see his discussion of "chair" in this light). Nevertheless, in this particular case, we feel that the political nature of community within current discourse, as well as what we perceive as the potential of a deep understanding of community, makes an interrogation of its definition (or lack thereof) a worthwhile endeavor.

18.   Again, Etzioni (1996) in addition to others, has described this as a "community of communities" (cf. Bookchin 1987, 1985) or a hierarchical nesting of allegiance or participation (cf. Bateson 1972).

19.   See the previous section "History as Disturbance" for a more detailed account of this argument.

20.   That is, we can measure the wave-length of refracted and subsequently reflected light, but we cannot empirically determine the *color* of any given object.

21.   Indeed, the famous drug-maker Eli Lily placed the following phrase on all of his drug bottles in the early years of his company: "a drug without side effects is not a drug at all" (McKnight 1995, p. 68).

22.   The term iatrogenic is usually associated with medical procedures that end up causing illness. Both Ivan Illich and John McKnight have extended the terms' usage to refer to services which cause what they are designed to prevent (McKnight 1995; Illich 1977, 1973).

23.   This is often illustrated with the example of the fish out of water: a fish only realizes what water is when it is removed from it. When we are embedded in contexts they are transparent (Evernden 1985).

24.   This term is borrowed from Henry Skolimowski who suggests that in current society economism is understood as "a philosophical doctrine which claims (implicitly or explicitly) that economics—the bottom line economics, that isDdetermines the structure and the ethos of society and should be unconditionally obeyed for it is our God" (1991, p. 123).

25.   John Ralston Saul has discussed the role of citizenship under what he calls "The Dictatorship of Reason in the West." This Dictatorship, Saul believes, creates the corporatist ideology in which we are currently embedded. Saul believes that

through the dictatorship of reason and the application of rationality above and
beyond other human qualities such as common sense, creativity and imagination,
ethics, intuition and memory, the West has become nothing more than a collection
of unconscious, corporate interest groups and managers rather than conscious
disinterested citizens capable of living an examined life based on the virtue and
acceptance of uncertainty and the celebration of doubt (Saul 1995, p. 190).

26.   While Laclau and Mouffe are critical of the communitarian view of politics,
which is similar (but not identical) to the view of community we have been
promoting, they likely would not speak directly to Baudrillard's notion of *the masses.*
We believe radical democracy understood as "a form of politics which is founded
not on dogmatic postulations of any 'essence of the social,' but, on the contrary,
on affirmation of the contingency and ambiguity of every 'essence,' and on the
constitutive character of social division and antagonism" (Laclau and Mouffe 1985,
p. 193), can help us to envision a community and politics in a way which frees us
from the constraints of the postmodern condition and the limitations of a premodern
communitarian notion of an objective common good.

REFERENCES

Bateson, G. 1972. *Steps to an Ecology of Mind.* New York: Ballantine Books.
Baudrillard, J. 1994. "Maleficent Ecology." Pp. 78-88 in *The Illusion of the End.*
    Stanford, CA: Stanford University Press.
————. 1983a. *Simulations.* New York: Semiotext(e).
————. 1983b. *In the Shadow of the Silent Majorities.* New York: Semiotext(e).
Bauman, Z. 1992. *Intimations of Postmodernity.* London: Routledge.
Bavington, B. 1996. Personal Communication with Dean Bavington, Toronto,
    Ontario, October 20th.
Bookchin, M. 1987. *The Rise of Urbanization and the Decline of Citizenship.* San
    Francisco: Sierra Club Books.
Bookchin, M. 1995. *Re-enchanting Humanity: A Defense of the Human Spirit
    Against Anti-humanism, Misanthropy, Mysticism and Primitivism.* New
    York: Cassell Books.
Buchsbaum, R. and M. Buchsbaum. 1957. *Basic Ecology.* Pacific Grove, CA:
    Boxwood Press.
Camus, A. 1955. *The Myth of Sisyphus:* New York: Vintage Books.Clark, J. 1993.
    "Utopian Dreams and Nightmares." In *Anarchism: Community and Utopia.*
    edited by L. Sekdj and V. Tomek. Praha: Filosoficky.
Clements, F. 1916. *Plant Sucession.* Washington: n.p.
Colinvaux, P. 1978. *Why Big Fierce Animals Are Rare.* New Jersey: Princeton Press.
de Saint-Exupery, A. n.d. *Pilote de Guerre,* 176. n.p.
Drury, W H. and I.C.T. Nisbet. 1973. "Succession" *Journal of the Arnold
    Arboreturm* 54(July): 331-368.
Etzioni, A. 1996. "The Responsive Community: A Communitarian Perspective."
    American Sociological Review. 61: 1-11.

Evernden, N. 1985. *The Natural Alien: Humankind and Environment*. Toronto: University of Toronto Press.

Gleason, H.A. 1926. "The Individualistic Concept of the Plant Association." *Bulletin of Torrey Botanical Club*. 53: 7-26.

Globe and Mail. 1996. "Vernon Massacre." April 13: D5.

Hardin, G. 1968. "The Tragedy of the Commons." *Science* 162: 1243-1248.

Heidegger, M. 1971. "Building, Dwelling, Thinking." In *Poetry, Language, Thought*. New York: Harper & Row, Publishers, Inc.

Illich, I. 1977. *Toward a History of Needs*. Berkeley: Heyday Books.

_____. 1973. *Tools for Conviviality*. New York: Harper & Row.

Jameson, F. 1991. *Postmodernism: The Cultural Logic of Lake Capitalism*. Durham, NC: Duke University Press.

Keller, E.F., and E. Lloyd. 1992. *Keywords in Evolutionary Biology*. Cambridge, MA: Harvard University Press.

Laclau, E., and C. Mouffe. 1985. *Hegemony & Socialist Strategy: Towards a Radical Democractic Politics*. London: Verso.

Luke, T. 1991. "Community and Ecology." *Telos*, 69-79.

McKnight, J. 1995. *The Careless Society; Community and its Counterfeits*. New York: Basic Books.

Miller, L.B. 1995. "Living Without Walls: The Idea of Community Control." Unpublished term paper, University of Victoria.

Mouffe, C. 1995. "Post-Marxism: Democracy and Identity." *Environment and Planning: Society and Space* 13: 259-265.

_____. 1993. *The Return of the Political*. London: Verso.

_____. 1992. "Discussion." *October* 61: 33-41.

Nietzsche, F. 1964. *Complete Works*, edited by O. Levy. New York: n.p.

Pearson, K. 1937. *The Grammar of Science*. London: Dent.

Pickett, S.T.A., and P.S. White. (eds). 1985. *The Ecology of Natural Disturbance and Patch Dynamics*. Orlando, FL: n.p.

Poerksen, U. 1995. *Plastic Words: The Tyranny of a Modular Language*. Trans. by J. Mason and D. Cayley. Pennsylvannia: Pensylvannia State University Press.

Rogers, R. 1996. Personal Communication to the authors, Toronto, Ontario, February.

Sachs, W. 1992. *The Development Dictionary*. London: Zed Books.

Sapp, J. 1994. "Symbiosis and Disciplinary Demarcations: The Boundaries of the Organism." *Symbiosis* 17: 91-115.

Saul, J.R. 1995. *The Unconscious Civilization*. Concord: Anansi Press Ltd.

Shepard, P. 1995. "Virtually Hunting Reality in the Forests of Simulacra." In *Reinventing Nature: Responses to Postmodern Deconstruction*, edited by M. Soule and G. Lease. Washington: Island Press.

Skolimowski, H. 1991. "Ecology, Education and the Real World." *The Trumpeter* 8(3): 123-125.

Taylor, D., and J. Wilson. 1994. "Ending the Watershed Battles: B.C. Forest Communities Seek Peace through Local Control." *Environments* 22(3): 93-102.

Worster, D. 1995. "Nature and the Disorder of History" In *Reinventing Nature? Responses to Postmodern Deconstruction,* edited by M.E. Soule and G. Lease. Washington: Island Press.

_____. 1994. *Nature's Economy: A History of Ecological Ideas.* Cambridge: Cambridge University Press.

PART III

ENVIRONMENTAL ISSUES AND COMMUNITY ACTIVISM/CHANGE

TECHNOLOGICAL CHANGE AND GLOBAL CHANGE:
TOWARD A FLEXIBLE ENVIRONMENT

Joel Novek

ABSTRACT

During the 1970s much of the environmental literature was highly critical of advanced technology as responsible for widespread ecological destruction. Limits to growth seemed to require a radical reorientation and downsizing of prevailing technologies. More recent theories of sustainable development, global change and ecological modernization, however, offer a more benign view of technology as a partner in managing environmental concerns rather than a destructive force. Changing perceptions of technology in the environmental movement are related to changing socio-political circumstances such as the rise of neo-conservatism, globalization, and distributional conflicts both within and among nations. These differing perceptions of technology and growth remain highly contested within the environmental movement. Two case studies are

Research in Community Sociology, Volume 7, pages 63-94.
Copyright © 1997 by JAI Press Inc.
All rights of reproduction in any form reserved.
ISBN: 0-7623-0272-0

presented illustrating the use of ecological modernization to manage
if not to resolve a politically divisive environmental dispute.

During the 1970s a growing environmental literature unleashed a
powerful critique of industrial technology as the villain in an ongoing
drama of ecological destruction. The solution to environmental
problems appeared to require a radical reorientation and downsizing
of prevailing technologies. More recent theories of sustainable
development and global change offer a more benign view of advanced
technology as a partner in managing environmental concerns rather
than an agent of destruction. It is part of the solution rather than
part of the problem. This essay will examine some of the changing
perceptions of technology in the environmental movement and relate
them to the broader social and political context in which ecological
concerns are debated. Two case studies are presented illustrating the
use of "green" technology to manage, though not necessarily to
resolve, a politically divisive environmental conflict.

Throughout the decades of post World War II consensus and
economic growth, especially the prosperous 1950s and 1960s, the
dominant tendency in the social science literature was to regard
advanced technology as progressive—as constituting a positive force
for good. Technological advancement meant economic growth and
that meant higher living standards, longer life expectancy and greater
quality of life for ever larger numbers of people. There were some
worms in the apple. Social critics such as Mumford (1961), who
warned of urban deterioration, and Carson (1962), who warned of
poisoned air, water and soil, drew attention to threats to human
health and well being contained within our technological expansion.
Nevertheless, the leading trend was positive. The ghost of Malthus
could be thwarted once again as higher levels of technology permitted
both population growth and rising living standards. The economist
Galbraith (1967) and the sociologist Bell (1965) agreed that advancing
technology would bring about a convergence of socio-cultural
systems and the emphasis would shift to using our knowledge to
manage common problems.

The prevailing point of view was that human domination of nature
was both possible and necessary. Our commitment to technological
progress and instrumentally-rational action, as elaborated in the
Marxist-Weberian tradition of political economy, gave us the tools

to manage and control nature in the interest of human development. The possibility that this commitment could have an ultimately destructive impact was either ignored, especially in the social sciences, or remained very much a minority point of view.

LIMITS TO GROWTH

Events of the late 1960s and 1970s delivered a serious setback to such dreams of a managed world. The energy crisis which resulted in a quadrupling of oil prices, heightened awareness of population growth, pollution and ecological deterioration, and the inreasingly visible activities of the environmental, peace and anti-nuclear movements all contributed to a sense of environmental insecurity. The publication of Limits to Growth by the Club of Rome in 1972 inaugurated a series of critical assaults on the impact and direction of industrial technology. In their computer model which examined the relationship among population, industrial production, pollution and resource consumption, the Limits to Growth researchers (Meadows 1972) were led to pessimistic conclusions. Rising population and economic growth would inevitably strain the carrying capacity of planet earth beyond the breaking point, ensuring that industrial society as we know it would be unsustainable. Although widely criticised for its assumptions and methodology, Limits to Growth did succeed in raising once again the Malthusian spectre of limits on unfettered technological expansion. It also represented a "catastrophist" prediction of doom backed up by the authority of science—a mode of environmental claim which remains popular, especially among disseminators of the theory of global warming.

In a similar fashion, biologist Barry Commoner (1971) criticized the "tunnel vision" inherent in the design of modern industrial technology in which narrow solutions are sought for specific problems and which often result in severe environmental impacts. The engineering approach tends to be segmented rather than wholistic and separated from and antagonistic to the environment. Commoner (1971) provided the example of petro-chemical based detergents containing phosphates which had been responsible for a considerable amount of water pollution in North America. In this case technological tunnel vision had dirtied our waters while trying to get our clothes clean. One problem's solution simply lead to the creation of a host of other problems which our relatively narrow technological focus is not designed to solve.

The growing concern with technology's environmental impact began to find its way into the social sciences. A small group of economists such as Henderson (1978) and Daly (1977) began to explore the economic implications of changing our institutional direction from an overarching commitment to economic growth to one of preserving nature while enhancing our quality of life. The new economics of the steady state emphasized redistribution rather than continued economic growth and the conservation of communities and social bonds as well as nature. The environmental impact associated with developments would be treated as a cost in an economic analysis rather than sidestepped as an externality. The tendency to reduce both nature and human beings to factors of production was now effectively challenged within economics.

Sociology also began to re-examine the relationship between human communities and the natural environment, spawning the new subdiscipline of environmental sociology. Catton and Dunlap (1978) proclaimed the end of "human exceptionalism" and the start of the "new enviromental paradigm" in which human beings would no longer be studied apart from nature. Instead, sociology must take into account our status as biological entities enmeshed in and dependent upon the natural world. However, Schnaiberg's (1980) notion of the "societal-environmental dialectic" would have more profound implications for the analysis of technological change. Drawing on the classical political economy of Marx and Weber, as well as ecological theory, Schnaiberg argued that there was a fundamental contradiction between the need of advanced capitalist and state socialist societies to expand versus the need of the natural environment for stability. Driven by the "treadmill of production" to produce more in order to avoid the inevitable distributional conflicts of a steady state, advanced economies must inevitably draw down their resource base through environmental additions and withdrawals which, in turn, must threaten their ability to maintain productive activity. In a more extreme version of the same Malthusian position, Catton (1980) held that human societies had already long exceeded the earth's carrying capacity by reckless pollution and resource extraction. Payback time was just around the corner.

The limits to growth perspective played a major role in raising questions about our continued commitment to economic growth and the energy and resource consuming technologies on which we depend. It stimulated thinking about possible political responses to a threatened eco-catastrophe. It also paved the way for a search for alternatives to the technology of advanced industrialism and this search generated an impressive amount of intellectual energy.

APPROPRIATE TECHNOLOGY

Appropriate technology or AT represented both an approach to the social contruction—or perhaps to the de-construction—of advanced technology and a social movement dedicated to the transformation of the basic processes of industrial production and personal consumption. AT held that modern technology was not an unalterable force of production but rather a socially and culturally-based design for living which could be changed in order to pursue less destructive ends. Human agency plays a vital role in the design of tools which should be positive and non-violent in their environmental impact. Ecological destruction and resource depletion could be avoided through the implementation of an alternative set of technologies which would be kinder and gentler to the environment as well as designed to promote more harmonious, less hierarchical social relations. The goal was self-limitation of our production and consumption democratically and cooperatively arrived at; this would obviate the need for some authoritarian political Leviathan to impose itself in the interest of environmental regulation.

Illich (1973) advocated "convivial" technologies such as bicycles and telephones which would promote personal transport and communication while being more environmentally benign than giant freeways crammed with polluting automobiles. Such technologies were also simple and cheap enough to be operated by individuals and families without requiring massive infrastructures based on large-scale investments by centralized pools of private or state capital. Thus, communities could flourish autonomously without dependence on expensive institutions of high technology such as modern hospitals, utilities and transportation systems.

Perhaps the most influential advocate of AT was Schumacher (1974) who was best known for his notion of "intermediate" technology as a middle way between the expensive energy and resource-intensive technologies of North America and Western Europe and the simpler technologies of the developing world. In his model, technology would not be designed to replace human labor with energy-consuming machines but rather to enhance a worker's productivity. Such tools would have the added virtue of being labor-intensive and thus able to contribute to employment in many communities in both the developing and developed world where good jobs were in short supply. As with Illich, individual empowerment and decentralization went hand in hand with moral exhortations to set realistic limits on production and consumption goals.

Another important aim of AT was to cement the connection between energy conservation and environmental protection. This was Lovins' approach in his work on "soft energy paths" (1977). Lovins laid out an alternative to increasing dependence on a fossil fuel and nuclear electric economy. He advocated a refocusing of our research and development priorities toward environmentally benign renewable resources with solar, wind, geo-thermal and bio-mass technologies being the most prominent. Although the short run transition from fossil and nuclear fuels might appear disruptive, in the long run we would gain from breaking our dependence on highly centralized, expensive and increasingly unstable sources of supply. A society based on soft energy would permit more local autonomy through energy self-reliance and would boost employment in the production and implementation of smaller-scale renewable technologies.

By the early 1980s, AT had become a social movement in many parts of North America and Western Europe dedicated to implementing the concepts outlined above (McRobie 1982; Nozick 1992). These included urban spaces freed from the automobile and oriented to maximizing human interaction, rural experiments in organic farming and workplaces specializing in environmentally friendly, labor-intensive technologies. Such themes had become popular among numerous non-profit, communal and progressive organizations in the voluntary/non-government (NGO) sector. AT themes had in fact become very influential in the wider environmental movement. Technologies were favored which were small in scale, decentralized in structure and attuned to local and community control. They would run, where possible, on renewable resources such as solar, wind and animate energy, would be enviromentally benign, and would maximize rather than supplant human skill.

These initiative were accompanied by a distrust of big business and the centralized welfare state as well as the dominant tendencies in science and technology in favour of bigness and expansion. Devolution, self-reliance and local autonomy were the preferred alternatives. Small businesses, voluntary organizations and community self-help groups were the favored institutions. In Ursula Franklin's (1992) terminology, technology should be "wholistic," promoting local autonomy and control, rather than "prescriptive" in which uses were externally imposed. Distributive dynamics favoured a transfer of power and wealth from corporate interests and centralized states to local communities which would be in a better position to gurantee both employment and environmental protection though labour-intensive technologies. Cuts in consumption necessary to preserve resources and the environment would be more effective because they were voluntarily rather than centrally imposed.

The AT perspective was not, however, without its problems. AT was wedded to the notion of the social construction of technology (Buttel and Taylor 1994) stressing human agency and cultural design as key factors in the conception and implementation of tools. This was necessary to open up the debate on technological alternatives but tended to exaggerate our degrees of freedom to override powerful economic, political and psychological forces which impose our technological structures. It is far from easy to transform the systems which feed us, clothe us, house us, transport us and in a multitude of ways guarantee our personal and economic security.

AT underestimated the extent of our commitment to the automobile, to mass production methods or to commercialized agribusiness. It also underestimated the continuing attachment of the majority population in the advanced industrial nations, and of growing numbers in the developing world, to the values of increasing economic growth and personal consumption. Voluntary restraints on consumption, thus, had only limited appeal. Finally, AT was largely detached from distributional and social class issues central to the political process. Industrial workers saw little future for themselves in smaller scale appropriate technology production units while leaders in marginal, rural and disadvantaged communities continued to see development in terms of large scale technology intensive projects.

NEW SOCIAL MOVEMENTS

Other environmental perspectives shared AT's concern with natural limits and an aggrandizing technology that refused to recognize those limits. Many of them came to be seen as new social movements organized against the dominant tendencies of industrial society such as consumerism and the welfare-warfare state. The anti-nuclear movement mobilized opposition both to weapons of mass production and the Cold War, and to civilian nuclear electric installations, much of whose technology flowed from the war effort (Nelkin and Pollack 1981; Babin 1985). The anti-nuclear movement was clearly a social movement whose efforts were mobilized episodically in relation to particular technical controversies such as sitings of reactors or nuclear missile bases. Anti-nuclear activists were issue driven—often they were identified with particular local contflicts—but did not offer a comprehensive program of social transformation equivalent to AT. Sometimes opposition was offered on a NIMBY basis: build your reactor elsewhere.

However, in addition to its success in opposing the proliferation of nuclear installations, the anti-nuclear movement was responsible for a critically significant contribution to the environmental movement: namely, the large scale introduction of scientific debates into environmental disputes. Whereas AT enthusiasts were often suspicious of mainstream science, anti-nuclear activists were more likely to immerse themselves in scientific analyses of nuclear fuel cycles, reactor designs, the disposal of radioactive wastes and technology/risk assessments. The anti-nuclear movement also became heavily involved in the political process and was able to take advantage of the growing popularity of public hearings into reactor licensings, and environmental reviews generally, in order to present its case. Although the anti-nuclear movement was single issue oriented, and thus of limited scope, it was able to make the case that the assessment of technological developments, and of the risks they might pose, could be subject to scientific debate and to the essentially political process of environmental review.

A growing proliferation of environmentally-oriented organizations could be grouped along a continuum according to their degree of integration into the political process, their acceptance of the findings of mainstream science and the distributional implications of their policies. At one end are the green political parties, mainly in Western

Europe, committed to achieving their agenda of environmental protection and limits on growth through formal involvement in politics. The political ecology they espoused was often aligned with other left of center community activist groups and was usually informed by scientific debates on ecological issues. They enjoyed some limited success in Western European politics (Dobson 1996) but never mounted a serious challenge to the dominant conservative and social democratic parties.

At the other extreme are a variety of radical "deep green" groups often alienated from or even hostile to the formal political process as well as environmental science. Deep ecologists, Earth First!ers and eco-feminists challenged the moral right of scientists and politicians to manage natural habitats. Direct action was often preferred to political debate and they drew on anarchist and anarcho-syndicalist traditions in their opposition to industrial society and its accoutrements. The middle ground reflects the expansion in the number and influence of environmental organizations in the voluntary and N.G.O. sector. This was especially the case in the United States where the two party monopoly effectively precluded European-style green politics but where the traditional strength of the voluntary sector offered a home for environmental groups. They range from powerful national and international organizations like Friends of the Earth, Sierra Club, Union of Concerned Scientists, and World Wildlife Fund to a multitude of locally-based community action and ecology networks. Many of these groups have enjoyed growing influence in environmental decision making (Dewar 1995) but this has come at the expense of considerable compromise on economic development issues (Gould, Weinberg, and Schnaiberg 1994).

The limits to growth perspective played an important role as a mobilizing force within the environmental movement. Predictions of eco-catastrophe in the face of business-as-usual inspired the search for alternatives to the present course. Limits to growth offered itself as the dialectical antithesis of the prevailing regime of technological expansion. Like the fable of the sorcerer's apprentice, out of control technology (Winner 1977) would surely lead to environmental disaster unless decisively checked. However, limits to growth ran into serious difficulties as a rallying cry for the Green movement seeking support in the broader political arena. Limits to growth was predicated on the assumption of a fundamental contradiction between economic growth and technological progress, on the one hand, and environmental health, on the other. This contradiction was its inheritance from its Malthusian ancestors.

At its heart was the conception of a natural environment which was a functionally integrated and closed system separate from and in opposition to human social and economic development. As in Schnaiberg's notion of a "societal-environmental dialectic" (1980), nature was static and pristine while human societies, especially advanced capitalist nation states, could only develop and grow. Human interaction with the environment was essentially destructive: the damage that we would inflict was countered by the even greater damage that a rigid and unforgiving environment would eventually impose on us.

This point of view had only limited appeal and failed to transform the fundamental commitment of the vast majority of citizens in Western societies, and of growing numbers in the developing world, to the goal of economic growth. During the early 1980s, environmental issues became less prevalent in the public agenda of most Western nations (Dunlap and Catton 1994) and limits to growth appeared as a fetter on progress, especially in the developing world. There was an important reason for this. As Schreker (1993) points out, growth remains central to the regulation of distributional struggles both within and between nation-states. Growth provides a means of generating resources to alleviate the stress on the increasing numbers of poor, unemployed and excluded in the embattled welfare states of North America and Europe. Without it, any economic resources desired to satisfy the needs of certain social segments must be conceded by other social segments or else commanded by an authoritarian state (Ophuls 1977; Paehlke and Torgerson 1990).

The same logic applies to North-South distributional issues. Limits to growth not only provoked both a "corporate veto" and trade union opposition in rich nations, it also aroused concern in poorer nations that their development efforts would be checkmated. Growth allows poorer nations to develop without seriously threatening the living standards in richer ones. Thurow's (1980) notion of the politics of zero-sum aptly describes the ferocious conflicts that can ensue when groups compete over their variable shares of a stagnant economic "pie." To the extent that a rising standard of living in developing nations would require corresponding cuts in consumption in the developed world, the stage would be set for an intensification of North-South distributional conflict.

If limits to growth had defined the environment as relatively rigid and static, ultimately hostile to human intrusion, it had also defined technology as rapacious, threatening and out of control. The critique of technology was quintessentially a critique of industrial technology: a technical system which grew by substituting resources and inanimate energy for human labor. However, the explosion of computers, networks, hardware and software over the past decade has changed the face of technology. There have also been major advances in energy conversion and materials science. These changes, along with a shift to services and information in employment activity, mean that doing "more with less" becomes a real possibility with mainstream technology. At the very least, environmentalists can no longer ignore or dismiss the significance of these developments which have spawned a growing literature in the social sciences on the shift to a post-industrial economy (Myles 1991) and to "ecological modernization" (Mol and Spaargaren 1993) as an important organizing principle of economic activity.

A further set of problems facing the environmental movement stemmed from its emphasis on local solutions to local problems. This was particularly the case for AT with its support of voluntarism and its suspicion of large scale organizations and centralized, externally-imposed controls on behavior. However, it had become abundantly clear that a new category of environmental problem had arisen, one which included the spread of acid rain and the depletion of the earth's ozone layer, and which was neither local in origin nor amenable to localized solutions. Environmentalism seemed to require a broader scale of analysis just as the expanding international division of labor and the integration of developing nations into the world market economy has changed the way we think about economics and trade.

Finally, environmentalism has had to come to terms with neo-conservatism which as a political ideology and as a social movement has had an enormous impact on the governance of the advanced societies over the past decade. With some notable exceptions (Paehlke 1989; Buttel 1992), environmentalists have not devoted much attention to the consideration of neo-conservative approaches. There appear to be some interesting parallels between the environmental and neo-conservative movements which are at least as striking as their obvious differences. Both movements have arisen in the vaccuum created by the weakening of the postwar welfare state regimes in the wealthy democracies of North America and Western

Europe. This weakening has been attributed to the decline of political coalitions led by labor or socialist parties; to the decline of the traditional blue collar working class in the transition to a post-industrial economy; to the emergences of a much more polarized class structure which has thwarted efforts to construct solidarities among competing occupational groups; and to the erosion of social protection in the face of globalized labor markets (Teeple 1995).

Environmentalists and neo-conservatives have been critical of the traditional post-war welfare states. Both have opposed centralized big government solutions and have favored decentralization with an emphasis on small business, voluntarism and individual and community responsibility. Here the similarities end. Neo-conservatism has maintained and reinforced a loyalty to the tenets of the capitalist system, to the marketplace as the solution to most distributional problems and to the imperatives of economic growth which goes well beyond what most environmentalists accept. The message of economic growth and privatization has proven politically popular to the extent that economic stagnation, rising costs and intractable distributional conflicts have hobbled so many government welfare policies (Mishra 1990).

The rise of neo-conservatism alongside the collapse of East European state socialism and the advent of a globalized market economy has constrained the future of the environmental movement in important ways (Buttel 1992; Buttel and Taylor 1994; Sklair 1994). Whether in governing coalitions, in opposition or outside the political process, environmentalists and green activists have had to come to terms with a political process strongly oriented to growth and the marketplace.

GLOBAL CHANGE

In the 1980s a new portrait of the environment began to emerge, one which was more dynamic, more flexible and more open to interchange with human society than what had previously been the standard. There was a de-emphasis on the functionalist or equilibrium view of the environment as a tightly integrated closed system frozen in space and time and unable to adapt to change (Odum 1971). Instead, a new paradigm developed out of the environmental sciences which was global in scope and based on change processes rather than homeostasis (Lewontin 1991). It was thus oriented to such issues as climate change, deforestation, desertification and biodiversity which are linked to very broad ecological transformations. They are also linked to human activities such as economic expansion, technological development and population growth (Burton and Timmerman 1989) which are seen as having a wide ranging and continuous impact on environmental change. In a break with the previous limits to growth perspective, human impact on the environment can in fact be positive in terms of sustainability and biodiversity (Hecht and Cockburn 1989).

Change processes themselves are conceived as complex, evolutionary and organic (Burton and Timmerman 1989; Christensen 1996). The focus is on disequilibrium, instability and non linear processes, rather than stasis, as normality. Chaos theory and open systems theory (Starkloff 1995), rather than equilibirium theory, are now exerting considerable influence on the environmental sciences. Starkloff (1995, p. 113) observes:

> Ecosystems are but the relationships and interactions of their participants. They are temporarily and spatially open, and thus volatile. They exhibit persitent change produced by multitudes of integrative and destructive forces.

A recent report on ecosystem management by the Ecological Society of America (Christensen 1996) makes the following points: ecosystems can be characterized by their complexity and connectedness, their dynamic character, their sustainability and their capacity to operate over a wide range of contexts and scales. Human impact on the environment is normal and can in fact be positive for maintaining sustainable activities. This is especially the case for sophisticated technologies and management techniques which would allow human societies to effectively "manage" the environment.

Just as the social sciences had earlier largely discarded theoretical models of equilibrium in favor of perspectives on disequilibrium and change, so too had the environmental sciences. However, it was environmental natural scientists rather than social scientists who were the first to impose this new perspective on the broader environmental movement. Social scientists largely followed the lead of natural scientists to redefine environmental thinking in the wake of newly perceived global realities (Vaillancourt 1995; Dunlap and Catton 1994). The publication of the Brundtland Report on sustainable development (1987) followed by the Tokyo Symposium on Climate Change in 1988 and the Rio Earth Summit in 1992 all played a major role in publicizing global environmental concerns. As Vaillancourt (1994, p. 18) observed:

> The participants' insistance on biodiversity, climate change, dwindling forests and desertification, and waste of all kinds, prodded the environmental social scientists to follow the example of the environmental natural scientists, in reorienting their research towards the larger global environmental problems of the day, and to better organize themselves at the international and national levels, in order to establish links among themselves and the natural science specialists and the social movement activists already established in these areas.

This new image of the environment as dynamic, flexible and open to interchange with human societies has had important social implications for the future of environmental politics. The break with limits to growth and the more positive role accorded economic development and technology in maintaining sustainability enabled environmentalists to get a better hearing in rich nations dominated by neo-conservatism and in developing nations which see no alternative to a strategy of growth. A rigid adherence to Malthusianism has been quietly jettisoned, though a more flexible "eco-catastrophist" variant has been retained. Nature may no longer impose sharp limits on human activities but potential disasters such as global warming, ozone depletion or deforestation remain a clear and present, even an increasing, danger unless appropriate steps are taken to manage our interchanges with the environment. Greater tolerance of the economic activities characteristic of advanced capitalist society coupled with threats of eco-catastrophe if suggested policies are not followed have given environmentalists more credibility in political debates.

The new perspective is global rather than local (Buttel 1992; Sklair 1994). The focus on environmental dynamics, on the interconnection of ecological components, and on problem areas such as acid rain or global warming has supported an outlook which is trans-national in scope. According to the new thinking, if problems develop at the regional or global level then solutions must be transnational as well. Environmental organizations have become active in national politics or lobbying in a number of major industrial nations as well as in key regional bodies such as the European Commission. Equally important, they have become influential in an administative role in leading international organizations such as the United Nations, World Bank, and International Monetary Fund (Dewar 1995; Buttel 1992). This has given environmental groups some limited influence over decisions affecting trade, aid and international development. However, it also means that the environmental movement no longer can unequivocally stand as the defender of local communities against the centralized power of trade flows, capital flows and development projects (Daly and Cobb 1989). The global environment becomes one more instance of the concept of globalization (Sklair 1994), along with a global economy (Teeple 1995) and a global system of stratification (Reich 1991).

The global point of view represents an important break with earlier environmental emphases on social and technological structures which were small in scale, decentralized and locally controlled. The AT vision of technology appropriate to a particular region, community or ecological niche has been de-emphasized in favor of an environmental role in policy development, technological design or regulation at the national or international level. Some environmentalists have even criticized community control in ecological matters as potentially dangerous because community leaders may not be sufficiently well educated in environmental matters to be able to truly judge the issues and might be too prone to compromise with developers, especially where local jobs are at stake (Gould 1991). The result, however, is a split in the environmental movement between the dominant global paradigm and the more communitarian perspective linked to the earlier AT and limits to growth orientation which insists that local control is essential for achieving environmental harmony (Shiva 1988).

If the environmental movement seems to be more attuned to the centers of political and economic influence, rather than the margins of local autonomy, one reason is the much greater prominence of scientific and technological advances in environmental thinking. It is very clear that recent developments in the natural sciences concerned with the environment, as discussed above, have played an important role in the social construction of the concept of global change (Buttel and Taylor 1994). Scientific expertise which was once rejected as the handmaiden of domination and destruction of the biosphere is now acknowledged as a necessary basis for an effective environmental policy. The claims which environmental groups make on the public policy process are increasingly scientific claims, supported or refuted by the evidence of environmental science. The ties between research and public policy are also becoming more evident in the environmental disciplines, similar to the well established ties between research and public policy in economics.

The global change perspective has also largely discarded the suspicion of advanced technology characteristic of AT and limits to growth. This is particularly the case with the commitment to sustainable development (Brundtland 1987; Ramphal 1992) which argues that economic development is compatible with environmental preservation if the rights of future generations to a healthy biosphere are not compromised. According to this point of view, technological advances enable human societies to support a given population at a higher level of affluence with less environmental damage than would be possible at lower levels of technological sophistication. "Green technologies" which enable us to do more with less resource extraction and waste handling can be a positive force for ecological health. Developing nations will be in a better position to manage their ecological endowments as they acquire the advanced techniques of energy conversion, materials processing and waste treatment characteristic of the advanced economies.

Not all environmentalists are happy with this newfound acceptance of science and technology as positive forces. For some, these forces are basically regressive and represent a return to an earlier era of "man over nature" (Clow 1995) in which an instrumentally-rational view prevailed and the environment was to be disposed of in the human drive for growth and mastery. This is really a split between "deep" and "shallow" shades of green (Sklair 1994). "Shallow green" environmentalists maintain that the biosphere can be effectively managed in the interests of present and future generations. "Deep green" environmentalists, on the other hand, take a more tragic point of view. For them, the relationship between the biosphere and a globalized economy and its counterpart, a global culture of consumption, remains contradictory and irreconcilable.

ENVIRONMENTAL MANAGEMENT

What is really at stake is the issue of whether or not the environment can be effectively managed in the interest of the vast majority of stakeholders. The new global change perspective assumes such management is not only possible but necessary and this assumption has been termed "environmental management" (Redclift 1987), "eco-managerialism" (Starkloff 1995), or the "management of global change" (Burton and Timmerman 1989). Modern environmental management is a socially constructed paradigm which seeks to control the interchange between ecological orders and human societies. Images of harmony and integration are established among human actors and between human and environmental systems. Nation-states, transnational corporations, labor unions, regional federations and local communities are all encouraged to cooperate in the interests of ecological order. The forces of disorder and conflict are to be controlled, appeased or mitigated.

Environmental management serves as a cognitive planning tool which is designed to accomplish the transformation of disorderly social reality into harmony and optimization (Starkloff 1995). It also serves as a potent ideological force to bring about the very cooperative forms of behavior it assumes are necessary and desirable. We are advised to behave in conformity with the new "global social contract" (Burton and Timmerman 1989). Behavior which does not conform to the new model threatens to bring into play the big stick of global eco-catastrophe.

Environmental management also represents a set of precepts which have much in common with contemporary theories of workplace management. Both employ consensus models which assume that problems can be managed through the cooperation of the human actors involved. Conflicts and contradictions are to be resolved or marginalized. Both rely on the authority of science. Workplace management has shifted from an earlier emphasis on scientific management to a much broader range of control theories such as cybernetics, human systems engineering, statistical process control and motivational theory. The "knowledge worker" (Drucker 1993) is at the center of the new scientifically based workplace. Environmental management is based on the disciplines of environmental natural science and engineering which have defined our understanding of such issues as global warning, forestry and waste management. Scientific credentials establish what is seen as a legitimate hierarchy of authority and power.

Finally, environmental management, like workplace management, is global in scope, concerned with adaptation to the problems of flux, uncertainty and change. Workplace management has become "post-Fordist" (Piore and Sabel 1984; Reich 1991), dealing with markets which are global rather than national, and dynamic and flexible rather than static. In an interesting analogy to the biological world, this change parallels the shift of environmental thinking to more dynamic open systems existing in complex and continuous interchange with human social orders. Success goes to those who know how to ride the tiger of global change rather than try to suppress it. Modern management accepts the inevitability of volatility and uncertainty instead of a futile attempt to force turbulent reality into a static Procrustean bed.

ECOLOGICAL MODERNIZATION

Of course, environmental management and the new "global social contract" are in keeping with a policy of capitalist-led economic growth as well as the neo-conservative mood prevalent in the majority of advanced nations and a growing number of developing ones. This growth will be maintained by a technological orientation which incorporates environmental concerns into advanced technology. Radical social change will be unnecessary because our major economic and political organizations will adapt themselves to changing requirements by gradually implementing environmentally friendly or "green" technologies. This policy of preserving our basic economic institutions by carefully transforming our technological infrastructure has been termed "ecological modernization" (Mol and Spaargaren 1993), "environmentalization" (Buttel 1992), "greening" (Yearly 1991) or "technical environmentalism" (Schnaiberg 1985).

   Ecological modernization contains several key elements. First is a commitment to sustainable development which means economic growth with the minimum possible environmental impact. Technology serves as a key intervening variable between human and ecological orders with the potential to significantly reduce or mitigate environmental harm. The goal of technological advances is to achieve more efficiency in the transformation of energy and materials into useful products and services (Clow 1995). This also means the production of more durable and recyclable products which generate less waste. Resources are to be extracted and wastes are to be disposed of in ways that do not disrupt the biosphere.

Secondly, "dematerialization" (Herman, Ardakani, and Ausubel 1989) refers to the positive environmental effects of structural change resulting from de-linking economic growth from its dependence on environmentally intensive inputs and outputs (Simonis 1989). A new branch of environmental engineering is devoted to a reduction in the resource inputs of production leading to a parallel reduction of emissions and waste. There is an emphasis on the development of integrated technologies which are more efficient and which do more with less rather than "end of pipe" technologies which tend to be costly add-ons designed to contain environmental damage once it has occurred. This process of structural change is well underway in most advanced nations which have seen more of their economic activity composed of information and services and less of resource-intensive transformations (Simonis 1989). In most rich countries the former strong correlation between economic growth and environmental additions and withdrawals is starting to diminish as the industrial mix gradually changes from resource-based to information-based technologies. However, in the developing world, progress is slower and far less evident.

A third component of ecological modernization involves an emphasis on risk analysis and prevention in environmental policy (Mol and Spaargaren 1993). The goal is to change the policy orientation from "react and cure" strategies designed to repair damage after it has occurred to more forward looking "anticipate and prevent" strategies (Simonis 1989). React and cure strategies may be too late to repair to repair severe damage to particular ecosystems once it has set in. They may also be very expensive to implement and raise important equity concerns about who pays the cost of any particular cleanup.

Preventive policies are superior in theory as they permit the anticipation and control of future impacts from particular technologies or development projects (Simonis 1989). They have, however, proven difficult to implement in practice. Environmental Impact Assessment (EIA) remains the form of technology assessment and damage prevention with the longest track record of experience in implementation, especially in North America (Koebberling 1990). EIA allows for the targeting of specific investment projects and imposes the burden of proving that the project is justified on the project initiator. EIA also represents an important instance of the growing focus on the social construction of technological risk (Clarke and Short 1993) which is perceived as the definition of acceptable risk in the face of economic benefits and environmental hazards. Implementation remains difficult because EIA cannot deliver certainty but is dependent on a balance among often competing scientific claims, changing societal notions of acceptable risk, and a variable political decision making process. The result is a set of compromises between shifting scientific and political currents.

Finally, ecological modernization requires the incorporation of ecological priniciples into the accounting systems on which a modern economy is run. This is difficult to achieve because nature has largely served as an exploited factor of production—a source for raw materials extraction and a sink for wastes to be deposited (Simonis 1989). The conflict between ecology and economy has largely been treated as a problem of negative external effects or "externalities" with the costs of technological developments transferred to future generations and to nature. The challenge is to reduce the impact of development by internalizing the negative externalities of production (Simonis 1989). This means an ecological accounting of our entire industrial metabolism (Herman, Ardekani, and Ausubel 1989) with its flows of energy, resources and waste materials. Resource use is to be sustainable while waste emissions are to be significantly reduced. However, ecological accounting appears to be dependent on further advances in dematerialization and green technologies which have yet to be made.

The enunciation of the global change paradigm coupled with the more specific policy tools of environmental management and ecological modernization have given environmental groups powerful new ammunition with which to assert their claims to be heard in national and trans-national political arenas. However, the dominance of the global change paradigm has raised serious concerns within the environmental movement. Critics, especially deep ecologists or "deep greens" who are skeptical that the environment can in fact be successfully "managed" by humans, have raised serious ecological and social equity concerns (Alexander 1990). They argue that fundamental contradictions in the ecological and social realms have been downplayed in the effort to craft a set of policy priniciples with positive implications for economic growth and technological expansion.

Critics claim that the compatibility between economic growth and environmental health has been asserted rather than proved and that the environment remains highly vulnerable to the destructive impact of human economic and technolgical initiatives (Rees 1990; Ekins 1989). In sum, the contradiction between economic and ecological processes has been glossed over, not resolved, and human economic activity on its present course will eventually destroy its ecological foundation (Dunlap and Catton 1994). Natural limits remain in force and growth cannot be relied on as a strategy to reduce the differentials between rich and poor. Critics worry that an over-concentration on the social construction of the global change paradigm, as opposed to real world instances of human-induced change, will mask the negative impacts resulting from the ongoing human project to manipulate nature (Murphy 1994). Limits to growth may have been de-emphasized but not entirely discarded.

A second line of attack charges that the new paradigm has failed to give adequate weight to social and political struggles over the appropriation and use of resources (Lohmann 1990). Discussions of a common future distort the extent to which the environment is a contested terrain in which conflicting political and social alliances assert competing claims to knowledge and to the implementation of their projects. Global change and environmental management seem to support the political and economic status quo of a globalized economy and transnational political processes. Critics worry that there is less concern with equity and distributional issues as influential elements within the environmental movement align themselves with politically powerful interests and are no longer able or willing to defend local communities against concentrated national and transnational power (Gould, Weinberg, and Schnaiberg 1993). At the same time, ecological modernization can be dismissed as a short term technological fix or else viewed as an inadequate means of resolving distributional issues given the limited progress made in developing "green" technologies (Simonis 1989).

A third point is that the very volatility, complexity and dis-equilibrium of open ecological systems render them resistant to efforts at environmental management and control (Starkloff 1995). Human efforts are subject to errors, incompetence and limitations of knowledge which may be magnified by the global reach of complex technological systems (Beck 1992). Furthermore, the impact of such efforts cannot be fully predictable in open, complex and dis-equilibrated systems. Risk remains an inherent component of all our interventions in nature despite the proliferation of technology assessments and EIA reviews. The increasing reliance on science is unlikely to resolve environmental disputes and more likely to become a point of contention among different groups competing for control over particular resources (Yearly 1991). Alternatively, science itself may be delegitimated as a source of uncertainty in a "risk society" obsessed by the potential for environmental disasters on a global scale (Beck 1992).

CASE STUDIES: PULP AND PAPER MEGAPROJECTS

The issue of whether or not environmental sustainability can be reconciled with economic development through the implementation of ecological modernization can be examined by means of two pulp and paper megaprojects in the Western Canadian boreal forest. In both cases, EIA and new integrated "green technologies" of pulp and paper processing were relied on in an attempt to resolve distributional conflicts surrounding the two projects. One project is the proposed expansion and conversion of the former provincially-owned Manfor mill located in The Pas in Northern Manitoba. Repap Enterprises of Montreal proposed to convert the mill into a bleached Kraft pulp operation and to expand production from 400 to 500 tons per day. The other is the Japanese-owned Alberta-Pacific (ALPAC) mill situated on the Athabasca River in Northern Alberta and claimed to be the world's largest pulp mill. It now has the capacity to produce 1,500 tons per day of bleached hardwood pulp. These projects reveal both the strengths and weaknesses of ecological modernization as a method of resolving competing claims dealing with issues of sustainability and development.

The case studies are based on two EIA reviews carried out in 1989. The one involving the Repap mill was conducted by the Manitoba Clean Environment Commission. The other, dealing with the ALPAC mill, was carried out by the Alberta Pacific Environmental Assessment Review Board. The details of the two projects and the issues at play in the EIA reviews have already been analysed (Novek and Kampen 1992; Novek 1995) and further elaboration along these lines would be unwarranted. However, it would be instructive to examine the outcome of the two EIA processes and the follow-up procedures designed to resolve the issues in dispute.

REPAP MANITOBA

Repap Enterprises of Montreal purchased the provincially-owned Manfor pulp mill in The Pas in 1989. Manfor was a money-losing operation that ran one of the few unbleached kraft mills in North America and which produced fiber for brown paper bags. Repap proposed to convert the Manfor mill into a bleached kraft operation and expand its output from 400 to 500 tons per day. The current employment level of 650 would be maintained. Bleached pulp would be shipped to Wisconsin where a Repap-owned paper mill would convert it into high grade magazine paper. However, because chlorine is normally used as the bleaching agent in the bleached kraft method of chemical pulp production, the potential environmental impact would be high. The converted Repap mill would discharge 750 kilograms of toxic adsorbable organic halogens per day into the North Saskatchewan River (Manitoba Clean Environment Commission 1989). In return for expanding the mill, Repap gained access to cutting rights over 10,400 square kilometres of forest in Northern Manitoba equivalent to about 20 percent of the province's land mass and 40 percent of its forest resources. Its annual allowable cut would be 3.2 million cubic meters or about 10 million trees, a 450 percent increase over current levels.

Manitoba has statutorily defined provisions for EIA review including public hearings before the Clean Environment Commission. However, the public hearings were divided into phases which limited the scope of what could be discussed at any particular hearing. Phase one hearings were devoted exclusively to pollution discharges from the mill which ensured that public discussion of other controversial issues such as Repap's logging practices could not be aired until a later date. Thus, Repap could obtain a licence to convert the mill before there were any public discussions of its plans to manage the 20 percent of Manitoba's land mass that had come into its possession. The phase one hearings were held in August and September, 1989, and, in November, the Clean Environment Commission recommended that Repap could proceed with its planned project (Manitoba Clean Environment Commission 1989). The provincial cabinet agreed.

However, the public hearings had aired substantial concerns about the Repap project from nothern aboriginal groups and urban environmentalists. Unlike the environmentalists, the northern aboriginals were not philosophically opposed to development but rather expressed concerns about the impact of logging and pulping on fishing, hunting, trapping and other key aspects of their livelihood. Their opposition, tentative at first, became more pronounced as testimony was presented on the potential threat posed by the mill to northern waters. In order to allay their concerns, a number of northern leaders advocated some form of community monitoring of Repap's performance in meeting environmental standards. Such monitoring would be designed to ensure that local communities, major stakeholders in the project, would have some influence over the mill's compliance with environmental regulations.

Environmentalists, on the other hand, raised concerns about over-consumption of paper and dependence on virgin timber as a source of fibre while no consideration was given to recycling as an alternative. In addition, concern was raised about the impact of large scale development on the relatively delicate ecology of the boreal forest and the lack of base line studies to provide any guidance in this area. These criticisms were widely reported. Repap, reacting to the negative publicity generated by the review process and to a downturn in the world pulp market, announced that it would not proceed with its planned expansion and conversion of the mill until all phases of the review were complete and all licenses granted. From 1990 to the end of 1995, Repap continued to manage its Manitoba operation as, essentially, a manufacturer of paper bags.

In December, 1995, Repap submitted a proposal to Manitoba Environment to construct a new mill, adjacent to its existing one in The Pas, starting in 1998 (Repap Manitoba 1995). The new mill would have a single fiber line capable of producing 500 tons of air dried pulp per day and would utilize a bleached chemical thermo-mechanical method of producing pulp. Most important, the bleaching process used to achieve the high brightness standards demanded in world pulp markets would be based on hydrogen peroxide rather than chlorine. Hydrogen peroxide is a standard bleaching agent in Scandinavian pulpmills and is now becoming more common in North America. Since no chlorine or chlorine compounds are involved, the mill design, based on advances in pulp mill technology, does away with chlorine effluent which is one of the major environmental objections to pulpmills. The new mill proposal represents a significant improvement in "green technology" over its predecessor because it relies on a more advanced integrated process which limits pollution as it produces pulp. The previous expansion and conversion proposal depended on a riskier and less elegant "end of pipe" approach under which the chlorinated effluent would be subject to primary and secondary treatment as it enters the North Saskatchewan River.

The new proposal is not foolproof. Demand on the boreal forest will be heavy as hardwood and softwood species will be logged up to a maximum of 600,000 cubic meters annually. Due to financial concerns, there are also questions as to when (and if) the mill will actually be built. Recently the existing mill in The Pas, as well as other Repap properties, have been put up for sale. Nevertheless, the new mill proposal is an instance of the principles of environmental management and ecological modernization being incorporated into a technical design.

ALBERTA PACIFIC FOREST INDUSTRIES

In Alberta, the provincial government put up 221,000 square kilometers of public forestlands covering about one third of the province for lease and seven major pulpmill developments were announced. The largest of these was the giant Alberta-Pacific (ALPAC) mill, a joint venture of two large Japanese multinationals, Mitsubishi Corp. and Honshu Paper Company. In return for agreeing to build a bleached kraft mill on the Athabaska River, ALPAC was granted cutting rights over 73,430 square kilometers of forests in the eastern Athabaska region with an annual allowable cut of 3 million cubic meters. It received $250 million in government loans and another $75 million in road and rail construction to aid logging.

In July, 1989, a joint federal-provincial assessment panel was announced to conduct a public review of the ALPAC proposal as well as the cumulative impact of other mills on the Peace-Athabasca River system (Alberta Pacific Environmental Assessment Review Board 1990). The provincial government agreed to this joint review panel in return for the right to select four of the seven panel members and to limit its terms of reference to water borne pollution to the exclusion of forestry and logging issues. Public hearings, however, were scheduled. These hearings were held in the fall of 1989 and, similar to the ones in Manitoba, generated much interest and considerable opposition to the mill from northern aboriginals and urban environmentalists.

Opposition from native groups was particularly intense due to the concentration of native communities in the vicinity of the Peace Athabaska Delta which would receive effluent from ALPAC as well as three other kraft mills. Aboriginal groups argued that their communities depend to a large extent on hunting, fishing and trapping and would be affected by widespread logging and pulping in the region. Concerns were raised about the scale of pulpmill developments planned for the Peace Athabaska region with ALPAC being merely the largest of several, and the resulting potential for damage from toxic efflluent dumping. Another important concern was the impact on native land claims of transferring large blocks of land to private management.

One of the most powerful critiques of the ALPAC proposal came from the federal Ministry of the Environment which raised the issue of the cumulative impact of pulpmill pollution on the Peace Athabaska river system. This submission to the review panel was important for several reasons. As a scientific document, the concise critique of the ALPAC proposal reduced the latter's credibility. As a political document, it brought a branch of the federal government into direct opposition to the economic development efforts of the Alberta government. Most important, the arguments presented in the Ministry of the Environment submission appeared convincing to the review panel. In March, 1990, the federal provincial review board issued a report recommending that ALPAC not proceed pending further study of cumulative pollution from existing and proposed mills (Alberta Pacific Environmental Assessment Review Board 1990).

After considerable debate, the Alberta cabinet reluctantly supported the board's recommendations. However, the pressures for development were too great to let the matter rest for any length of time. ALPAC soon released a revised proposal under which toxic emissions would be mitigated through some improvements in "green technology." The most important changes occured in the bleaching process. The bleaching tower was increased in size so that chlorine dioxide could be substituted for chlorine as a bleaching agent. The oxyen extraction stage was redesigned to accommodate hydrogen peroxide rather than chlorine. The amount of toxic adsorbable organic halogens discharged into the Athabaska River would be reduced from 1.3 kilograms per ton of pulp in the first proposal to 0.35 kilograms per ton of pulp in the second. As in the Repap case, the model was the Scandinavian experience in developing integrated technologies to reduce emissions in the pulp bleaching process, rather than "end of pipe" devices to clean up toxic wastes after they have been dumped in the river.

A second Alberta Pacific Scientific Review Panel (1990) was convened by the Alberta government with a mandate to study the feasability of the revised proposal. No other concerns could be considered within this second panel's mandate. After two months of deliberation the Scientific Review Panel recommended in favor of the revised proposal in a report which was issued in October, 1990, and quickly accepted by the Alberta cabinet. ALPAC received its licence to proced along with a modicum of scientific legitimacy. The mill is now fully constructed and has been successfully put into operation.

CONCLUSIONS: TOWARD A FLEXIBLE ENVIRONMENT?

The Repap and ALPAC case studies reveal some of the strengths and limitations of the approach based on environmental management and ecological modernization which seeks to reconcile the desire for economic growth with some degree of environmental sustainability. The goal of this aproach is to achieve social harmony through the resolution of distributional conflicts over resource use. The image is that of a flexible environment: an environment flexible enough to accommodate diverse though responsible demands on its resources without suffering unsustainable damage. Wise management and sophisticated technology precludes the need for severe limits on consumption and growth.

The Repap and ALPAC cased illustrate the partial success of this approach. The techniques of ecolgical modernization were introduced to try to resolve the toughest disputes: those between the pulpmill developers and the northern aboriginal communities concerned about their livelihood. EIA provided a forum in which scientific standards for environmental regulation could be debated and revised. It also provided a political arena in which various interested groups could assert competing claims on resource utilization and environmental management. Provincial governments responded to their contradictory roles as development promoters and as protectors of northern communities and resources by invoking EIA as a dispute resolution mechanism but then attempting to limit its scope to the relatively narrow issue of effluent discharge. This gave EIA a specific mandate on which to focus its conclusions but excluded from consideration broader questions dealing with the disposition of forest resources or even the need for the industrial development of the boreal region in the first place.

The advances in ecological modernization asked for and implemented were positive in that they assured that the mills would be based on state of the art technology designed to reduce pollution in the processing and production stage. More sophisticated technological design means less environmental stress. These improvements were, however, relatively narrow in range and technical in scope. Even from the point of view of "dematerialization" they represented only a partial advance. The implementation of full dematerialization should obviate the need for increased consumption of paper in an electronically-based information society, and thus the need to construct more pulp and paper megaprojects. The information superhighway should not be littered with paper.

Pressing social concerns were avoided rather than addressed. The role of northern Canadian communities as resource hinterlands exporting their wood fiber as pulp to the information processing centers of southern Canada, the United States and Japan was not questioned. The access of native communities to the immense forest management areas remained unresolved. Unlike the AT perspective, the new consensus in support of the global change and sustainable development points of view does not oppose a globalized economy. Technological improvements leading to a reduction of environmental damage are designed into development projects but the desirability of such projects and the escalation of needs and wants which drive them are not questioned.

In the end, certain environmental accommodations are incorporated into our basic institutions promoting economic growth and technological advance. Flexibility is the key word. We assume that our markets, transnational corporations, political systems and technological structures are flexible enough to incorporate a modest amount of green procedures into their operating systems and still remain on track for economic growth and profitability. We also assume that the environment is flexible enough to accommodate a reasonable degree of growth mitigated by scientific knowledge and environmental management techniques. If we do not accept these assumptions, then we must assume that our environment and our commitment to capitalist-led economic growth and technological advance are on a collision course.

REFERENCES

Alexander, D. 1990. "Left Ecology, Deep Ecology and Shallow Environmentalism." *Canadian Dimension* 24(1): 16-18.

Alberta-Pacific Environmental Impact Assessment Review Board. 1990. *The Proposed Alberta Pacific Pulp Mill: Report of the EIA Review Board.* Edmonton: Alberta Environment.

Alberta-Pacific Scientific Review Panel. 1990. *A Review of the Modified Wood Pulping and Bleaching Processes Proposed for Alberta Forest Industries Pulp Mill.* Edmonton: Alberta Environment.

Babin, R. 1985. *The Nuclear Power Game.* Montreal: Black Rose Books.

Beck, U. 1992. "From Industrial Society to the Risk Society: Questions of Survival, Social Structure and Ecological Enlightenment." *Theory Culture and Society* 9(1): 97-123.

Bell, D. 1985. *The End of Ideology*, Rev. ed. New York: Free Press.

Brundtland, G.H. 1987. *Our Common Future.* World Commission on Environment and Development. Oxford: Oxford University Press.

Burton, I., and P. Timmerman. 1989. "Human Dimensions of Global Change: A Review of Responsibilities and Opportunities." *International Social Science Journal.* 121: 297-313.

Buttel, F. 1992. "Environmentalization: Origins, Processes and Implications for Rural Social Change." *Rural Sociology* 57(1): 1-27.

Buttel, F., and P. Taylor. 1994. "Environmental Sociology and Global Change." Pp. 229-255 in *Social Theory and the Global Environment*, edited by Michael Redclift and Ted Benton. London: Routledge.

Carson, R. 1962. *Silent Spring.* Greenwich, CT: Fawcett.

Catton, W. 1980. *Overshoot: The Ecological Basis of Revolutionary Change.* Urbana, IL: University of Illinois Press.

Catton, W.R., and R.E. Dunlap. 1978. "Environmental Sociology: A New Paradigm?" *The American Sociologist* 13:41-49.

Christensen, N. et al. 1996. "Report of the Ecological Society of America Committee on the Scientific Basis for Ecosystem Management." *Ecological Applications* 6(3): 665-691.

Clarke, L., and J. Short. 1993. "Social Organization and Risks: Some Current Controversies." *Annual Review of Sociology* 19: 375-399.

Clow, M. 1995. "Meeting the Challenge of the 21st Century: Sociology and Environmental Degradation." Pp. 83-97 in *Environmental Sociology: Theory and Practice*, edited by Michael Mehta and Eric Ouellet. North York, Ontario: Captus Press.

Commoner, B. 1971. *The Closing Circle: Nature, Man and Technology.* New York: Knopf.

Daly, H. 1977. *Steady State Economics.* San Francisco: W.H. Freeman.
Daly, H., and Cobb, L.J. 1989. *For the Common Good.* Boston: Beacon Press.
Dewar, E. 1995. *Cloak of Green.* Toronto: James Lorimer.
Dobson, A. 1996. "The Green Scene: Academics on the Environment." *Sociology* 30: 395-403.
Drucker, P. 1993. *Post Capitalist Society.* New York: Harper Business.
Dunlap, R., and W. Catton. 1994. "Struggling with Human Exemptionalism: The Rise, Decline and Revitalization of Enviromental Sociology." *The American Sociologist* 25(1): 5-30.
Ekins, P. 1989. "Beyond Growth: The Real Priorities of Sustainable Development." *Environmental Conservation* 16(1): 5-12.
Franklin, U. 1992. *The Real World of Technology.* Concord, Ontario: House of Anansi Press.
Galbraith, J.K. 1967. *The New Industrial State.* Boston: Houghton Mifflin.
Gould, K., A. Weinberg, and A. Schnaiberg. 1993. "Legitimating Impotence: Pyrrhic Victories of the Modern Environmental Movement." *Qualitative Sociology* 16: 207-246.
Gould, K. 1991. "The Sweet Smell of Money: Economic Dependency and Local Environmental Mobilization." *Society and Natural Resources* 4: 133-150.
Hecht, S., and A. Cockburn. 1989. *The Fate of the Forest.* London: Verso.
Henderson, H. 1978. *Creating Alternative Futures.* New York: Berkley Publishing.
Herman, R., S. Ardekani, and J. Ausubel. 1989. "Dematerialization." Pp. 50-69 in *Technology and Environment,* edited by Jesse Ausubel and Hedy Sladovich. Washington: National Academy Press.
Illich, I. 1973. *Tools for Conviviality.* New York: Harper & Row.
Koebberling, U. 1990. "Problem Areas in the Management of Technology: Technology Assessment." Pp. 165-183 in *Managing Technology: Social Science Perspectives,* edited by Liora Salter and David Wolfe. Toronto: Garamond Press.
Lewontin, R. 1991. *Biology as Ideology: The Doctrine of DNA.* Don Mills, Ontario: Stoddart Publishing.
Lohmann, L. 1990. "Whose Common Future?" *The Ecologist* 20(3): 82-84.
Lovins, A. 1977. *Soft Energy Paths: Toward a Durable Peace.* San Francisco: Friends of the Earth International.
Lynn, W. 1989. "Engineering our Way Out of Endless Environmental Crises." Pp. 182-191 in *Technology and Environment,* edited by Jesse Ausubel and Hedy Sladovich. Washington: National Academy Press.
Manitoba Clean Environment Commission. 1989. *Report on Hearings Repap Manitoba, Inc.* Winnipeg: Manitoba Environment.
Meadows, D. et al. 1972. *The Limits to Growth.* New York: Universe.
McRobie, G. 1982. *Small is Possible.* London: Abacus.
Mishra, R. 1990. *The Welfare State in Capitalist Society.* Toronto: University of Toronto Press.
Mol, A., and Spaargaren, B. 1993. "Environment, Modernity and the Risk Society: The Apocalyptic Horizon of Environmental Reform." *International Sociology* 8 (4): 431-459.

Mumford, L. 1961. *The City in History 1961*. New York: Halcourt Brace & World.

Murphy, R. 1994. "The Sociological Construction of Science Without Nature." *Sociology* 28: 957-974.

Myles, J. 1991. "Post-Industrialism and the Service Economy." Pp. 351-366 in *The New Era of Global Competition*, edited by Daniel Drache and Meric Gertler. Montreal-Kingston: McGill-Queen's University Press.

Nelkin, D., and M. Pollak. 1981. *The Atom Besieged: Anti-nuclear Movements in France & Germany*. Cambridge MA: MIT Press.

Novek, J. 1995. "Environmental Impact Assessment and Sustainable Development: Case Studies of Environmental Conflict." *Society and Natural Resources* 8: 145-159.

Novek, J., and K. Kampen. 1992. "Sustainable or Unsustainable Development: An Analysis of an Environmental Controversy." *Canadian Journal of Sociology* 17(3): 249-273.

Nozik, M. 1992. *No Place Like Home*. Ottawa: Canadian Council on Social Development.

Odum, E. 1971. *Fundamentals of Ecology*. Orlando FL: Saunders College Publishing.

Ophuls, W. 1977. *Ecology and the Politics of Scarcity*. San Francisco: W.H. Freeman.

Paehlke, R. 1989. *Environmentalism and the Future of Progressive Politics*. New Haven, CT: Yale University Press.

Paehlke, R., and D. Torgerson. (eds.). 1990. *Managing Leviathan*. Peterborough, Ontario: Broadview Press.

Piore, M., and C. Sabel. 1984. *The Second Industrial Divide: Possibilities for Prosperity*.

Ramphal, S. 1992. *Our Country, The Planet*. Washington DC: Island Press.

Redclift, M. 1987. *Sustainable Development*. London: Methuen.

Rees, W. 1990. "The Ecology of Sustainable Development." *The Ecologist* 20(1): 18-23.

Repap Manitoba Inc. 1995. *Environmental Act Proposal*. Winnipeg: Manitoba Environment, December 14.

Reich, R. 1991. *The Work of Nations*. New York: Alfred B. Knopf.

Schnaiberg, A. 1985. "The Retreat from Political to Technical Environmentalism." Pp. 19-36 in *Social Responses to Technological Change*, edited by Augustine Brannigan and Sheldon Goldenberg. Westport CT: Greenwood Press.

Schnaiberg, A. 1980. *The Environment: From Surplus to Scarcity*. New York: Oxford University Press.

Schrecker, T. 1993. "Missing the Point About Growth." Pp. 535-541 in *Crosscurrents: International Relations in the Post Cold War Era*, edited by Mark Charlton and Elizabeth Riddel-Dixon. Scarborough Ontario: Nelson Canada.

Schumacher, E. 1974. *Small is Beautiful: Economics as if People Mattered*. London: Abacus.

Shiva, V. 1988. *Staying Alive: Women, Ecology and Development*. London: Zed Books.

Simonis, U. 1989. "Ecological Modernization of Society: three strategic elements."
    International Social Science Journal 12: 347-361.
Sklair, L. 1994. "Global Sociology and Global Environmental Change." Pp. 205-
    227 in *Social Theory and the Global Environment*, edited by Michael Redclift
    and Ted Benton. London: Routledge.
Starkloff, R. 1995. "Nature: Adversary or Victim?" Pp. 99-123 in *Environmental
    Sociology: Theory and Practice*, edited by Michael Mehta and Eric Ouellet.
    North York, Ontario: Captus Press.
Teeple, G. 1995. *Globalization and the Decline of Social Reform*. Toronto:
    Garamond Press.
Thurow, L. 1980. *The Zero-Sum Society*. New York: Penguin.
Vaillancourt, J.-G. 1995. "Sociology of the Environment: From Human Ecology
    to Ecosociology." Pp. 3-32 in in *Environmental Sociology: Theory and
    Practice*, edited by Michael Mehta and Eric Ouellet. North York, Ontario:
    Captus Press.
Winner, L. 1977. *Autonomous Technology: Technics out of Control as a Theme
    in Political Thought*. Cambridge, MA: MIT Press.
Yearly, S. 1991. *The Green Case*. London: Harper Collins Academic.

TOXIC CONTAMINATION AND ALIENATION:
COMMUNITY DISORDER AND THE INDIVIDUAL

Stephen R. Couch, Steve Kroll-Smith and
John P. Wilson

ABSTRACT

Sociologists are making important contributions to understanding how environmental contamination affects community institutions. The effects of this institutional change on the person, however, remain matters of speculation. A review of the literature on contamination and institutional change reveals a stepwise pattern of social disruption. The concept of alienation is introduced to connect contamination and community disruption to individual distress. Data on a contamination event permits a limited test of the utility of alienation in accounting for the personal experiences of institutional change in response to toxins in a local environment. Indicators that alienation is related to psychological distress in the contamination event suggests the

Research in Community Sociology, Volume 7, pages 95-115.
Copyright © 1997 by JAI Press Inc.
All rights of reproduction in any form reserved.
ISBN: 0-7623-0272-0

importance of this line of inquiry in future studies of environmental toxins, communities, and individuals. A concluding discussion comments on the continued relevance of alienation to sociology and the importance of sociologists in accounting for the deleterious effects of environmental hazards and disasters.

INTRODUCTION

Social science research consistently reports on the deleterious consequences of toxic contamination for social institutions. A wealth of evidence is now at hand documenting the adverse effects of industrial and military pollution on governments, religious organizations, and friendship networks. A number of studies examine problems of local governments overwhelmed by the demands of toxic contamination (Wolensky 1984; Reich 1991). Other studies document the emergence of factious citizens' groups that collide with sufficient friction to create what Freudenburg and Jones call "corrosive communities" (Freudenburg and Jones 1991; Cutherbertson and Nigg 1987; Kroll-Smith and Couch 1990). Still other studies account for the extraordinary difficulties of cleaning-up hazardous materials (Edelstein 1991; Couch and Kroll-Smith 1992). Finally, at least one study examines the failure of local and regional religious organizations to curb destructive community conflict in response to poison gas contamination (Kroll-Smith and Couch 1987). Indeed, it is routinely argued that the adverse effects of toxins on local social structures contrasts dramatically with community responses to natural disasters, which often lead to a strengthening of community ties, as illustrated by such concepts as "amplified rebound," the "democracy of stress," and the "therapeutic community" (Erikson 1976, 1991; Kutak 1937; Fritz 1961).

Faced with this convergence of conclusions, it is worth noting that to date there are no studies that attempt to account for the relationship between toxic contamination, problems with local and extra-local social institutions, and their effects on the individual. If one purpose of institutions is to routinize the life course, creating a predictable, if not necessarily nurturing, sense of order, institutional problems in responding to environmental toxins should result in some noticeable problems for individuals, above and beyond those posed by a poisoned environment. This paper is a first and modest attempt to introduce this timely topic and suggest its theoretical, empirical, and applied importance for sociologists.

The concept alienation is introduced to account for the separation of people from social institutions during contamination crises. Aided by the insightful work of Melvin Seeman (1975, 1983, 1991), we argue that alienation is a conceptual bridge between the social and psychological responses to toxins in local environments; it is a means of operationalizing the disillusionment with the social system felt by many residents of affected communities. Moreover, and important for this discussion, there is ample evidence that alienation itself is related to psychological difficulties for individuals. Therefore, in cases of contamination, we suggest that psychological distress resulting from the contamination itself is amplified by distress due to alienation.

For logistical reasons we do not have longitudinal data, which is arguably important for an argument that uses causal reasoning. We do, however, have suggestive survey data from a case of chemical contamination in a small community in the United States. We present these data, comparing levels of alienation in a contaminated community with those in a nearby comparison community. We also examine the relationship between levels of alienation and psychological distress in the contaminated community. Finally, we consider some theoretical and applied implications of this type of work and suggest some fruitful lines for further research.

A short discussion introduces the common results found in a wide array of social science accounts of collective responses to toxic contamination, each study documenting some particular deterioration in local community organization. With these studies in mind, the concept alienation is introduced and defined in a manner that conceptualizes and operationalizes this social process and its attendant individual responses.

CONTAMINATION AND INSTITUTIONAL DISORDER

While the potential danger to health and physical well-being is a critical factor in a toxic contamination event, institutional responses to exposure are also likely to provide profound distress in people's lives. Seeking redress from public and private institutions and the more informal friendship and neighborhood affiliations, victims of toxic exposure discover that the social structures they assumed were in place to protect them are not adequate, and indeed may resist their requests for assistance. In their struggle to bring their problem to public awareness and seek medical attention, compensation and cleanup of their environment, victims of toxic pollution are likely to see themselves victimized twice: once by the toxic exposure itself, and once again by the formal and informal social institutions they assumed were available to offer help and assistance (Kroll-Smith and Couch 1990; Reich 1991; Dyer, Gill, and Picou 1992).

Aggregating the literature on institutional responses to pollution events, we can discern a predictable political pattern, akin to a natural history model. It begins with the recognition by some community residents that they are now at risk from the willful or negligent acts of others, and quickly proceeds to the next stage: a realization that not everyone in the community or region perceives the same or approximate level of danger stemming from the pollution. The emergence of divisions within a community over the appropriate definition of contamination dangers is complemented by the next stage: the discovery that local social institutions are ill equipped to initiate ameliorative actions. Lastly, it becomes painfully clear to victims that corporations, government agencies, and so on are unable to assume, or worse, actively resist assuming responsibility for abating or cleaning-up the contamination and offering fair compensation (Brown 1991; Clarke 1989; Reich 1991; Couch 1996).

We begin with the first stage. Willful or negligent releases of hazardous chemicals are likely to violate people's expectations that business or government willingly assumes responsibility for their personal safety. Simply put, hazardous chemicals are not supposed to end up in human habitats—in air, in food, in backyards or potable water; and human communities are not supposed to be part of the environment that other people contaminate for economic or political gain. Thus, a marked sense of betrayal is likely to follow the unintentional or negligent poisoning of the environment (Erikson 1991; Davidson and Baum 1991; Freudenburg and Jones 1991).

Moreover, exposure to contamination is rarely uniform. Some neighborhoods are likely to be at more risk than others. The uneven and often erratic distribution of toxins invites multiple interpretations of the dangers and possible remedial strategies for reducing them. Stage two is thus a highly charged context of uncertainty wherein friends and neighbors find themselves unable to agree on a course of action (Kasperson and Pijawka 1985; Walsh 1981). Freudenburg and Jones (1991) suggest that toxic exposure is likely to create a "corrosive community." Borrowing from Simmel, Kroll-Smith and Couch (1990) argue that hazardous waste controversies are likely to generate "social hatred." One side believes the other side is underestimating the probability of loss or endangerment; likewise, those accused of underestimating the risks are themselves accusing others of exaggerating the threats. Each side is supported by an array of contradictory and confusing evidence, frequently coming from the same sources. A recent paper that considers this and related literature concludes that communal civility, that delicate filigree of interpersonal courtesies, is itself at considerable risk when toxins enter local environments (Kroll-Smith 1995).

Revealed in this intense intra-community conflict is the common adage that extraordinary events are most likely to occur within ordinary social institutions. What is lacking in most communities is a crisis resolution structure coupled with an active civic life adequate to respond to this type of controversial event. It is this problem that typifies the third stage. Wolensky, for example, examines the difficulties small town governments encounter when they are forced to respond to local pollution events (Wolensky 1984, 1991; see also Edelstein 1988). Another study of small town responses to contamination found that pastoral leadership and local church organizations were unable to stem the tide of community divisions and rancor (Kroll-Smith and Couch 1987).

Finally, if toxic contamination exposure forces people to acknowledge the weaknesses of their communal attachments, it also brings into stark relief the quality of their relationships with government and corporations, revealing a little something about the nature of power (Molotch 1970). In the fourth and final stage, parties potentially responsible for the pollution are likely to deny that any off-site release occurred. Unable to sustain this denial in the face of mounting evidence, potentially liable parties are likely to provide figures that the off-site releases that did occur are not sufficient to endanger surrounding populations. If they fail to make a convincing claim for their no-risk argument, responsible parties are likely to blame the release on operator error, subcontractor malfeasance or engineering flaws in machinery purchased from non-related companies (Perrow 1984; Clarke 1989). And, in many cases, responsible parties possess sufficient resources to fight long and protracted law suits, often spending more money in the courts than they would in an out-of-court settlement.

Likewise, the government's regulatory agencies mandated to respond to unplanned toxic releases are frequently understaffed, uninformed and dedicated to preserving bureaucratic operating procedures in crises that require accurate knowledge and adaptive response capabilities (Perrow 1984; Shrivastava 1991; Couch and Kroll-Smith 1992; Levine 1982; Edelstein 1988). In a comparative study of three major toxic exposure incidents, Reich found the polluting industries and responsible government agencies working to "maintain the problem as a nonissue" in spite of insider knowledge that in each case the exposure was severe. "Contradictions between a corporation's (and government agency's) private knowledge and its public actions created in victims a sense of moral outrage" (Reich 1991, p. 165).

In summary, then, the discovery of toxic exposure is likely to trigger feelings of profound doubt and disenchantment with the institutional fabric of modern society. Fundamental issues of power and civil rights are arbitrated in a highly charged political context that leaves many people embittered and angry.

Toxic Contamination and Alienation

One way to conceptualize and operationalize the link between this social process and individual responses is through the concept of alienation. Marx's treatment of alienation as arising from the relations of production under capitalism is fundamental. For Marx, capitalism is "the domination of living men by dead matter" (Marx 1956, p. 5; see also pp. 167-177). Alienation is caused by the structural conditions of capitalism which separate humans from their work, the state, and each other. Empirical research on alienation has focused on how individuals experience this separation, and on how that experience differs, depending on one's social location and life circumstances.

While use of the concept of alienation has waxed and waned, its themes—among them, power and powerlessness, the quest for community, and the search for life's meaning—continue to inspire research. Melvin Seeman argues that the reason for the continuing popularity of these themes is their critical importance as analytical tools in the study of the individual and of social life:

...the ideas involved in the alienation tradition are indispensable for sociological and psychological analysis....The thrust is that the themes that are classically brought together under the alienation rubric refer to the fundamental ways in which the individual is related to the social structure (Seeman 1983, p. 172).

We theorize that the onset of feelings of alienation is part of the personal experience of estrangement from social institutions resulting from toxic contamination. These feelings represent personal responses to a perceived breakdown in the social fabric in which individuals are embedded. The commonly accepted norms and assumptions of civil social behavior are inadequate for solving the problem at hand. One's friends, neighbors and government will not help and cannot be trusted. People feel at the mercy of forces beyond their control and comprehension, threatened by a physical world which used to provide security and sustenance, and also by their social world which once gave them comfort, solace and meaning.

If this is the case, there is good reason to believe that the social process set in motion by contamination will have negative psychological consequences. Summarizing the relationship between alienation and psychological distress, Mirowsky and Ross wrote: "powerlessness, self-estrangement, and the other subjective forms of alienation are not just 'in your mind'. They are realistic perceptions of objective social conditions. They are the link between social conditions and emotional well-being or distress" (1989, p. 12).

In fact, the literature clearly indicates a link between alienation and psychological distress (Mirowsky and Ross 1986). For example, powerlessness (or very similar concepts) has been linked to demoralization (Wheaton 1980), lack of coping ability (Wheaton 1983), stress (Pearlin et al. 1981), depression (Mirowsky and Ross 1989, pp. 116-118), problem drinking (M. Seeman, A.Z. Seeman, and Budros 1988), and emotional distress following a natural disaster (Lima et al. 1989). And normlessness has been found to be correlated with such problems as mistrust, paranoia, brooding, and worrying (Mirowsky and Ross 1989).

TOXIC CONTAMINATION AND ALIENATION IN SUNBURST

At present, there are no quantitative studies which test the relationships between contamination, the separation of people from key social institutions, subjective alienation, and psychological distress.

Ideally, in order to conduct such a study, a longitudinal analysis of the specific social and political events following the discovery of contamination is needed. While we do not have longitudinal data specific to a particular case, we have reviewed the literature on several cases and identified what appears to be an expected pattern of social and political responses. Those results were summarized above. In addition, we have carried out a cross-sectional survey of litigants in a chemically contaminated community in the United States. A history of this case suggests that it typifies the social and political processes that separate the individual from key social institutions in contamination crises. To the extent to which this is true, these data support the hypothesis that alienation is a secondary stressor resulting in amplified levels of psychological distress.

"Sunburst" is the pseudonym for a residential subdivision of single family units located on the outskirts of a city of about 50,000 inhabitants. Located on the western plains, most of Sunburst's residents are married, working class and middle-aged, and most are high school graduates. At the southern edge of the community is a dense area of industrial and commercial activity with over 20 chemical blending, petroleum refining, truck maintenance, and petroleum service operations.

During the summer of 1986, a few Sunburst residents noticed acrid odors in the air accompanied by foul smelling water. In response to a complaint by a Sunburst resident, the U.S. Environmental Protection Agency (EPA) sampled two wells in the subdivision. Additional water sampling was conducted by the County Health Department and the State Department of Environmental Quality. The primary contaminants identified in the drinking water supply were trichloroethylene, tetrachloroethylene and benzene. Trace amounts of toluene and xylene were also found in two wells.

At the request of the EPA, the Agency for Toxic Substances and Disease Registry examined the water sampling data in December of 1986, and the EPA began investigating several local industries to determine who was responsible for the contamination of the subdivision. Among the problems identified in their inquiry was a hydrocarbon plume moving from a refinery located on the western edge of the subdivision onto residential property.

On June 21, 1988, the EPA proposed that the Sunburst subdivision be placed on the Superfund National Priority List for cleanup, officially designating it as among the 1,200 most seriously contaminated sites in the country. Many families voluntarily relocated and a lively controversy between many residents and the chemical companies ensued. This led to a law suit against the companies by over 80 percent of the subdivision's adult population of about 200 residents. The suit was settled out of court in 1993 with generous awards to the litigants. The site is now undergoing a cleanup.

Evidence for the erosion of community life among Sunburst residents was plentiful throughout the contamination controversy. Similar to the experiences of the Love Canal residents in Niagara Falls, New York, city government quickly distanced itself from the claims of the Sunburst residents, refusing their repeated requests for local government assistance in holding responsible industries accountable for a cleanup or buy-out. The steadfast refusal of city government to acknowledge the problems of Sunburst forced the EPA to negotiate with the county Board of Supervisors, bypassing the city entirely.

In addition, more than half of Sunburst homeowners received notices from their insurance agents that their homeowners' policies would either not be renewed, or would be renewed at a substantially higher rate. Local banks would not hold the contaminated houses as collateral for those residents who wanted to borrow money to relocate before the settlement. Finally, local and state industry groups publicly accused Sunburst residents of seeking personal gain at the expense of the state's economy.

Within the neighborhood itself, schisms quickly emerged among former friends and acquaintances. One group pressed its neighbors to hold out for a court hearing rather than simply settle. Another group emerged that wanted to settle quickly, but soon fell apart when its members could not agree on a fair settlement figure. Several open-ended interviews conducted with Sunburst residents revealed a common conclusion that the fabric of social life was unraveling. "I'm at a loss for words," remarked one man. "I thought all we had to do was tell people our backyards were poisoned by chemicals and help would be on the way. I'm disappointed with everybody—my former friends, neighbors, the city, the state, you name it."

METHODS

In the summer of 1988, the first and second authors attempted to obtain a completed self-administered survey instrument from all of

Sunburst's present and former adult residents who were involved in litigation against the chemical companies. A total of 97 questionnaires were returned; this represents a response rate of 63 percent of those adults involved in the law suit.

In order to consider the effect of contamination on alienation while controlling for other factors associated with alienation, the instrument was also administered to a group of respondents who had not been exposed to contamination but who were similar on other characteristics believed associated with alienation. Ideally, the best test of the influence of contamination would have been both a pre-exposure and a post-exposure examination of the subjects. As this is impossible in almost all cases of toxic contamination, the posttest-only control design (Hartsough 1985) was used, as it is frequently in the study of human response to industrial contaminants (Smith et al. 1986).

Specifically, the results of the Sunburst survey were compared with results from a comparison group of adults drawn from a nearby community which was not affected by environmental contamination. The comparison community is a subdivision of the same city, but located on the opposite side of the city from Sunburst. It was selected because of its structural, cultural and demographic similarity to Sunburst (see Table 1).[1] Both communities are composed of a largely married, middle income population of white homeowners. Since both communities are subdivisions on the outskirts of the same city, both are part of a similar western, suburban cultural milieu. Questionnaires were distributed to all of the approximately 600 adult residents of the comparison community. A total of 308 questionnaires were returned.

Table 1.   Sunburst and Comparison Community Demographic Variables

	Sunburst (N = 97)	Comparison (N = 308)
Mean Family Income	$29,100 (SD = 14,200)	$29,200 (SD = 13,000)
Mean years of Education	12.3 (SD = 2.2)	13.5 (SD = 2.1)
Mean Age	43.3 (SD = 12.0)	34.8 (SD = 9.7)
Married	81%	81%
Female	52%	50%
Homeowners	81%	84%

We measured respondents' experience of social breakdown using Dean's alienation scale (Dean 1961; see also the discussion of the subscales in Seeman 1991). Contained within the scale are three subscales—one for social isolation (the degree to which one feels isolated from other people), one for powerlessness (feeling that one lacks control over one's life and over events), and one for normlessness (feeling that following the rules will not lead to desired goals). A sample item for each subscale (in turn) is:

> "Sometimes I feel all alone in the world."
> "We are just so many cogs in the machinery of life."
> "The only thing one can be sure of today is that he can be sure of nothing."

The total scale score is composed of the sum of scores for all items, with the range for each item being from "0" (low alienation) to "4" (high alienation).

Independently of this survey, the third author administered batteries of psychological tests to the adult Sunburst litigants. Included among them was the Symptom Check List 90 (SCL-90R), an objective, 90 item self-report scale that measures general psychiatric symptoms on a five-point Likert scale (range 0-4). The SCL-90R contains a widely accepted summary measure of distress, the Global Severity Index, as well as a series of sub-scales measuring such things as anxiety, depression, and somaticism (Derogatis 1973).

The third author also administered the Impact of Events Scale, a generic measure of avoidance/denial and intrusion/re-living aspects of stress response syndromes. It consists of sixteen statements which assess the subject's feelings of denial and the occurrence within the past seven days of intrusive thoughts in regard to a previously stressful life event.

RESULTS

In order to examine the proposition that the discovery of toxins in a local habitat triggers a process of social breakdown that is likely to result in elevated levels of alienation, mean scores for the alienation scale for the Sunburst respondents and comparison group members were computed. These mean scores are given in Table 2.

Table 2. Means and Standard Deviations for Alienation Scale and for Powerlessness, Normlessness and Social Isolation Subscales

Alienation Scale	Sunburst	Comparison	Significance	Range
	51.2	44.1	<.001	0-96
	(SD = 13.8)	(SD = 12.3)		
Subscales:				
Powerlessness	20.8	17.4	<.001	0-36
	(SD = 6.5)	(SD = 5.5)		
Normlessness	11.4	9.7	.002	0-24
	(SD = 4.5)	(SD = 4.4)		
Social Isolation	19.0	17.0	.028	0-36
	(SD = 5.4)	(SD = 4.9)		

As can be seen by comparing the mean scores, in the case of the scale and each of its subscales, the Sunburst respondents score significantly higher than the comparison group.

In order to see if location in a contaminated community is still a significant factor causing alienation even after controlling for the effects of socio-demographic factors, we ran a multiple regression on the alienation scale and the three subscales. Included as independent variables were two dichotomous variables ("location," where "1" = Sunburst and "0" = the comparison community; "gender," where "1" = female and "0" = male), along with education, age, and family income. The results are presented in Table 3.

Table 3. Regressions, Alienation Scale and Subscales, with Location and Demographic Variables: Standard Regression Coefficient (Betas) and Multiple Correlation Coefficient (R^2).

Dependent Variable:	Alienation Scale	Powerlessness Subscale	Normlessness Subscale	Social Isolation Subscale
Education	-.278**	-.279**	-.301**	-.148**
Age	-.191**	-.096	-.213**	-.183**
Family Income	.010	.024	.002	.018
Gender	-.036	-.046	-.060	.003
Location	.234**	.224**	.143**	.203**
$R^2 =$	.153	.138	.139	.080
F value	13.843	12.259	12.360	6.683
Prob.	<.001	<.001	<.001	<.001

Notes: *$p < .05$
　　　**$p < .01$

The results clearly show that location in a contaminated community remains an important part of the explanation. Location and education, and to a lesser extent age, are statistically significant predictors of alienation. Examination of the subscales indicates that lower education and younger age are associated with higher normlessness and social isolation, with education being the only demographic variable which is a significant predictor of powerlessness. Most importantly, location is found to be significant for all three subscales.

Unfortunately, since psychological testing was not carried out in the comparison community, we cannot compare levels of psychological distress in Sunburst with those in the comparison subdivision. However, on the basis of comparisons with the literature, it appears that Sunburst respondents did experience elevated levels of psychological distress. Specifically, high levels of depression, anxiety, somatic concerns, and post-traumatic stress disorder symptoms were found.

Using only the Sunburst data, we can look at the relationship between alienation and psychological distress. Zero order correlations between the alienation scale, its subscales, the SCL-90R Global Severity Index (the overall measure of distress), SCL-90R subscales for anxiety, depression, somatic concerns, and post-traumatic stress disorder, are found in Table 4. With only two exceptions, the correlations between the alienation measures and the psychological distress measures are substantial and statistically significant. The exceptions both involve the somaticism subscale, a measure of concern over physical problems. It is not surprising that somaticism would be less strongly linked to social isolation and

Table 4. Correlation Matrix, Psychological and Alienation Measures

	Alienation Scale	Powerlessness Subscale	Normlessness Subscale	Social Isolation Subscale
General Severity Index	.586**	.587*	.429**	.438**
Anxiety Subscale	.472**	.493**	.306**	.360**
Depression Subscale	.595**	.571**	.439**	.468**
PTSD Subscale	.560**	.523**	.386**	.483**
Somaticism Subscale	.237**	.312**	.195	.073

Notes: *p < .05
**p < .01

Table 5. Regression, General Severity Index: Standard Regression
Coefficient and Multiple Correlation Coefficient

	Model 1	Model 2	Model 3
Education	.153	.113	.012
Age	.158	.103	.002
Family Income	-.032	-.030	-.056
Gender	.100	.055	.035
Powerlessness	.471**	.425**	.358**
Normlessness	.016	.010	-.023
Soc. Isolation	.303*	.202*	.179*
Impact of Events		.420**	.387**
Grassroots Groups			.335**
R^2	.472	.629	.720
F	9.565	15.708	20.854
Prob.	<.001	<.001	<.001

normlessness, both measures of social estrangement, than would the other subscales, which measure perceptions of more purely psychological problems.

It appears, then, that in Sunburst, alienation is strongly related to measures of psychological distress. But might this relationship be caused by other factors? Or might certain aspects of alienation be more important predictors than others? A series of regression models were developed and run for each psychological measure. Table 5 reports the results for the Global Severity Index, our overall measure of distress. The first model includes four demographic variables (education, age, family income, and gender) and the three alienation subscales. The powerlessness and social isolation subscales are the only significant variables, with powerlessness being an especially powerful predictor. Controlling for the other variables, normlessness does not make a significant independent contribution.

The strength of the powerlessness measure is not surprising, given the literature and the specific type of situation under consideration here. In their extensive survey of social causes of psychological distress, Mirowsky and Ross wrote: "The sense of powerlessness can have two effects on distress. It can be demoralizing in itself and it can hamper effective coping with difficult events or situations.... Of all the things that might explain the social patterns of distress, one stands out as central: the sense of control over one's own life" (1989, pp. 134, 167). Residents in contaminated communities must cope with a loss of control over their environment, their social community, and their own lives, and for a seemingly interminable period of time. The psychological effects can be grueling.

The other significant relationship was between social isolation and psychological distress. This is interesting in that, as is typical of contaminated communities, Sunburst experienced an increase of social activity within the community as a result of contamination. Community meetings were held; neighbor talked with neighbor over what to do about the problem; a grassroots environmental group was formed. Yet feelings of social isolation were apparently increased in the community (see Table 2), and those feelings were associated with heightened psychological distress. Perhaps the feelings of social isolation are indicative of the type of social activity taking place, activity which broke down the ties people felt to the larger community and to their social institutions, thereby increasing feelings of isolation in the midst of a whirl of social activity.

Perhaps, however, the impact of feelings of powerlessness and social isolation on psychological distress are not caused by any social process, but only by the worries associated with the contamination itself. Model 2 in Table 5 adds the Impact of Events Scale as an independent variable. This scale measures the impact of the contamination itself on the thoughts of the respondents. This scale is significant, but, while diminishing their effects somewhat, powerlessness and social isolation remain significant also.

One final social variable was considered—the relationship of grassroots group membership to psychological distress. While we are aware of no empirical studies directly on this subject, there are interesting and contradictory approaches to it in the literature. Some argue that grassroots group participation is empowering and liberating (Edelstein 1988; Cable and Walsh 1991; Levine and Stone 1986). If so, one might predict that grassroots group members would have lower psychological distress than non-members. However, another line of reasoning leads to the opposite conclusion. In extensive research on the long-term response to the Three Mile Island nuclear accident, Baum and his colleagues found that those who applied "instrumental" coping strategies (e.g., who blamed others and tried to change something about the situation) had higher levels of stress than those who used "emotional" coping (blamed themselves and tried to change their own responses and reactions) (Davidson and Baum 1991). It would follow that those joining a grassroots group bent on changing the situation (a form of instrumental coping) would have higher levels of psychological distress than those who did not join.

Model 3 adds whether or not a respondent was involved with Sunburst's local anti-toxics group as an independent variable. The results indicate that membership in the grassroots group is a significant predictor of psychological distress.

This would seem to support Baum's position. Some caveats, however, are in order. The measure of involvement in the group is very crude, only ascertaining if the respondent had been involved in any of the group's activities, and coded "yes" or "no." Moreover, the data are not longitudinal, and therefore the direction of any causal relationship cannot be established. Theory is of little help here, either. Do people who are more psychologically distressed join grassroots groups to try to solve the problem plaguing them? Or do people join grassroots groups, become frustrated, and experience increased levels of psychological distress? Or both? Or would characteristics of grassroots groups affect psychological distress? We cannot tell from these data. Nevertheless, these findings, however tentative, are provocative, and suggest the need for further research in this area.[2]

DISCUSSION

Our research has shown the Sunburst situation to be a typical example of what takes place when toxic exposure occurs. The direct experience of toxic exposure was exacerbated by the long-term social process set in motion by the exposure, resulting in adverse social and psychological effects. The residents of Sunburst became alienated, feeling powerless over their lives and isolated from social support. This alienation, in addition to emotional reactions to the contamination itself, was found to be related to psychological distress. These findings are consistent with those of the majority of qualitative studies of human response to toxic contamination (e.g., Cuthbertson and Nigg 1987; Kroll-Smith and Couch 1990; Reich 1991; Couch and Kroll-Smith 1994).

Additional research is needed in the area of grassroots group involvement. Research on the social psychological motivations for joining anti-toxics grassroots groups, and on the social psychological consequences of membership, would be beneficial toward increasing our understanding of the relationship of these groups to psychological well-being. In doing so, however, it is important to guard against the value assumption that automatically views a lack of psychological distress as the ultimate goal; a certain amount of psychological distress may be necessary for longer-term beneficial personal and social change.

Theoretically, this paper contains some implications concerning the production of alienation in modern society. Marx argued that social structural conditions that produce estrangement, powerlessness, and so on, are, to a greater or lesser degree, constantly present in capitalist society. But these objective conditions may not always be experienced subjectively as alienating. Rather, the alienating nature of those structures may be obscured to most people most of the time. The fact that the emperor has no clothes may not always be noticed; the realization of this fact may be situationally emergent. If this is the case, then toxic contamination may be one kind of situation which is likely to lead to an "unmasking" of objective alienation, thereby raising the degree of subjective alienation.

Viewing the experience of alienation as situationally emergent counters one problem in the way the concept is often used. There is a tendency to see alienation as a personality trait formed by one's experiences in various social statuses (Perkins 1982). Seeman argues strongly against this view, crediting Goffman (1957) for making "clear the fact that (social psychological) alienation was not intrinsically a matter of 'personality' or 'attitude' but could readily be discerned as a specifically situational emergent" (1983, p. 172 and p. 173, note 2; see also Seeman 1959). Confirmed in this study is the idea that a person's statuses do not translate into subjective alienation without the situations, processes and real-life events which are influenced by, but not mechanically or inevitably produced by, those statuses.

On a final note, this paper suggests the important role of social scientists in assessing the losses that people and their communities incur when toxins enter local biospheres. Damage is not limited to the biosphere or the built and modified environments, nor is it confined to human health. Toxins in the biosphere are likely to disturb the predictable and assumed relationships between people and key social networks and organizations. The severity of these community-level disturbances is likely to affect the capacity of individuals to successfully cope with an environmental danger. One analyst goes so far as to conclude that community-level variables might prove more important than the type of disaster itself in predicting how individuals will adapt to the event (Golec 1983). Risking the charge of hyperbole, another researcher introduces the idea of "secondary disasters" to account for disorganized, inept or corrupt institutional responses to technological disasters (Erikson 1976, p. 254). The convergence of social science studies on the deleterious effects of environmental contamination on local and extra-local social structures invites sociologists to consider research strategies that assess how the disordering of social life affects the well-being of men and women, age groups, ethnic and religious groups, rural and urban residents, and so on.

NOTES

1.   While similar on most demographic variables, the comparison group has a somewhat higher mean number of years of school than the Sunburst sample, and the average age is younger in the comparison group. Further analysis indicated that these factors did not affect the results discussed in the paper.

2.   Similar analyses were performed for the four SCL-90R subscales discussed in the text. While there were some specific differences for some subscales and models—for instance, women scored higher on the anxiety subscale than men, and the alienation subscales were not significant predictors of somaticism—the overall pattern of results was nearly identical to those found for the Global Severity Index.

REFERENCES

Brown, P. 1991. *No Safe Place: Toxic Waste, Leukemia and Community Action.* Berkeley, CA: University of California Press.

Cable, S., and E. Walsh. 1991. "The Emergence of Environmental Protest: Yellow Creek and TMI Compared." Pp. 113-132 in *Communities At Risk: Collective Responses to Technological Hazards,* edited by S.R. Couch and J. S. Kroll-Smith. New York: Peter Lang.

Clarke, L. 1989. *Acceptable Risk? Making Decisions in a Toxic Environment.* Berkeley: University of California Press.

Couch, S.R. 1996. "Environmental Contamination, Community Transformation and the Centralia Mine Fire." Pp. 60-85 in *The Long Road to Recovery: Community Responses to Industrial Disasters,* edited by J.K. Mitchell. New York: United Nations University Press.

Couch, S.R., and J.S. Kroll-Smith. 1992. "Controllability, Social Breakdown and the Centralia Coal Mine Fire." Pp. 337-349 in *Natural and Technological Disasters: Causes, Effects and Preventive Measures,* edited by S.K. Majumdar, E.W. Miller, G.S. Forbes, and R.F. Schmalz. Easton, PA: The Pennsylvania Academy of Science.

_____. 1994. "Environmental Controversies, Interactional Resources, and Rural Communities: Siting Versus Exposure Disputes." *Rural Sociology* 59: 25-44.

Cuthbertson, B.H., and J.M. Nigg. 1987. "Technological Disaster and the Nontherapeutic Community: A Question of True Victimization." *Environment and Behavior* 19: 462-483.

Davidson, L.M., and A. Baum. 1991. "Victimization and Self-Blame Following a Technological Disaster." Pp. 33-52 in *Communities At Risk: Collective Responses to Technological Hazards*, edited by S.R. Couch and J.S. Kroll-Smith. New York: Peter Lang.

Dean, D.G. 1961. "Alienation: Its Meaning and Measurement." *American Sociological Review* 26: 753-758.

Derogatis, L.R. 1973. "SCL-90: An Outpatient Psychiatric Rating Scale." *Psychopharmacology Bulletin* 9: 13-28.

Dyer, C., D. Gill, and S.J. Picou. 1992. "Social Disruption and the Valdez Oil Spill: Alaskan Natives and a Natural Resource Community." *Sociological Spectrum* 12: 105-126.

Edelstein, M.R. 1988. *Contaminated Communities*. Boulder, CO: Westview Press.

_____. 1991. "Ecological Threats and Spoiled Identities: Radon Gas and Environmental Stigma." Pp. 205-226 in *Communities At Risk: Collective Responses to Technological Hazards*, edited by S.R. Couch and J.S. Kroll-Smith. New York: Peter Lang.

Erikson, K. 1991. "A New Species of Trouble." Pp.11-30 in *Communities At Risk: Collective Responses to Technological Hazards*, edited by S.R. Couch and J.S. Kroll-Smith. New York: Peter Lang.

_____. 1976. "Loss of Communality at Buffalo Creek." *American Journal of Psychiatry* 133: 302-305.

Freudenburg, W., and T.R. Jones. 1991. "Attitudes and Stress in the Presence of Technological Risk: A Test of the Supreme Court Hypothesis." *Social Forces* 69: 1143-1168.

Fritz, C.E. 1957. "Disaster." Pp. 651-694 in *Contemporary Social Problems*, edited by R.K. Merton and R.A. Nisbet. New York: Harcourt Brace.

Goffman, E. 1957. "Alienation From Interaction." *Human Relations* 10: 47-60.

Golec, J.A. 1983. "A Contextual Approach to the Social Psychological Study of Disaster Recovery." *International Journal of Mass Emergencies and Disasters* 1: 255-276.

Hartsough, D.M. 1985. "Measurement of Psychological Effects of Disaster." Pp. 22-61 in *Perspectives on Disaster Recovery*, edited by J. Laube and S. Murphy. Norwalk, CT: Appleton-Century-Crofts.

Kasperson, R.E., and K.D. Pijawka. 1985. "Societal Response to Hazards and Major Hazard Events: Comparing Natural and Technological Hazards." *Public Administration Review* 45: 7-18.

Kroll-Smith, S. 1995. "Toxic Contamination and the Loss of Civility." *Sociological Spectrum* 15: 377-396.

Kroll-Smith, J.S, and S.R. Couch. 1990. *The Real Disaster Is Above Ground: A Mine Fire and Social Conflict*. Lexington, KY: University Press of Kentucky.

_____. 1987. "The Chronic Technical Disaster and the Irrelevance of Religious Meaning: The Case of Centralia, Pennsylvania." *Journal for the Scientific Study of Religion* 26: 25-37.

Kutak, R.I. 1937. "Sociology of Crises: The Louisville Flood of 1937." *Social Forces* 17: 66-72.

Levine, A.G. 1982. *Love Canal: Science, Politics and People.* Lexington, MA: Lexington Books.

Levine, A.G., and R.A. Stone. 1986. "Threats to People and What They Value." Pp. 109-130 in *Advances in Environmental Psychology*, Vol. 6, edited by A.H. Lebovits, A. Baum, and J.E. Singer. Hillsdale, NJ: Lawrence Erlbaum Associates.

Lima, B.R., H. Chavez, N. Samaniego, M.S. Pompei, S. Pal, J. Santacruz, and J. Lozano. 1989. "Disaster Severity and Emotional Disturbance: Implications for Primary Mental Health Care in Developing Countries." *Acta Psychiatrica Scandinavica* 79: 74-82.

Marx, K. 1956. *Selected Writings in Sociology and Social Philosophy.* Trans. by T.B. Bottomore, edited by T.B. Bottomore and M. Rubel. New York: McGraw-Hill.

Mirowsky, J., and C.E. Ross. 1989. *Social Causes of Psychological Distress.* New York: Aldine de Gruyter.

_____. 1986. "Social Patterns of Distress." Pp. 23-45 in *Annual Review of Sociology*, edited by A. Inkeles. Palo Alto, CA: Annual Reviews.

Molotch, H. 1970. "Oil in Santa Barbara and Power in America." *Sociological Inquiry* 40: 131-144.

Pearlin, L.I., M.A. Lieberman, E.G. Menaghan, and J.T. Mullan. 1981. "The Stress Process." *Journal of Health and Social Behavior* 22: 337-356.

Perkins, H.W. 1982. "On the Specificity of Social Alienation: An Exploratory Investigation in England and the United States." *Sociology and Social Research* 66: 399-417.

Perrow, C. 1984. *Normal Accidents: Living with High-Risk Technologies.* New York: Basic Books.

Reich, M. 1991. *Toxic Politics: Responding to Chemical Disasters.* Ithaca, NY: Cornell University Press.

Seeman, M. 1959. "On the Meaning of Alienation." *American Sociological Review* 24: 783-791.

_____. 1975. "Alienation Studies." Pp. 91-123 in *Annual Review of Sociology*, edited by A. Inkeles. Palo Alto, CA: Annual Review Press.

_____. 1983. "Alienation Motifs in Contemporary Theorizing: The Hidden Continuity of the Classic Themes." *Social Psychology Quarterly* 46: 171-184.

_____. 1991. "Alienation and Anomie." Pp. 291-372 in *Measures of Personality and Social Psychological Attitudes*, edited by J.P. Robinson, P.R. Shaver and L.S. Wrightsman. New York: Academic Press.

Seeman, M., A.Z. Seeman, and A. Budros. 1988. "Powerlessness, Work, and Community: A Longitudinal Study of Alienation and Alcohol Use." *Journal of Health and Social Behavior* 29: 185-198.

Shrivastava, P. 1991. "Organizational Myths in Industrial Crises: Obfuscating Revelations." Pp. 263-290 in *Communities At Risk: Collective Responses to Technological Hazards*, edited by S. R. Couch and J. S. Kroll-Smith. New York: Peter Lang.

Smith, E.M., L.N. Robins, T.R. Przybeck, E. Goldring, and S.D. Solomon. 1986. "Psychosocial Consequences of a Disaster." Pp. 50-76 in *Disaster Stress Studies: New Methods and Findings*, edited by J.H. Shore. Washington, DC: American Psychiatric Press.

Walsh, E. 1981. "Resource Mobilization and Citizen Protest in Communities around Three Mile Island." *Social Problems* 29: 1-21.

Wheaton, B. 1980. "The Sociogenesis of Psychological Disorder." *Journal of Health and Social Behavior* 21: 100-124.

————. 1983. "Stress, Personal Coping Resources, and Psychiatric Symptoms: An Investigation of Interactive Models." *Journal of Health and Social Behavior* 24: 208-229.

Wolensky, R. 1984. "Power, Politics and Disaster: The Political-Organizational Impact of a Major Flood." National Science Foundation, Final Report. Grant #CEE8113529.

————. 1991. "POWER: Collective Action and the Anthracite Region Water Crisis." Pp. 229-261 in *Communities At Risk: Collective Responses to Technological Hazards*, edited by S. R. Couch and J. S. Kroll-Smith. New York: Peter Lang.

MUNICIPAL BOUNDARIES AND PROSPECTIVE LULU IMPACTS

William Michelson

ABSTRACT

This chapter explores the extent that municipal boundaries focus the potential impact of a locally unwanted land use (LULU) onto a more definite and identifiable collectivity. A telephone survey was taken during 1994 of a random sample of 904 adults in three regional municipalities within the Greater Toronto Area. The results indicate that people observe qualitative differences among municipalities, with considerable impact on their everyday lives and on their life chances. People are indifferent to LULUs except when these are physically located within their own municipalities. In the latter case, they react strongly and usually negatively, regardless of where they live within the municipality. Yet, the LULU plays a small part in expected mobility. These data suggest that fixed borders, even when the municipality is of as large scale as a regional municipality, amplify the impact of a prospective LULU, making the NIMBY syndrome more understandable.

Research in Community Sociology, Volume 7, pages 117-140.
Copyright © 1997 by JAI Press Inc.
All rights of reproduction in any form reserved.
ISBN: 0-7623-0272-0

The not-in-my-back-yard syndrome (NIMBY) occurs frequently when residents of a local area reject in advance a new land-use as inappropriate for this location. Such a land-use might be needed by society at large (or at least by other factions within it), but the residents don't want it close to themselves. In this regard, Raymond Vernon once commented in a public lecture that, "Everybody wants the water, but nobody wants the reservoir." The land-uses in this case are increasingly referred to (cf. Edelstein 1988, chap. 7; Szasz 1994, chap. 3; Gould, Schnaiberg, and Weinberg 1996, p. 136) as LULUs: locally unwanted land-uses.

Conflicts often arise between proponents and opponents of newly planned LULUs. The former, a mixture of special interest groups, decision makers, and professionals, typically blame opponents pursuing a NIMBY argument for being selfish—for carrying out a particularistic, emotion-laden campaign to obstruct "progress." The thrust of this accusation is that there is no basis for NIMBY other than narrowly-defined self interest. However, dismissing the merit of a NIMBY-based opposition on these grounds does not explain the geographic distribution and tenaciousness of local feelings, well beyond what people normally suppose correspond to the dangers involved.

In this paper, I shall explore the place of the municipality as a mediating factor which focuses the prospective impact of a LULU onto a geographically-defined population and embeds the issue into a more inclusive substantive context. When a LULU is placed in a particular political entity, it will be assessed by those who share the entity because this place is in part theirs. And they will evaluate it according to the diversity of criteria which they find meaningful for the municipality itself. This takes the issue away from a more narrow, technology-oriented matter confined to a specific catchment area and to a more general one relating to quality of life and environment for a municipality and all its residents.

But are municipalities currently worthy of this crucial place in my explanatory scheme? The network school of thought within Urban Sociology suggests that the importance of bounded local territories in contemporary human life has declined. Advances in communication "liberate" people from the need for local support systems (Wellman and Leighton 1979). People, in any case, are highly mobile in terms of residence and occupation, gaining valuable contacts at many levels of scale. Neighborhoods are still seen to have residual functions, but of "limited liability" (Janowitz 1967). But what about municipalities? Many suburban municipalities are parallel to central-city neighborhoods in terms of relative internal socio-demographic homogeneity—and differences from one another. Comparatively less attention has been paid to the place of municipalities in people's lives and thoughts.

MUNICIPALITIES

Research by Weiher (1991) makes a strong argument in favor of the salience of the municipality in people's lives. Weiher argues that municipalities have the benefit of explicit boundaries as cues for people to identify and compare them. They also have governments, with the mandate to deliver a specific set of goods and services. Municipalities take on unique identities according to the decisions they make and the milieu which takes shape over time. To the extent, as in the suburbs, that social areas approximate the size of municipalities, potential residents are drawn to a municipality by their image of who lives there, further reinforcing the special characteristics of the municipality, both socially and in terms of policy directions.

Some criteria that people have for their municipal place of residence, according to Weiher, include quality of housing, provision of services, the kinds and levels of fees and taxes, the amenities, security, quality of life, social status, and other population characteristics of residents. All these are placed in relief by the existence of municipal boundaries, for observation and comparison.

The municipality is but one of several levels of government making decisions on behalf of citizens. Depending on time and place, there is a complicated combination of division of labor among levels of government regarding specific functions pursued and hierarchies or duplication concerning specific functions. There is no universal opinion about which is the most important level of government. But what Weiher points out is that most people feel that they have more control over what happens at the municipal level, further increasing the salience of municipalities and the municipality as a distinct place of residence. As another observer put this point in a comparison of different types of influence on "life quality," "... the potential for the community as a focus for improving life quality is the potential for meaningful change and improvement that exists at the community level" [emphasis by the original author] (Lyon 1987, p. 241).

One link between people and their municipal place of residence is that the latter serves as a form of identification, to oneself and to other people. Feldman (1990, p. 184), for example, notes from her research that "...the vast majority of respondents indicated that they identified themselves with a type of settlement, lived in that type of settlement in the past and present, and intended to maintain their residence in that type of settlement in the future."

Philosophers have recently applied a phenomenological approach, "uncovering hidden meanings already in place in the rich and complex relation of humans to the spaces in which they seek to dwell" (Stefanovic 1992, p. 151).

The bond and identity are not only personal, but interpersonal in how they are used and experienced. According to Abu-Lughod (1991, p. 338), "...the larger neighborhood or even the city can take on an important symbolic and social meaning, serving as a source of identify ("I come from Grosse Pointe")..."

In *A World of Strangers* (1985), Lofland addresses the question of how people can deal with each other in an orderly way when, under urban conditions, so many are strangers to each other. As cited by Karp, Stone, and Yoels (1991, p. 121), Lofland expresses her argument for order based on identify by place of residence as follows: "In the pre-industrial city a man was what he wore. In the modern city a man is where he stands." Municipality of residence is frequently used at present as a proxy to personal acquaintance in dealing with other persons: with limited circulation publications, the availability and cost of automobile and home insurance, a prestigious mailing address for corporate images, and, of course, people's own self-presentations of propriety and lifestyle.

A magazine article about a musical group called Barenaked Ladies gives an informal view of these phenomena (Jennings, 1993, p. 55): "Scarborough has always had a really low self-image. Growing up, we were ashamed to come from there. But I think that's where our humor comes from."

Agnew (1981) connects people's identification with particular settings to the perceived desirability of control over local municipal decisions. "People not only live in houses, they also live in local communities or neighborhoods.... It is necessary, therefore, to be concerned with events which threaten any or all of these symbolic and material interests" (p. 473).

While identification and bonds with places of residence, not to speak of actions to exercise control over their nature and change, occur in connection with varying scales of surroundings, as reflected in the citations above, their application to municipalities is both strengthened and made clearly recognizable by the formal status of municipalities, including legal boundaries. As Weiher put it in his book (1991, p. 60): "Indeed, because of...the interaction that such precise boundaries encourage between geography, political power and publicly provided services, economic activity, and the social characteristics of residents, political boundaries are quite instrumental in creating place identity."

One of the consequences of something as formal as municipal boundaries is that the type of identification which occurs typically expands beyond the very specific area in which it is generated, to apply to residents of adjacent areas who include themselves as part of the same area. Postal address boundaries, for example, are often used to convey prestige to a wider range of residents and enterprises.

MUNICIPALITIES, LULUS AND STIGMATIZATION

One variety of this identification process which people do not seek or cherish is stigmatization. A stigma is a label placed on a person or group of persons, based on a criterion which other people dread. There are many criteria which can arouse stigmatization. A literature has grown which documents the dynamics of siting of LULUs: "...facilities and infrastructural construction projects (halfway houses, prisons, housing projects, hospitals, airports, highways, power plants, and the like) that provide a good for society as a whole but concentrate all the undesirable costs in the host community" (Szasz 1994, p. 41).

A recent emphasis of research has been on the impacts of toxic waste disposal sites. Edelstein (1987) has studied a number of communities so affected. Typical reactions are in terms of "fears, stigma, stress, disablement, and community mobilization" (p. 170). Particularly relevant is the fact that this occurs at a municipality-wide level. This results from a legacy of information about such situations indicating that technical judgments by professionals about the boundaries of direct impact are typically underestimated. The extent of actual impact is greater, but the indefiniteness and often secrecy of information about it means that the associated impact area expands to the boundaries of the municipality. Once a potential or existing threat becomes known, the stigma associated with it applies to every resident, regardless of degree of absolute distance or exposure.

Stigma also extends beyond the technically-derived impact area in ways that exceed human feelings. With stigma, the municipality becomes a pariah area in terms of real estate values. This has an extremely tangible impact on residents, to go along with their physical symptoms and mental malaise. According to McClelland and associates (1990), research has shown that there is customarily a difference of opinion about the *degree* of health risk involved (in addition to the size of the area of risk), and that real estate values typically follow public opinion, not expert opinion, on health risks. According to Fitchen (1989), "The effects upon people will be greater than could be explained simply by the 'facts' of actual or projected health problems and financial costs" (p. 321).

A process of stigmatization that ends up seriously eroding the identification and general situation of residents as a class makes the actions of NIMBY-like responses more rational. Reacting against nearby LULUs is not viewed by these people as personal selfishness. It is a reaction to usually externally-generated forces which inflict a stigma with objective consequences. According to Milroy (1991), "Some professionals accuse property owners of narrow-mindedness.... However, the resistance to public facilities could be interpreted as an effort by property owners to keep some control over their immediate environment" (pp. 538-539).

Protests and attempts to exercise more citizen influence on local political decisions have become both active and widespread. In the face of an increase in activism, project proponents have taken to the conscious siting of unwanted land-uses in those municipalities where the residents are relatively powerless and hence less likely to organize in protest (Bryant and Mohai 1992; Szasz 1994).

Furthermore, such discrimination is not restricted to the selection of municipalities on the basis of demographic profiles. As people have observed and learned more about the impacts of LULUs and have become more likely to take actions to influence decisionmaking at the municipal level, authorities at higher levels have devised policies to preempt local decision making. As Szasz (1994, p. 108) put it: "The answer seemed straightforward enough: state 'preemption' of local control promised to neutralize local resistance by taking authority from the political institutions most responsive to it."

One of the startling findings in studies of exposure to toxic waste is that people typically do not move when undesirable land-uses are found or created nearby (Edelstein 1987; Brown and Mikkelsen 1990). The book by Brown and Mikkelsen, which places the situation of Woburn, Massachusetts within the accumulating literature, is entitled *No Safe Place*, because residents in such municipalities add to the factors which make many reluctant to move a belief that alternative places have their own unique perils; hence, there is "no safe place" to live.

American Demographics reported a study by Bernard Cohen, who "calculates that average Americans spend about 70 percent of their lives in their final area of residence.... Americans may have a far greater attachment to place than was previously thought" (Waldrop 1991, p. 10).

These findings are substantiated by Canadian data. A national study conducted by York University Survey Research Centre in 1981 (with data available for computation in the University of Toronto Research Library) indicated that respondents had lived a mean of 21.5 years in their current metropolitan/regional area and that 64 percent of those answering would like to remain there the rest of their lives.

Low mobility rates make the matter of locally unwanted land uses in a municipality much more serious. Residents of municipalities impacted and stigmatized by LULUs are also subsequently exposed to the full consequences of living there.

Therefore, the largely-American literature provides a paradigm in which municipalities are at once a long-term, meaningful reference point for residents and for the locational dynamics of LULUs and their subjective and objective impacts.

PROBLEMATIQUE

The greater Toronto area is filling its current sites for waste disposal. Governments have been trying in vain to find disposal sites within the region which are both environmentally suitable and acceptable to local residents. Finally, in 1992, the Government of Ontario wrote and passed Bill 143, which, among other provisions, legislated two ways of resolving the Toronto waste disposal problem.

(1) A new landfill waste disposal site capable of handling waste generated in both Metro Toronto and the Regional Municipality of York for at least 20 years would have to be located in one or the other municipality (or across the line joining them). In reality, since Metro Toronto is mostly built-up, the site would have to fall in York, which is not. Subsequent work by the Interim Waste Authority placed the prospective site near the town of Maple in Vaughan Township, both within York Region. Vaughan is currently the site of the Keele Valley dump site, run by Metro Toronto and with relatively few years of capacity remaining. Compared to neighboring areas, Vaughan gives less evidence of land-use regulation and enforcement.

(2) A number of provisions of the Environmental Assessment Act would not apply, limiting the scope and content of any environmental assessment done on the single site to be put forward by an Interim Waste Authority.

Thus, a major prospective LULU was slated for a site in a regional municipality through pre-emptive legislation by the provincial government, which at the same time waived provisions of the Environmental Assessment Act which might have given local residents the chance to provide empirical evidence in support of alternative plans.

As part of evidence for legal processes raised in this context, it was considered desirable to gather data to assess the extent that the substance of the largely-American literature applied to the case of York Region. More specifically, the following hypotheses from this literature were tested:

1. People treat municipalities as distinct entities, with differing attributes and bases of attraction.
2. The structure of a municipality is perceived to impact upon the daily life of residents and on their life chances.
3. People's views of the potential impacts of prospective LULUs are a function of the municipality in which they live, but not of where they live within the municipality in which the LULU will be sited.
4. The siting of a prospective LULU does not significantly affect considerations of future mobility.

METHODOLOGY

A telephone survey of 904 randomly selected households in the Municipality of Metropolitan Toronto, the Regional Municipality of York, and the Region of Durham was carried out in February, 1994, by Environics Research Group Ltd. Stratified sampling was used to ensure nearly equal numbers of respondents from each metropolitan/regional municipality for comparative purposes. Within each household, one person 18 years or older was selected by the randomizing factor of most recent birth date. A comparison of the socio-demographic characteristics of the sample drawn with similar distributions found for these areas by Statistics Canada in 1986 and 1991 and by Environics in its regular Metropolls showed that the respondents in the current sample are highly representative of the actual distribution of the population in the three areas.

The basic unit for aggregation and comparison in the study design was the metropolitan/regional government, because this level was adopted for the various considerations in Bill 143. If we wonder whether municipalities are relevant to the lives of citizens, we wonder even more about the relevance of even-larger, regional municipalities. A question widely-debated regarding municipal restructuring is whether the regional level of government is meaningful to the average citizen. People often treat uncritically the old saying that "the best government is the one closest to home," and they argue that democracy is diluted among too many people over a large territory when functions of local government are carried out at the metropolitan or regional levels. But reactions to Bill 143 raised the question as to whether or not the regional municipality is sufficiently important in the lives of its residents that a LULU in one part of it would be a threat to all residents. Indeed, legal proceedings were started by the Mayor of the township within York Region located most distant from Vaughan, acting as an individual.

RESULTS

Distinctiveness Among Regional Municipalities

Respondents were asked, "Consider the following factors. Compared to the other nearby regions, would you rate [yours:

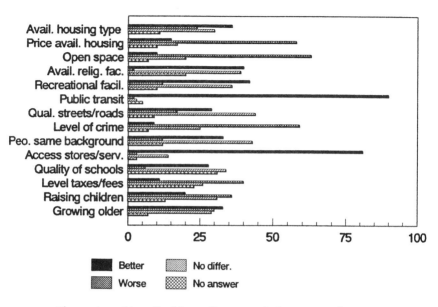

Figure 1a. How Residents Compare their Municipality to Others Nearby: Metro Toronto (*n* = 303, in percent)

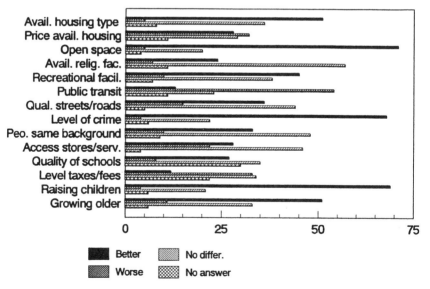

Figure 1b. How Residents Compare their Municipality to Others Nearby: York Region (*n* = 300, in percent)

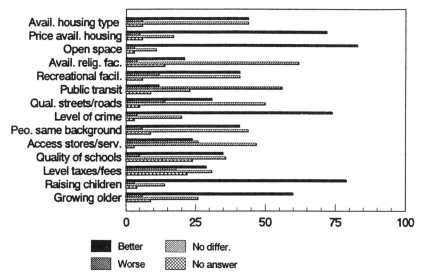

Figure 1c. How Residents Compare their Municipality to Others Nearby: Durham Region (*n* = 301, in percent)

Metropolitan Toronto/York/Durham] as better, worse or no different .....?" The distribution of answers for respondents in each of the municipalities on the 14 factors is found on the respective pages of Figure 1. This chart can be examined in several ways.

First, one can look at differences among the three municipalities in how their residents rate their municipality on a given factor. Quite apart from whether a municipality is seen as better, worse, or no different on, for example, the type of housing available, are the distributions of ratings for the three municipalities on housing type significantly different from one another? Chi-square analysis was done on each of the fourteen criteria, on a contingency table containing the number of responses for evaluations by municipality.

Of the fourteen factors, only three—recreational facilities, the quality of streets and roads, and the quality of schools—are rated equivalently in the three municipalities. On the eleven other criteria, residents see their contexts as significantly distinct. The patterns of difference are so great that the responses on "local people with the same background as you" could only occur by chance at or less than 5 times in a hundred, "availability of religious facilities for you," once in a hundred, and the nine other factors, no more than once in a thousand samples. These responses indicate an ample basis for distinct municipal contexts.

Looking at the pattern of responses across all the factors for each given municipality enables the construction of a unique profile for each of the three.

Metropolitan Toronto, for example, is viewed as better than other nearby municipalities by a great majority of respondents on public transit and access to stores and services. More than a majority of respondents view it as worse in terms of the price of available housing, the amount of open space, and the level of crime.

A majority of the respondents from the Regional Municipality of York see their municipality as better in terms of housing types available, open space, the level of crime, raising children, and growing older. They see York as worse only with regard to public transit.

Durham resembles York in many of the positive ways, as well as the deficit in public transit, but it differs in one significant way. Durham is viewed by most as better in terms of the *price* of available housing rather than regarding the *type* of housing available. This one difference can be a basis for a milieu distinct from that of York.

Survey responses indicate not only that the municipalities are seen as different but that respondents do feel that they can have an impact on the future of their own municipality. This does not suggest that municipalities are the only institutions with an impact on people. Table 1 suggests that residents of all three municipalities agree that their provincial government "has the most impact on [their] everyday living conditions," compared to their own metropolitan or regional government or to the federal government.

Table 1. Answers to Question on, "Which of the Following Levels of Government Do You Think Has the Most Impact on Your Everyday Living Conditions?", by Municipality of Residence (in percent)

Government with most impact on everyday living conditions:	Metro Toronto	York Region	Durham Region
metro/regional	24%	28%	29%
provincial	48	43	45
federal	21	21	19
don't know/no ans.	7	8	8
n =	303	300	301

Table 2. Answers to Questions on, "At Present, if You Wanted to Have a Say in a Policy Decision which Affected You, on Which Level of Government do You Think You Could Have the Most Impact?", by Municipality of Residence (in percent)

Most impact on:	Metro Toronto	York Region	Durham Region
metro/regional government	51%	58%	52%
provincial gov.	25	22	27
federal gov.	16	11	13
don't know/no ans.	8	9	8
n =	303	300	301

Nonetheless, Weiher's findings (1991) are unambiguously supported by the data in Table 2. A clear majority of residents in all three municipalities agree that they could have the most impact on a policy decision made at the municipal level, more than selected the provincial and federal levels combined.

These data therefore support strongly the findings in the general literature that municipalities are distinct, salient entities for the people who reside in them. People do feel some degree of control over decision making in metropolitan and regional municipalities, indeed more so than at the provincial level of government, despite the perceived potency of the latter. While people see clear differences between regional municipalities, there is no difference in feelings of access to decisionmaking by municipality.

Impact on Daily Life and Life Chances

Respondents were asked, "Which of the following 2 statements better represents your point of view? (1) I happened to find a place to live in [my regional municipality], but it wouldn't matter to me and members of my household, which municipality in the greater Toronto area we lived in. (2) The fact that I live in [my regional municipality] makes a difference in terms of the kind of life members of my household and I can lead." Figure 2 shows very clearly that the overwhelming majority of people in each of the three metropolitan/regional municipalities feel that the municipal place of residence makes an impact upon them as individuals. Variation in response by municipality is extremely small, with support for municipal impact on individuals ranging from 72 percent in Metro to 80 percent in Durham.

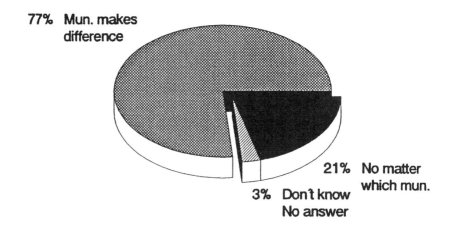

77% Mun. makes difference

21% No matter which mun.

3% Don't know No answer

Figure 2. Impact of Municipal Place of Residence on
Respondents (*n* = 904, in percent)

In what aspects of daily life and life chances does this kind of
municipality make an impact? Some answers are found in response
to a series of direct questions: "Would you say that the fact that you
live in [your metropolitan/regional municipality] has a lot of impact,
some impact, a little impact or no impact at all on..." a series of major
outcomes which vary by municipal structure and institutions. This list
included: "(a) The amount of beauty or tranquillity which enters your
everyday life, (b) Your personal safety, (c) How easy or hard it is to
get to where you need to go on an average day, (d) The kind of people
with whom you get together on a regular basis, (e) your children's
development, (f) Your self image, [and] (g) Your future wellbeing."
Insofar as the answers were of degree of current impact *per se*, not
a quality rating, it is not surprising that the distribution of differences
between municipalities was trivial. What the results show, however, is
that, with one exception, these Toronto area residents see their
metropolitan/regional municipalities as having a major impact on these
personal outcomes. The majority of respondents feel that their
municipalities have either some or a lot of impact on each of the
outcomes except "Your self image." The category of impact chosen
most often on each of the positive-impact outcomes is "A lot of impact."
These findings are presented in Figure 3.

The one exception, "Your self-image," is an interesting anomaly. In
one respect, it serves a useful function in correcting any possible

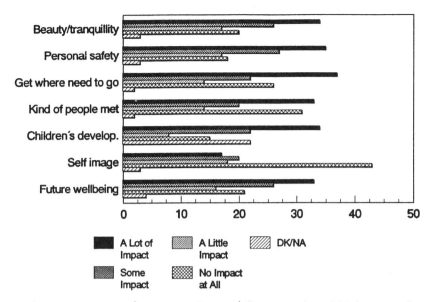

Figure 3. Municipal Impact on Personal Outcomes (*n* = 904, in percent)

thoughts that respondents were employing simply a positive response-set bias. Second, the use of "Your self image" was perhaps a mistake of wording, on theoretical grounds; the literature suggests that self image is a potential basis for selecting place of residence, rather than an impact of it. When self-image and municipal characteristics are congruent, there is a bond. One may gain an identity regardless. But it is not certain that municipality impacts strongly on self image.

These indications of marked impacts of municipal place of residence on specific personal outcomes could be an outcome of the feelings and experiences of just one subgroup in the sample, a reflection of that characteristic. Analyses of such data customarily ask there are competing variables which contribute a stronger explanation of the outcome variable(s)—for example, gender, home ownership status, or ethnicity. Is it really women who give a certain answer? or predominantly homeowners? Or people of British background? In the present case, however, and throughout the analyses reported in this document, the relationship of all the outcomes was analyzed with regard to a battery of conventional (and often useful) explanatory variables and found NOT explained by them. Men and women, for example, answered with extreme similarity, as did people of different social class, residential tenure, and the like.

Municipality of Residence and Impact of Selected LULUs

Respondents were asked, "What impact would each of the following
[hypothetical or discussed projects] have on *your life* [emphasis in
original]?" The answers ranged on a five-point scale from very positive
to very negative. Tables 3a.-d. show, among other things, that the
salience of a potentially intrusive land-use to people is directly a
function of whether it is to be found in their regional municipality, *even
if the effects might be more general to the greater Toronto area.*

For example, Table 3a. presents responses (collapsed into three
categories, plus don't know/no answer) to the hypothetical situation,
"if Metro Toronto were to build a new expressway from Pearson Airport
to Downtown?" The clear majority of residents of York and Durham
feel that this would have neither positive nor negative impact on
themselves. Exactly half of Metro respondents, however, feel this would
have a positive impact on their lives, 12 percent see a negative impact,
and only 36 percent see neither. This difference is statistically significant
at the level of chance occurrence of less than once in a thousand.

When such a project is located in Durham, however, "if a major
new power line were to be built in Durham Region?" The table turns
in a predictable direction. Table 3b shows that the clear majority of
Metro and York residents see no positive or negative impacts for
themselves. Durham residents, in contrast, line up with 39 percent
negative and 22 percent positive; even the positive response in
Durham is greater than the total non-neutral response in Metro! This
degree of inter-municipality differences is again significant at the
probability level of .001.

Table 3a.   Impact "if Metro Toronto Were to Build a New Expressway
from Pearson Airport to Downtown,"
by Municipal Place of Residence (in percent).

Impact on life:	Metro Toronto	Region of York	Durham Region
Very/somewhat positive	50%	36%	25%
Neither positive nor negative	36	57	69
Somewhat/very negative	12	5	5
No answer/don't know	3	2	1
n =	303	300	301

Table 3b. Impact "If a Major New Power Line were to be Built in Durham Region," by Municipal Place of Residence (in percent)

Impact on life:	Metro Toronto	Region of York	Durham Region
Very/somewhat positive	13%	17%	22%
Neither positive nor negative	72	61	33
Somewhat/very negative	7	16	39
No answer/don't know	7	6	7
n =	303	300	301

Table 3c. turns the focus onto York Region: "if a major new waste disposal site for Metro Toronto were to be located in York Region?" Insofar as this project has somewhat more than hypothetical status and has been the subject of considerable publicity, it is not surprising that negative responses are higher than in response to the other projections mentioned. Nonetheless, respondents from York Region are much more likely to give an answer reflecting negative impact (indeed nearly all "very negative" impact), as do 80 percent of them, while just about half of the Metro and Durham respondents are neutral—the majority neutral after taking away the no answer/don't know responses. The differences are as extremely significant statistically as the preceding tables, indeed, technically, even more so. Of the 241 York respondents who provided a negative impact answer, 30 percent rooted this feeling in terms of pollution, noise,

Table 3c. Impact "If a Major new Waste Disposal Site for Metro Toronto were to be located in York Region," by Municipal Place of Residence (in percent)

Impact on life:	Metro Toronto	Region of York	Durham Region
Very/somewhat positive	12%	8%	15%
Neither positive nor negative	49	11	48
Somewhat/very negative	35	80	34
No answer/don't know	5	1	3
n =	303	300	301

Table 3d. Impact "If More Runways Were to be Built at
Lester B. Pearson International Airport," by
Municipal Place of Residence (in percent)

Impact on life:	Metro Toronto	Region of York	Durham Region
Very/somewhat positive	37%	28%	27%
Neither positive nor negative	51	61	65
Somewhat/very negative	10	8	8
No answer/don't know	2	2	1
n =	303	300	301

or smell, while 29 percent noted that their house values would decline, and another 23 percent spoke of threats to their health. These are textbook responses to this situation. The disposal site would be relatively localized, and the regional municipality is huge in size; but the responses from a sample representing the whole region are unambiguous.

Finally, Table 3d. represents answers to the situation, "if more runways were to be built at Lester B. Pearson International Airport?" This is an interesting case, insofar as the airport is located in Peel region (i.e., in none of the regions sampled), but yet the landing patterns of aircraft overfly both Metro and York, depending on conditions. The importance of municipality, however, is underlined by the responses. The majority in all three of the municipalities sampled cite a neutral impact response, and among those who do imagine an impact, more are positive than negative. There is no significant statistical difference among the municipalities sampled when the offending land-use is (literally) across the street, into an adjacent municipality!

But what happens when a prospective LULU is located in one's own regional municipality? A special analysis of the data within York Region on answers to the section on "if a major new waste disposal site for Metro Toronto were to be located in York Region?" sheds light on the extent that residents within a municipality feel impacted by a proposed project regardless of their proximity or distance to it. Respondent postal codes were used to differentiate them by distance from the current disposal site and the nearby (in regional terms) site given widespread publicity as the potential future

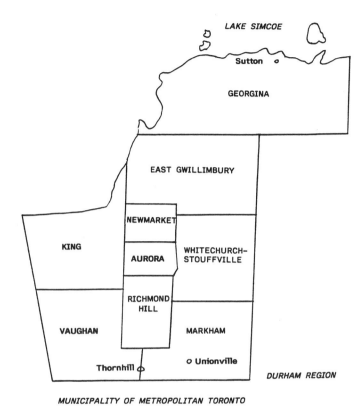

Figure 4. Map of the Regional Municipality of York

Table 4. Impact "If a Major New Waste Disposal Site for
Metro Toronto Were to be Located in York Region," by Distance Zones
from Present and Discussed Future Waste Disposal Sites (in percent)

Impact on life:	Zone 1 (closest)	Zone 2	Zone 3	Zone 4 (farthest)
Very positive	6%	4%	3%	5%
Somewhat positive	5	4	7	1
Neither pos. nor negative	6	13	17	12
Somewhat negative	10	16	33	22
Very negative	73	62	40	60
n =	63	68	30	138

Note: missing data = 1

one for Metro Toronto disposal. The closest category included respondents from Vaughan and King. Next proximate included those from Aurora and Richmond Hill. Next more distant included Thornhill and Newmarket. The most distant category included other parts of Markham, Stouffville, Whitechurch, Sutton, Unionville, East Guillembury, and Georgina. Figure 4 shows on a map the respective locations of these places, as well as the situation of York with respect to Metro Toronto and Durham.

Table 4 illustrates this phenomenon within York. The patterns of response to this question are similar and strongly negative within the borders of the regional municipality, regardless of distance from the existing and apparent target sites. For example, 83 percent in the most proximate category foresee a negative impact, as do 82 percent in the most distant category. Amongst the largely negative impact responses in all the distance categories (which range from 73 percent to 83 percent), the heavy weight of responses is on "very negative impact" in every case.

Qualitative comments given in response to, "How would this affect · you?" are remarkably similar regardless of location.

"...lowering of value of land nearby" (Richmond Hill).
"It would ruin the image of the place I'm living" (Richmond Hill).
"I think it would affect everybody" (Stouffville).
"Real estate values would go down, financial effect, and social standing" (Markham).
"It would lower the quality of the region" (Markham).
"Negative image for area" (Markham).
"Real estate value would decrease" (Thornhill).
"Because it's our lives they're polluting" (Sutton).
"Would be very close" (Sutton).
"Quality of life in region" (King).
"Decreased value of land" (King)

Thus, the survey data confirm exactly conclusions in the literature more generally about how locally unwanted land-use activities within municipal boundaries have a wide-ranging stigmatizing impact upon residents throughout the municipality involved and not as a direct function of distance.

Expected Future Mobility

In the current survey in Metro, York, and Durham, only 28.7 percent of the respondents expect to move away from their metropolitan/regional municipality within the next five years. The greatest percentage, at 34.3 percent, is among the Metro Toronto respondents, with York second at 30.7 percent, and Durham lower yet at 20.9 percent. It should be noted that, in a previous study (Michelson 1977), answers to this question had extremely high predictive power for subsequent behavior.

Table 5 shows the more frequently cited reasons people give in the respective areas for considering such a move. Every reason attracting at least 10 percent of respondents within one of the areas is cited, as, for comparison, are the distributions of people whose moves would be prompted by either the waste disposal site or other perceived environmental threats. The data show that some of the most frequent reasons for such a move are common to all the municipalities. Real estate costs and/or taxes are greatest in both Metro and York, and also mentioned significantly in Durham. Proximity to job opportunities, and a change in job or school location account for many prospective moves out of all the areas. Metro Toronto has a nearly unique set of move precipitants which include escaping the local milieu and/or population mix, the crime rate, a desire for a more remote and/or rustic area, wanting to leave the province, Canada, or the geographic region, and wishes for more space in and around the dwelling unit. Just under 10 percent of York respondents also would prefer to escape their local conditions, to live in a more remote/rustic area, or to move to be closer to their relatives and friends. Respondents from Durham were somewhat likely to base future moves away on a departure from the larger political or geographic area or to be closer to friends or relatives.

In contrast, only three percent in York Region out of the 300 in the sample suggested that they would leave York because of the "dump site," and the same percent in Durham had the same intention due to other environmental hazards.

The reasonable but not great level of mobility expected among the respondents in the next five years has largely to do with commonplace reasons for changing residence, quite apart from the unwanted land-uses shown to be extremely salient within

Table 5. Percentage of Respondents Giving Specific Reasons
for Somewhat or Very Likely Moves Outside their
Metropolitan/Regional Municipality within the Next Five Years

Why consider move:	Metro Toronto	Region of York	Durham Region
Real estate costs/taxes	17%	21%	11%
Closer to work/ availability of work	12%	16%	13%
Escaping local milieu/pop. mix	12%	9%	*
Job/education children	11%	12%	19%
Crime rate	11%	*	*
Leaving province/ Canada/geog. area	11%	*	13%
Towards more remote/rustic area	10%	9%	*
More space in/around home	10%	*	*
Closer to relatives and friends	*	9%	10%
"The dump site"	*	3%	*
Other environmental hazards	*	*	3%
n =	104	92	63

Note: * mention very low or absent

municipal boundaries in the previous section. People may be worried about the impact of such land-uses on their lives, but they do not contemplate moving on that account. Their place of residence will remain stable, and therefore their exposure to whatever occurs will eventuate. As the previous literature documents, municipal place of residence is an even more serious human context with respect to unwanted land-uses because of its stability in people's lives.

CONCLUDING REMARKS

The data presented clearly support the hypotheses derived from the literature: that people find their regional municipalities as distinct entities which have an impact on daily life and life chances and that municipal boundaries tend to frame prospective LULUs as salient to all municipality residents, not least because they are not likely to move away in response.

This linked set of phenomena help to explain why NIMBY responses are as strong and widespread as they are.

That this is the case, however, does not mean that large projects and interventions should cease once and for all. The public good is frequently served by land-uses which are unwanted locally. Certainly, sociologists are aware that conflict in decisionmaking is a regular part of social systems. Some LULUs might be avoided through alternative forms of transportation and by the three R's of resource management. But others convey a known good, and the real question is the optimal location for them, in social and environmental terms. Local opposition may be natural, but is not necessarily the final word.

Social and environmental impact assessment procedures are intended to deal rationally with allocation procedures, following determination of the necessity of the project or intervention. If these are carried out and administered objectively—extremely big "ifs"— then LULUs will land in the least disruptive locations. But when and where LULUs are forced upon a local area through unreasonable processes and without recourse, NIMBY reactions are not only natural but entirely justifiable and worthy of support by the wider public.

ACKNOWLEDGMENT

An earlier draft of this paper was presented to the Section on Environment and Technology, American Sociological Association, August 16, 1996. I am grateful to Environics Ltd. for undertaking the data collection. This study was conducted in part fulfillment of a contract with Cassels Brock & Blackwell, Barristers and Solicitors, Toronto, but the substance reported is entirely the undertaking of the author. Boxu Yang provided helpful research assistance. Two anonymous reviewers provided useful suggestions.

REFERENCES

Abu-Lughod, J. 1991. *Changing Cities*. New York: Harper Collins.

Agnew, J.A. 1981. "Homeownership and the Capitalist Social Order." Pp. 457-480 in *Urbanization & Urban Planning in Capitalist Society*, edited by Michael Dear and Allen J. Scott. New York: Methuen.

Brown, P., and E.J. Mikkelsen. 1990. *No Safe Place: Toxic Waste, Leukemia, and Community Action*. Berkeley: University of California Press.

Bryant, B., and P. Mohai. (eds.). 1992. *Race and the Incidence of Environmental Hazards*. Boulder: Westview Press.

Edelstein, M., 1987. *Contaminated Communities: The Social and Psychological Impacts of Residential Toxic Exposure*. Boulder: Westview Press.

Feldman, R. 1990. "Settlement Identity: Psychological Bonds with Home Places in a Mobile Society." *Environment and Behavior* 22: 183-229.

Fitchen, J. 1989. "When Toxic Chemicals Pollute Residential Environments: The Cultural Meanings of Home and Homeownership." *Human Organization* 48: 313-324.

Gould, K.A., A. Schnaiberg, and A.S. Weinberg. 1996. *Local Environmental Struggles*. New York: Cambridge University Press.

Illidge, P. 1994. "Confessions of a Scarberian." *The Toronto Star* (May 27), p. A25.

Janowitz, M. 1967. *The Community Press in an Urban Setting*, 2nd ed. Chicago: University of Chicago Press.

Jennings, N. 1993. "Naked Ambition." *Maclean's* (March 8), p. 55.

Karp, D., G. Stone, and W. Yoels. 1991. *Being Urban*. New York: Praeger.

Lofland, L. 1985. *A World of Strangers*. Prospect Heights, IL: Waveland Press.

Lyon, L. 1987. *The Community in Urban Society*. Chicago: Dorsey.

McClelland, G. et al., 1990. "The Effect of Risk Beliefs on Property Values: A Case Study of a Hazardous Waste Site." *Risk Analysis* 10: 485-497.

Michelson, W. 1977. *Environmental Choice, Human Behavior, and Residential Satisfaction*. New York: Oxford University Press.

Milroy, B.M. 1991. "People, Urban Space, and Advantage." Pp. 519-544 in *Canadian Cities in Transition*, edited by Trudi Bunting and Pierre Filion. Toronto: Oxford University Press.

Stefanovic, I.L. 1992. "The Experience of Place: Housing Quality from a Phenomenological Perspective." *Canadian Journal of Urban Research* 1: 145-161.

Szasz, A. 1994. *EcoPopulism: Toxic Waste and the Movement for Environmental Justice*. Minneapolis: University of Minnesota Press.

Waldrop, J. 1991. "The Powerful Lure of Home." *American Demographics* 13(7): 10.

Weiher, G. 1991. *The Fractured Metropolis: Political Fragmentation and Metropolitan Segregation*. Albany: State University of New York Press.

Wellman, B., and B. Leighton. 1979. "Networks, Neighborhoods, and Communities: Approaches to the Study of the Community Question." *Urban Affairs Quarterly* 14: 363-390.

Wireman, P. 1984. *Urban Neighborhoods, Networks, and Families*. Toronto: Lexington Books.

SACRED SPACE IN THE CITY:
COMMUNITY TOTEMS AND
POLITICAL CONTESTS

Scott Swearingen

ABSTRACT

In this paper I use concepts from Durkheim and Eliade to show how
the implicit religious processes of integration, totemism, and sacred
space function to establish group connection to space and create a
sense of community. A case study of a social movement in Austin,
Texas, illustrates these processes. At the local level, these universal
social processes revolve around certain key environmental features of
Austin, and are conditioned by the political contestations that occur
within the political economy of Austin's growth. Analyzing a political
campaign run by this social movement, I illustrate how these processes
operate in Austin to sacralize a particular space as totemic of the larger
community, and define an alternative meaning of the city. I conclude
with some thoughts on the relevance of these processes to issues of
planning and development.

Research in Community Sociology, Volume 7, pages 141-169.
Copyright © 1997 by JAI Press Inc.
All rights of reproduction in any form reserved.
ISBN: 0-7623-0272-0

INTRODUCTION: COMMUNAL ATTACHMENT TO SPACE

Social Theories of Space

One of the enduring interests of urban sociology has been the relationship between urban space and group formation. The socio-biotic theories of the early Chicago school (Park, Burgess, and McKenzie 1925) with its interest in natural areas and concentric zones, and demographic explanations of the effects of urban space on human interactions (Wirth 1938) established research in the topic. Later sociological research has shown that urban spaces come to have cultural meanings for groups who dwell within them, meanings conditioned by the roles of those groups in their society. The works of Firey (1945) and Gans (1962) stand out as exemplars of this research, while contemporary urbanists such as Zukin (1982) and Mock (1993) continue this interest. Contemporary urban theory notes that historical and cultural mechanisms of local social groupings shape contests over the creation of urban space (Castells 1983; Orum 1991; Gottdiener 1985; Gottdiener and Feagin 1988), as well as the symbolic understandings of that space (Gottdiener and Lagopoulos 1986). Such symbolism has been termed "urban meaning," the notion that urban space means something symbolic to residents. Some symbolic meanings of space, especially the hegemonic meaning of the city as "growth" organism, are ideological in nature, and can be deployed by elites in political contests to shape the terms of discourse over the meaning of the city. However, opposing meanings can arise, and can serve as bones of contention between contesting social groups in the city (Gottdiener 1985; Orum 1987, 1991).

In addition, social geographers theorize that a mixture of geography, architecture, and socio-cultural processes produce symbolic and representational meanings of the spaces human societies create. Working primarily within the phenomenological tradition of social theory, cultural geographers have shown that people attach psycho-social meaning to spaces (Tuan 1974; Relph 1976; Gold and Burgess 1982; Carter et al. 1993). The specific meanings which are created are mediated by the social institutions of the culture, for example religious ideologies (Duncan 1990; Kong 1993), political contests (Beauregard 1995), social class (Duncan 1973) and the contemporary post-modern capitalist system (Shields 1991).

The uses to which people put their spaces are the principle means of defining the meaning of their places. Such uses are often inherently political, occurring in contestations for social power between groups (Duncan 1990; Western 1993). Other uses are part of the daily round of living; buying food, going to school, relaxing (Ley 1983). Both sociologists and cultural geographers call attention to the ways in which geographic and architectural space interact with human activity and cultural ideologies to create meanings of space for particular groups (e.g., Rotenberg and McDonogh 1993). Left unanswered, however, are several questions about that interaction. How is it that groups claim space, instilling in it their own meanings? How does a particular type of space come to be made symbolic of a particular group? How can certain types of spaces become representative of a community?

In this paper I use concepts from the sociology of religion to answer these questions. I describe a set of implicit religious processes that establish both group connection to space and a sense of community related to that space. An implicit religion is a seemingly secular phenomenon that nevertheless contains one or several religious overtones; that is, it might answer supernatural questions, may employ some ritual to attain a particular goal, or might deify some object not traditionally understood to be religious. Such beliefs or behaviors are implicitly religious because they do not seem to be religious in the sense of church attendance or spirituality but, upon closer scrutiny, resemble traditionally religious beliefs or behaviors. Implicit religious processes often function as a surrogate for what are traditionally understood as religious values or actions. In this paper, I describe the implicit religious processes of integration, totemism, and sacred space to illustrate how group attachment to space and community formation occur. Using a case study of Austin, Texas, I try to show how these implicit religious processes are imbedded in the political economy of urban growth, and how they are conditioned and even created out of the conflicts inherent in that political economy.

After a brief description of the sociological processes of integration, totemism, and sacred space, I describe the most recent grassroots political campaign to protect a local creek and swimming pool as an example of these processes. A content analysis of the literature produced by the coalition who organized the campaign, and a series of in-depth interviews with leaders and activists of the coalition, are used to illustrate the process at work. I conclude with a description of how these ritualistic processes create and amplify a community represented by a particular environmental feature in Austin.

Quasi-Religious Processes: Integration, Totemism, and Sacred Space

One of the seminal sociological concepts discussed by Durkheim (1965) is the operation of what he calls "religious facts." According to Durkheim, all human societies create Sacred and Profane objects and behaviors. The Sacred is created through a process whereby common ritual and symbolism bond an individual to a group, making the individual feel part of an abstract ideal. For example, religious rituals make their participants feel a connection to some god-like force as the sacred. The secular practice of pledging allegiance to a flag creates the nation itself as the abstract, or sacred, ideal. A sports team can represent the ideal of its college. But Durkheim claims that any of these sacred categories are simply a representation of the society itself. They are, "[i]n short, ... a *principle of grouping and unification*" (Durkheim 1975, p. 87, my emphasis). In human society, states Durkheim, what humans believe to be an abstract force, be it God, University, or Country, is simply a symbolic representation of the moral force of their group or society itself. Although social customs, laws, and traditions are the observable forces that socialize and constrain human action, people do not consciously analyze the effects of these social forces upon themselves. Instead,

> ... men know well that they are acted upon, but they do not know by whom. So they must invent by themselves the idea of these powers with which they feel themselves in connection, and from that, we are able to catch a glimpse of the way by which ... [people] transfigure them by thought (Durkheim 1915, p. 253).

There are two kinds of "transfiguration by thought" that I will discuss in order to show the interaction between environmental space and sense of community. The first is what we now call social integration. Through their shared religious, familial, and political activity, the bonds of humans are formed. These activities integrate individuals into their groups by occupying the individuals in the common practices of the group (Durkheim 1951). The greater the degree of common experience, the higher the degree of integration.

The second transfiguration I discuss is Totemism. Durkheim (1965) described the way that groups represent themselves in the form of physical objects, called totems. However, according to Durkheim, the totem of the group is more than simply a physical symbol. It represents what Durkheim calls the Totemic Principle, the essence of the group. Durkheim's discussion of totemism will be used to explain how groups within a city can define themselves in relation to environmental features in the city. In addition, the idea of totemism helps understand how a meaning of a particular city can be expressed.

Extending Durkheim's notion of Sacred and Profane, Eliade (1961) suggested that space itself can become sacred to groups of people, acting as a break between people's secular lives and their sacred realm. What Eliade terms "heirophanic" and "theophanic" spaces allow group members to experience the cosmogony of their group. Heirophanic spaces are spaces which allow experience of the sacred. Theophanic spaces are spaces that allow access to that experience. Such space defines the relationship of that group to the larger universe. By allowing a connection to a larger cosmos, sacred space symbolizes the group's relationship to a larger cosmic order, further defining the group as a distinct community.[1]

In this paper, I illustrate the ways that integration, totemism, and sacred space operate as mechanisms that define a community for one set of protagonists in an ongoing battle over growth in a Southwestern U.S. city. In Austin, Texas, a natural spring-fed pool called Barton Springs has emerged over the past two decades as the symbolic focus of a larger meaning of Austin as a special kind of place (Swearingen, forthcoming), a meaning in opposition to the ideology of growth. Protecting the Springs from the damages of urbanization has fueled a two decades long political movement between these two groups that has established a public discourse where "environmentalists" battle "developers" over the kind of city that Austin will become.

As part of this ongoing battle, Barton Springs has been promoted by environmentalists as a symbol of their meaning of Austin. As this battle has developed, Barton Springs has come to function as both a sacred space and the totem of this environmental group. The latest political contest in this battle illustrates the sacralization of Barton Spring as sacred space, and the use of the totemic symbolism of the space as communal representation by the environmental group.

These processes have occurred within the context of the political
economy of growth in Austin, the geography that shapes political
struggle over that growth, and larger cultural ideas about "nature"
that are reflected in this struggle.

Methods

Data for this study are culled from a larger ongoing case study
on the meanings of urban space (Swearingen, forthcoming). For
this paper, I use in-depth interviews with leaders of local
environmental groups and a content analysis of campaign
literature to analyze implicit religious processes about Austin and
Barton Springs.

In-depth interviews with environmental activists were conducted
between 1994 and 1996. Activists were defined for this purpose as
either present or past leaders of local environmental organizations
which are members of the SOS Coalition (described below), or
political operatives who donated their time to operate the SOS
referendum campaign of 1992 (described below). Thirty-five activists
were interviewed. The interviews are composed of roughly equal
numbers of men and women ranging in age from their late 20s to
early 60s, all of whom are college graduates, most of whom are
professionals, and all but two of whom are white. Interviews were
conducted as semi-structured discussions. A few general questions
were asked of the respondent, with specific targeted probes used to
illuminate statements about the relationship between specific
environmental features and the city of Austin. Interviews were then
coded using an emergent themes technique whereby issues salient to
the respondents were cross referenced with other respondents to
generate the analysis used in this paper.

Content analyses are taken from the literature produced by the
SOS Coalition in its referendum campaign of 1992. All press releases,
campaign literature, and fund raising letters issued by the Coalition
in this campaign were collected. Relevant sections of this literature
are used in the present paper to illustrate what Snow and associates
(1986) call "frame alignment processes." Frame alignment processes
are used by organizations to garner support for their cause by aligning
their own interpretations of events (Snow, et. al 1986, p. 467) to
attitudes in the larger population.[2] One frame alignment technique
is Frame Bridging, whereby Social Movement Organizations attempt

to reach out to "unmobilized sentiment pools or public opinion clusters. These sentiment pools refer to aggregates of individuals who share common grievances and attributional orientations, but who lack the organizational base for expressing their discontents and for acting in pursuit of their interests" (Snow, et al. 1986, p. 467) In this paper, I use the campaign literature of the SOS Coalition for two purposes. The SOS literature helps to illustrate how implicit religious mechanisms create attributions of Austin as a certain kind of place and foster attachment to that place. At the same time, the frame bridging of SOS literature can be seen as an indirect measure of public sentiment. The Coalition successfully framed their issue in a way that would mobilize existing public attitudes for their cause, suggesting that the public perception of the problem matched the SOS definition of the problem.

THE SOCIAL AND GEOGRAPHIC CONTEXTS
OF THE ENVIRONMENTAL CITY

The Social Geography of an Environmental City

Austin is built around three principle geographic features. The Colorado River runs through the center of town, providing drinking water and recreation to the citizens. A dam on the river creates a lake around which extensive parkland has been built. The second principle feature incorporated into Austin's design are its creeks. Running through the central city, many creeks have been established by the city as greenbelts—linear parks with trails for walking and bicycling. Finally, the Hill Country to the west of Austin has historically served as a boundary for the city, providing a natural semicircle on the west side of the city. In the past Austin was known as the "City of the Violet Crown" for the spectacular effect of the sunsets over the Hill Country.

As geographic spaces, these features have historically defined the character of Austin. Stephen F. Austin, the city's founder, chose the location of Austin because of its location; nestled against the Hill Country on the river between the creeks. His original map plattes of the city are bounded by these features, and nineteenth century maps of the town illustrate how the town's growth was shaped by these features. The symbolic importance of water is represented in

Mr. Austin's choice of street names: he named the east-west streets for trees, and the north-south streets for the rivers in Texas.

The rivers and creeks have caught the attention of modern Austinites as well. The Austin master plan of 1928 called attention to the fact that the "natural beauty of the topography and the unusual climate [made Austin] an ideal residential city, [so that] it is only natural that the chief characteristic of greater Austin will continue, as at present, essentially a cultural and educational center" (Koch and Fowler 1928). That plan established a detailed system of parks, encouraging the city to buy property along the lake and creeks to build the system. While the city did purchase some of this land, the major implementation of the creeks-as-parks idea was implemented by two of the city's wealthy residents, who used their own money to build the first gravel pathway along Shoal Creek, the western boundary of Austin's original city. The couple coined the term Hike and Bike for their trail, and the name stuck. The master plan of 1961 synthesized the Hike and Bike idea with the parks system, planning a system of greenbelts along the major inner city creeks. These greenbelts with hike and bike trails were to serve as both park space and transportation node for pedestrian traffic within the city. Illustrating how important the creeks and lakes are to Austin's sense of its self as a place, Austin's Bicentennial Gift to the Nation (part of the National Bicentennial Celebration) created the Creeks Project that used all the city's creeks as multimodal park and transportation spaces. The committee of prominent citizens which put that plan together wrote that the waterways of Austin defined the city both physically and symbolically. "When we speak of the natural endowment of Austin, we are inevitably talking about the Colorado River and all the creeks and waterways that flow into it" wrote the committee (Horizons Committee 1976).

Along with the lake and creeks, one particular water feature stands out as special to many Austinites. Located at the end of the largest southern creek, in the central park next to the lake, there is a natural formation of springs that pumps out 26 million gallons of water a day. This formation has been a central swimming facility for Austin since the late 1800s. In the 1920s the city built a dam 1/8 mile below the springs, creating Barton Springs Pool, which presently serves as a natural swimming area and recreation center for the city. Since the pool is in the bottom of a creekbed, it flows through a shallow canyon surrounded by huge pecan and oak trees, acres of grass, and rock formations eroded by the creek. The canyon slopes are maintained as grassy open spaces, which for eight months of the year are occupied by hundreds of swimmers and sunbathers as a kind of hillside beach. This mix of "natural" and human constructed topography creates a peaceful relaxation experience away from the noise and bustle of daily urban activity. Staying at the pool for any length of time creates the type of experience one usually finds only on camping or hiking trips, yet the experience can be had in the middle of a large city.

The water from Barton Springs emerges from an aquifer underneath the Hill Country to the southwest. That aquifer is recharged by rain that seeps through the ground via unbuilt land and the creeks that run through its recharge zone. In the 1970s, a city master plan named Austin Tomorrow was drawn up by city staff, citizens, neighborhood groups, and developers. The plan specified that the recharge zone was an area to be protected by limiting development of large projects (City of Austin 1980). However, this very zone was chosen by many real estate developers for land speculation, primarily because it is one of the prettiest areas near the city. As Austin grew in the 1980s, developers began large scale suburban development in the recharge zone, electing and lobbying city councils who extended the urban infrastructure into the Hill Country on top of the aquifer in contradiction to the Austin Tomorrow plan. This development has begun to cover the Hill Country, directly threatening the water quality of the aquifer and the creeks coming into town from the south-west, and eroding the quality of the water that emerges in Barton Springs pool.

Cultural Ideas of Nature

The geography of Austin lends itself perfectly to the larger cultural ideals of "nature" in North American culture.[3] In much of U.S. culture there is an inherent anti-urban bias (Lees 1985; Warner 1972; White 1963) that defines a dichotomy between urban spaces and a more "natural" realm of non-urban living (Graber 1976; Lane 1988), creating a definition of "nature" as retreat from the degrading qualities of the city (Schmidt 1969; Wilson 1992). Thus many U.S. urbanites are already conditioned in some respects to expect that the "urban" is inherently different from the ideal of "nature," which may contribute to the positive correlation often found between urban residence and environmental sentiment (e.g., Howell and Laska

1992). This cultural conditioning, along with the way Austin has been built into the geography of the area, has created a structural "fit" between larger cultural predispositions and local sentiment about place. As a former Mayor related during our discussions, "when the [national] environmental movement started, it caught on big here—it had meaning here." This structural fit shapes the kind of space that is capable of being sacralized in Austin; as I describe below, Barton Springs has become a sacred space due in large part to its distinctive "natural" qualities that separate it from the increasingly urban environment.

Because of the synthesis of larger culture ideals of nature and its geographical setting, the waterways of Austin help structure the kinds of political contestations and symbolism that arise as a response to the effects of urban growth. The social geography of Austin, added to the cultural predispositions toward "nature" as wholesome and "urban" as dirty, have created a structure where Barton Springs could *become* salient as a symbol of purity and community. It is in this structure that Barton Springs has become a central symbol for many Austinites who oppose the environmental degradation and changes in the lifestyle of Austin brought by its growth. As they have made Barton Springs pool into a symbol of a meaning of Austin defined by its "natural" qualities, environmentalists have created a totemic feature that represents their meaning of Austin. Through their use of Barton Springs as totem, they identify themselves as "Austinites" by their desire to maintain Austin as a place defined by its environmental features instead of urban growth.

The Political Economy of Austin

Orum (1987) details how the growth of Austin into a big city was created by a set of actors who deployed the ideology of growth as the guiding vision of what Austin could be. There have always been challengers to that vision, however, organized around various grievances that were heightened by that growth. By the 1990s, the challengers had become reorganized around a loose coalition of environmental groups called the Save Our Springs Coalition (SOS).

As have many before them, the members of the SOS coalition feel that the natural environmental features of Austin give the city its special meaning. They feel that the creeks and springs should be protected for the use and enjoyment of the citizens rather than private profit taking by individuals. These opposing views of land presently shape the political contestation in Austin between groups who want to preserve the "natural" feel of Austin as defined by its waterways and unbuilt Hill County environment, and pro-growth actors who define those same spaces as places for private profit.

Throughout the 1980s, neighborhood and environmental groups fought to make the city follow the Austin Tomorrow Plan for the city's growth. Environmentalists successfully enacted a series of creek ordinances and urban water quality ordinances that placed some limits on development in areas surrounding creeks and watersheds. Because multiple exemptions from the ordinances were often granted by the city's planning commission, however, these ordinances were largely ineffective at curtailing development. In addition, a Texas law allows developers to build their projects as Municipal Utility Districts (MUDs). MUDs are exempted from regulations imposed on other city developments. Many MUD's were built in the aquifer recharge zone from the late 1970s through the 1980s. Citing the need to service the MUDs that had already been built, Austin's utility departments continued to build utility services and roads out to new MUDs in the recharge zone. Thus the actions of developers and city ran contrary to the stated goals of the AT plan, infuriating many segments of Austin who had worked on that plan, and mobilizing neighborhood and environmental groups into political coalitions. These coalitions won an occasional bond election, and got a few of their members elected to the City Council. But the combination of Texas laws, city staff, and developer friendly Councils during the 1980s kept them from being able to stop the growth that was occurring in the recharge zone.

Then, in 1991 Freeport Properties, a subsidiary of the large multinational corporation Freeport-McMoran, proposed a huge suburban development on top of the aquifer and Barton Creek. When Freeport Properties asked the city to grant it a Planned Unit Development (PUD) with multiple exemptions from the 1980s water quality ordinances, the environmental groups publicized the fact with flyers and media ads, encouraging people to attend the City Council meeting where the PUD proposal would be discussed. Over 900 citizens opposed to the PUD rallied at the City Council meeting, sparking the longest council meeting in the city's history, and convincing the Council to reject the proposed PUD. The council even passed a new ordinance strengthening water quality controls for new developments. But FP continued to work on plans that would allow it to develop its property, promising to return for another try.

The impact of that meeting carried over into the Council election the next year, and all the major candidates held press conferences at Barton Springs promising to strengthen city water codes for the safety of Barton Springs. Once elected, however, the new Council wrote an ordinance that was weaker than the one the previous council had passed. The new Council's ordinance would have allowed denser development in the PUD than had been permissible in the initial plan. The ordinance written by the new councilmembers who had campaigned on promises of environmental protection further energized the environmental and neighborhood groups. Local environmental groups, along with the local offices of national environmental and citizen action groups, formed a coalition called Save Our Springs (SOS).

The local groups such as Save Barton Creek Association had been active in Austin for several years, were the primary proponents of following the Austin Tomorrow growth plan, and had led the efforts which forced the city to create the creeks and water quality ordinances. Many of their members had sat on the task forces that drafted these ordinances, and several of their members had become City Councilmembers during the 1980s, voted into office through the strength of their organizations. All had worked through political action or public education programs to publicize the delicate nature of the Hill Country ecosystem that feeds Barton Springs (see Swearingen, forthcoming, for details). They were joined by the local Sierra Club, and Audubon society, both of whom had pressed for environmental protection in Austin since the late 1960s. The local offices of national organizations included Clean Water Action and Texas Citizen Action joined because they saw the Environmental causes in Austin as the most likely vehicles around which effective citizen's groups could emerge.

The coalition wrote its own water quality ordinance, and gathered enough signatures on a petition to place their ordinance on a city-wide referendum. However, the newly elected council refused to call an election for the referendum, delaying for three months until a previously scheduled bond election. During this delay, developers filed numerous motions for development in the recharge zone so that they would not have to develop under the restrictions imposed by SOS should it pass. Public anger was palpable, and the council's tactic may have backfired. It energized negative feelings towards the council, and gave the SOS coalition more time to campaign for their ordinance.

THE SOS CAMPAIGN AND IMPLICIT RELIGIOUS PROCESSES

Political Ritual and Integration

Political ritual in the United States has long been held to be a secular ritual that has all the components of religious ritual, and the SOS campaign was no different. Durkheim argues that large social rituals serve an integrative function in social groups, by creating "collective states of mind." The more numerous and strong these collective states of mind, the stronger the integration (1951, p. 170). Social rituals also integrate groups by creating nationalistic feelings when "...great social disturbances...rouse collective sentiments, simulate partisan spirit...and concentrating activity toward a single end...[Such disturbances] force men to close ranks and confront the common danger, [where] the individual thinks less of himself and more of the common cause" (1951, p. 208). According to Durkheim, by creating a psychological bond between individuals through social action, society recreates itself;

> Through the very fact that these superior forms of human activity have a collective origin, they have a collective purpose. As they derive from society they have reference to it; rather *they are society itself incarnated and individualized in each one of us* (1951, pp. 210-121, my emphasis).

As the latest battle in this ongoing contest between "environmentalists" and "developers," we can view the SOS political campaign as an integrative process. As environmentalists acted with "collective purpose" in the partisan spirit Durkheim described to pass the SOS ordinance, they helped define the larger "society" of Austin. In order to "rouse collective sentiment," the SOS campaign literature framed the issue as fight which defined the collective society of Austin. For example, one SOS handbill read in part:

> This Saturday, August 18th, we can write the last chapter in the fight to preserve the springs...and fight to preserve the quality of water and the quality

of life that makes living and working in Austin so special.... Because Save
Our Springs is our story. It's Austin's story.

This public frame was essentially a simplified expression of the
feelings of many who have worked to safeguard Austin's
environmental features from degradation brought by urban growth.
As the latest eruption of this ongoing effort, several of the SOS
organizers believed the SOS campaign itself represented the society
of Austin coming together in a political expression. "We tried to focus
on Barton Springs as a symbol, and the water is a common resource[4]
[for] the health of the community," mentioned one. "Things I heard
people saying at the office was that the voters saw it as an Austin
thing—the myth that Austin is different, the old Austin spirit coming
alive." Others noted that SOS was simply one more manifestation
of the continuing effort to safeguard the society of Austin. To some,
like this long time environmental leader, Austin is defined by the
political action of its citizens to save its hills, creeks, and springs:

> ...you know the SOS election in a way defined Austin. The fact that we did
> turn out those people stamped us a certain kind of a city. And Im proud of
> that. Experiences mold character, and the SOS experience helped mold
> Austin... the *doing* of that define[d] the kind of place we are.

The insider-outsider dichotomy was also highlighted to emphasize
that support for SOS was support for the collective of Austin.
Freeport-McMoran was defined by the campaign as the outsider
intent on destroying Austin's communal resources. This was not hard
to do; Freeport McMoran is consistently listed by the United States
Environmental Protection Agency as one of the top water polluters
in the United States, a fact noted frequently in SOS literature. Its
Chief Executive Officer, Jim Bob Moffet, in a meeting with
environmentalists and city staff, had threatened to bankrupt the city
with lawsuits should the SOS ordinance be adopted. Moffet was used
in the campaign as the enemy against whom the city needed to band
together. The same handbill emphasized that:

> We can close the book on greedy developers who pollute our water and make
> us pick up the tab. Save Our Springs is a story that began when citizens took
> a stand against greedy developers like Jim Bob Moffet... And if we don't write
> the last chapter, Jim Bob Moffet and a few greedy developers will.

Such insider/outsider definitions framed the election as a struggle to protect "us" from "them." The use of insider/outsider symbology shows the integrative function that Barton Springs possesses: those who will protect the springs are "us," the society of Austin. In framing a campaign based on this simple dichotomy, the organization succeeded in getting the majority of Austinites who voted to "close ranks and confront the common danger" (Durkheim 1951, p. 208).

As political ritual, the framing of the SOS campaign reified the concept of Austin as the society, and defined that society by its natural environmental features. In the SOS frame, destruction of those features will destroy the society of Austin. In Durkheim's sense, the political act of saving those features integrates those who are members of that society into the group "Austinites," forming a community of concerned citizens defined by their efforts to save the kind of place Austin means to them. The outsiders, the "greedy developers," were framed as the threat to that society, further elucidating the idea of an Austin community by identifying the opposite of that community.

Barton Springs, Totemism and Community

Durkheim distinguishes what he calls a "totem" from what he defines as "the totemistic principle." The totem of a clan is a class of objects in the world, such as wolves or mango trees, which defines the clan because the members of the clan believe themselves to share in the same essential characteristic as that which animates the totem. Members of the clan hold physical attributes of this class of objects as symbols of their totem; hides, hair, bark, carvings, and so forth. However, these are simply physical reminders that the group member shares some similar basic qualities as the totem:

> This is what the totem really consists in: it is only the material form under which the imagination represents this immaterial substance, this energy diffused through all sorts of heterogeneous things, which alone is the real object of the cult... what the native means when he says that the men of the Crow phratry, for example, are crows. He does not mean to say that they are crows in the vulgar and empiric sense of the term, but that the same *principle* is found in all of them, which is their most *essential characteristic* (Durkheim 1915, pp. 217-218, my emphasis)

The political fight over Barton Springs is, at its essence, a fight over the kind of city Austin will be. To the leaders of the SOS coalition, this is a fight over the "essential characteristic" of Austin—will it be a place that means a high quality of life defined in large part by its natural environment? Or will it be a place like any other city, defined by the kind of urban sprawl that causes the destruction of community resources such as Barton Springs?

One of the principal reasons that respondents give for protecting the areas which contribute to Barton Springs Pool has to do with their notions of the way all the natural environmental features of Austin, and Barton Springs in particular, shape the image of the city. To them, the creeks, hills, lakes, and springs of Austin define its essential characteristic, its quality of life. It is a place that has a quality others do not have, a quality defined in large part by its natural environment. To these activists, then, saving Austin's environmental features conserves this essential characteristic.

This essential characteristic of Austin gives activists a sense of place, and they have made Barton Springs itself into one of the most potent symbols of that place. Interviews with the activists showed that they thought about the Springs in two interrelated ways. They see Barton Springs as a natural feature that should be protected because it represents Austin's "principle" as an environmental place. They also see the pool as a feature that promotes a sense of community. The two things are inseparable to the respondents. To them, public use of this unique environmental feature creates a community. The community is therefore defined by a particular environmental feature, just as the sense of Austin as a place is defined by environmental features. Without Barton Springs, they feel, both will disappear. As one activist puts it,

> Barton Springs is a symbol of community. The struggle really is a symbolic struggle to retain a sense of self that is a unique community that can have a quality of life and the environment....Folks get sustenance, a sense of well being, from feeling a sense of place, of having a tie to a place....If we destroy these things, we as a society are doomed. So it is self preservation—protecting a sense of connection: a family issue, a citizenship issue.

> This open space defines a community, it literally draws boundaries around a space so that you can get a sense of community. The nicest communities have some natural environmental boundary that draws this line.

According to many respondents, one of the things that makes this natural environmental feature a positive community focus is its accessibility to everyone as place apart from the normal social stratification present in daily life. Because it is a place to swim, for example, it has the leveling effect of making people remove their clothes, which are always a status symbol in themselves. In addition, people don't wear jewelry, hair styles, and so forth, when in the water, and several respondents noted that these stratifying symbols are replaced by a shared use of the pool as a communal resource. Many activists point out that all races and economic groups use the pool in a "natural" setting—naked but for a swim suit. They think the common use of a space that downplays stratifying symbols is one of the things that creates a sense of community. For example, a relatively new resident to Austin describe how

> Barton Springs is a symbol about what is great about Austin, It has a cross section of town. It's nature's gift-Da place that people love...what community is supposed to be. You take off the clothes, strip to the essentials of a human being. The place inspires a true community...it feels healthy here....You always run into people here....Barton Springs is a big park in the middle of town where everyone from the community comes together to talk. There's nothing like it anywhere else I have ever lived.

> This place represents all that is good about Austin. Austin prides itself on being a progressive/liberal town, and shafts the lower class and racial groups—it's hypocrisy. But here everyone is kind of equal. [Local events that are held here] are ways to relate and celebrate what this place means through time. It is building community ties to this sense of place.

Because this sense of community is generated by the use of a specific place, the sense of community and Barton Springs as physical space become dialectically related. Many activists who feel a sense of community do so by *using* the pool in conjunction with others from Austin. For them, the pool serves as the locus of this communal feeling.

Only about half of the respondents are regular users of the pool, the rest range from weekly visitors to infrequent users. But even in the infrequent users, the pool represents a *symbolic* attachment to the community of Austin for many respondents. Using Durkheim's concepts shows how both the use and symbolism of Barton Springs creates a sense of community for these activists. This community is defined by the "principle" of Austin, the quality of life found there. In its function as a shared symbol, Barton Springs has become what Durkheim would call totemic, a representation of the underlying principle of the group. A response by one of the organizers of the campaign (himself and infrequent user of the pool) illustrates this symbolic attachment on a conscious level;

> [Barton Springs] is a symbol of quality of life and the power of government to disrupt what people want. Are we trying to protect a mythology? But isn't that all there ever is? One of my favorite word groupings is modern mythology—so much of what I see is myths we carry around rather than reality.
>
> Q. Then what is the relationship between people and the city?
>
> A. A community that allows people to have a happy life, all concerned with others' well being...basic health, safety, and financial support so all can be psychologically healthy...It should give people a common vision. People should know what they are alive for, and this should dictate how they should live.

In a Durkheimian analysis, protecting the totem, the collective representation of the group, is equivalent to protecting the group itself. Barton Springs as totemic space was used in the SOS campaign as the focus of this "common vision," and many activists think using Barton Springs as a symbol of the community was one reason the SOS referendum was passed by such a strong margin. The SOS campaign used this symbology of Austin to mobilize support for the referendum by creating in-group consensus for action. The name Save Our Springs includes all these elements: "Saving" some special place, "Our" community resource, the "Springs" that define this community. During the SOS campaign, the activists used Barton Springs as totem to bridge their frame of the essential characteristic of Austin to the electorate. For example, SOS literature frequently referred to Barton Springs as the "Soul of the City." Fund raising letters referred to Barton Springs as "ours springs," "Austin's heritage," and the "Jewel in the Crown of Austin." SOS fund-raisers always featured well known local musicians who helped define the campaign as a local community event. And the symbolizing of Barton Springs as community center is an ongoing project of the SOS Coalition. The group currently holds activities and fund-raisers around the pool. The latest activity is the Barton Springs Diving Championships, an event sponsored by the Hill Country Foundation that includes local bands playing, and local celebrities as emcees who give the event what one organizer calls an "Austin feel." Through these uses of the pool, the SOS campaign framed their efforts to protect Barton Springs as efforts to protect the collective representation of the community of Austin.

Sacred Space and Group Totem

In addition to Durkheim's ideas about totemism, Eliade's concept of sacred space helps understand how attachment to space occurs as a communal undertaking. Bartkowski and Swearingen (forthcoming) describe these in more detail, but the following brief account of sacred space is germane to the present analysis. According to Eliade, certain spaces are chosen or built by humans as a means of experiencing the sacred. A space that is built or chosen to allow humans to glimpse what Eliade (1961) calls the "ultimate reality" provides a theophany. A theophany is a space that acts as a "vehicle of passage from one space to another" (Eliade 1961, p. 25). Theophanies are places where humans pass from profane space to sacred space. Such transitional spaces allow humans to feel a connection to the "ultimate reality" of the universe. The actual perceived connection to the divine is labeled a hierophany by Eliade.

Eliade notes that in order to provide such connections, theophanic space must be distinct from surrounding space, and be sacralized by the people who use it. Barton Springs provides such a distinction because its "natural" characteristics (spring water, trees, canyon) make it distinct from the urban milieu that surrounds it (concrete, buildings, cars). Many respondents note that the use of Barton Springs creates a different kind of experience because it is a "natural" spring fed pool, surrounded by quiet parkland setting, in the middle of a growing urban area. These physical qualities match the cultural predispositions of North American culture to distinguish between nature and urban, seeing nature as somehow pure, urban areas as somehow corrupted.

Because of the synthesis between its physical characteristics and the larger cultural ideas about nature, the pool is a kind of space that is ripe for sacralizing processes among people who perceive it as a threshold between the "natural" world and the "urban" world. Several respondents report that the use of Barton springs as a swimming place offers an empirical bonding between human activity

and some different reality. This different reality is what Eliade calls
an experience of an "absolute reality." In this way, Barton Springs
provides a physical connection with something greater than humans.
For many, like this long time resident, Barton Springs is thought of
directly in terms of a spiritual realm:

Q. What makes Barton Springs so special?

A. well, its no swimming pool—its a swimming hole! (laughing)....It's like
heaven, you know, it's perfect. There's just something about it, a spirit of the
thing that prevails among the swimmers of Barton Springs, there's something
that's just different. And my saying is that Barton's is like heaven—more a
state than a place.

Q. What kind of state is it?

A. A state of being, a state of mind...

This state of mind is what Eliade would describe as a hierophany.
Since the use of Barton Springs as space allows that transcendent
reality to be experienced, Barton Springs functions as a theophany.
For example, a long-time resident and SOS organizer notes that

To me, genetically, we have a spiritual need to have spiritual values. For some
it's religious values. For others, when you have something so undeniably
magnificent, so undeniably refreshing, it's part of the human mind to seek
parts of natural beauty... Each area has a cherished symbol... something that
people can identify with, but that they can empirically bond to.

Q. Why Barton Springs here in Austin?

A. I don't know. Because it's natural, because it is so cold, refreshing in
summer time....Its a symbol of purity, of times gone by....There is a sense
of something so wonderful, also, that humans can't change, or have no right
to change. Part of it is a realization, not with human insignificance, maybe
more of a Platonic idealism, that there is a world outside human endeavors.

Because of its physical and symbolic traits, the world "outside
human endeavors" can be accessed through the use of Barton
Spring. This empirical bonding with a natural feature is important
in creating the sense of community felt by respondents. Eliade noted
that theophanic space serves the function of situating the community
within the larger universe. Such spaces represents not only the
sacred, but the ties of the community to the sacred. In perceiving
sacred spaces within their community, people sacralize their
communities because they are perceived to exist in close relation to

the universal forces represented by the sacred space (Eliade 1961). Since the pool is a totemic representation of Austin, the state of mind associated with using this space is related to Austin, making Austin distinct because of the theophanic space of Barton Springs. "I think that's, in a way, of saying why people have a quasi-religious feeling of nature. And in the springs they have a symbol here" explains one SOS organizer.

Adding together Eliade's and Durkheim's ideas about the sacred and society allows an understanding of how Barton Springs as space can function both to define community and integrate individuals into that community. Eliade shows that as theophany, the use of the springs allows these individuals a window into the sacred. Durkheim claims that experience of the sacred is actually an experience of the moral force of the society itself, where society is represented by the totemic principle. In the case of Austin, that principle is the "quality of life" essence already defined by the geography of the city and the cultural understandings of "natural" places. By providing a theophany to that essence, the use of Barton Springs as sacred space allows environmentalists to associate themselves with the principle of Austin, further integrating them into the Austin community; making them feel that they are part of the community of "Austinites."

A cogent statement by a long-time resident and activist illustrates all of these elements, when she relates the reasons for the uproar over the planned development on the aquifer that threatens the purity of the water in the pool:

Q. What makes a community?

A. Symbols like the capital, UT tower, Barton Springs create a sense of being. What they have to say to the urban community is: remember your past. It's not just the high rise buildings, but water coming pure bubbling out of the earth—a *gift*!... You need those shared symbols, the place needs to *mean* something, to be understood by the people there, in order for it to be a community (respondent's emphasis).

DISCUSSION: SPACE, IMPLICIT RELIGIOUS PROCESSES, AND COMMUNITY

Although both urban sociologists and social geographers have documented the fact that groups define themselves relative to urban space, and have established the fact that institutional forces such as the economy shape this relationship, there are still some fertile questions left unanswered. I began this paper by asking three questions about the ways in which group attachment to space occurs. How is it that groups claim space, instilling in it their own meanings? How does a particular type of space come to be made symbolic of a particular group? How can certain types of spaces become representative of a community? To answer these questions, I have attempted to show how certain implicit religious processes can serve as the social mechanisms by which such attachments occur.

A methodological note is in order at this point. As with any research method that uses a case study with a small sample of respondents as its unit of analysis, generalizing the results of this study is problematic. The fact that environmental activists report the feelings they have about Barton Springs and Austin does not necessarily mean that others in the city have those same feelings, or that other citizens act upon those feelings.[3] But an indirect measure of public alignment with environmentalists' ideas can be found in the analysis of the campaign literature used by the SOS Coalition. The ways in which the Coalition tried to bridge their meaning of the city to a wider public is indicative of the pool of public sentiment about Austin. In the case of the SOS initiative, the environmentalists' frame seems to have aligned fairly well with popular sentiment; the vote was 2-1 in favor of the initiative. Thus there is room to infer that some of these same processes are operating in what Snow, et al. (1986) call larger "sentiment pools" throughout Austin.

While such a design can not generalize its claims to the larger population, it does have the very positive benefit of providing "thick" descriptions of particular mechanisms of social action. I have used this case to illustrate how the implicit religious mechanisms of totemism, integration, and sacred space, shaped by the larger structural contexts of a given society, can create group attachment to space. It is to a discussion of these mechanisms, and the contexts in which they emerge, that I now turn.

First and foremost, this particular study suggests that group attachment to space, and the notion of community, are shaped by the kinds of conflicts which inhere in social institutions. In the case of Austin, rapid growth from a town into a big city has brought to the fore social conflicts inherent in the creative destruction of contemporary capitalism. As they struggle against the growth groups to protect the unbuilt "natural" qualities of creeks, lake, and springs in Austin, environmentalists as a group have emerged from this conflict as the main opponents to unregulated growth. Their understandings about Barton Springs, and their efforts to sacralize that space and make it totemic of Austin, should be understood in this context. It is the very conflict over the city's growth that shapes the need of environmentalists to define their totems as a way of defining their community .

Secondly, attachment to space is channeled by the relationship between social factors and the geography of an area. In Austin, the geography and terrain of the city, coupled with a North American culture that has traditionally distinguished between the purity of "nature" vs. the decadence of the "city," has provided a context within which people who are opposed to growth as a meaning for their city find fertile grounds for the creation of an alternative meaning. Environmentalists probably emerged as the predominant challengers to growth because the alternative meaning of space they promote— "quality of life" instead of quantity of built space—has a certain fit with the geography of the area. Historically, Austin has been seen by its residents as a place that has a high quality of life due to its natural environment. The actual design of the city, built into and around its prominent creeks, rivers, and hills, allows direct use of those features by residents. To the leaders of the SOS coalition, Barton Springs and other natural environmental features help to define the meaning of Austin by its quality of life. In Durkheim's terms, this meaning can be understood as the "principle" or "essence" of Austin.

Thirdly, Durkheim notes that the moral bonds of social groups are re-created through shared totems and shared ritual experience. Through their political activity, environmentalists have made Barton Springs into the totem of the "principle" or "essence" of Austin. As environmentalists seek to frame their meaning of Austin through the literature and discourse of political campaigns, their meanings are bridged to the wider urban constituency. The SOS referendum described here is just the latest such campaign. In their efforts to bridge this meaning to others, environmentalists use the symbology of Barton Springs to represent the quality of life meaning. As they promote their symbology of Barton Springs through frame bridging techniques, they create Barton Springs as a totem. Barton Springs as totem allows environmentalists to communicate a symbolic meaning of the city to other residents, thereby reifying the uniqueness, the "essential characteristic," of Austin.

This two decade battle by environmentalists and others to channel growth away from the most environmentally sensitive areas of Austin has created a discourse in the public realm of "developers" v. "environmentalists." This discourse has further refined the difference between those groups who pursue growth as the meaning of Austin and those who seek to define the city by its quality of life. As the "environmentalists" who created the SOS organization frame "developers" as outsiders who threaten to ruin Barton Springs, the distinction between themselves and the "developers" becomes more pronounced. This distinction functions as what Durkheim calls a "principle of unification"; those opposed to unregulated growth are defined by themselves and others as a group, unified by their meaning of Austin. Political activity to promote that meaning, such as the SOS referendum, is one of the integrative rituals that forms the moral bonds between environmentalists. Participation in the unifying ritual of the campaign to protect this totem further integrates people who act to protect that essence of Austin, creating a sense of unity and community.

Lastly, Eliade defines theophanic space, space that provides a transition point to a an "absolute reality" (Eliade 1961). To many respondents, Barton Springs as space is a theophany to a different reality. Some of them call this reality "nature," others call it the "community." In either case, since Barton Springs has also been symbolized by these same people as representative of the meaning of Austin, I suggest that those who experience "nature" and/or "community" through Barton Springs conflate that experience with the totemic meaning of Austin. Durkheim's insight was that the forces men feel to be sacred are often really the moral force of the larger society itself. His insight can be seen in operation in this case. I suggest that part of the theophany experienced at Barton Springs is essentially an experience of the larger society of Austin itself, the sense of what "Austin" is, with all the emotional and symbolic meanings attached to that society. By making its physical and symbolic space the totem of Austin, environmentalist have made Barton Springs the central symbol of a community, the community they call "Austin."

CONCLUSION

I have used this case study to try and show how the implicit religious processes of totemism, integration, and sacred space act as the mechanisms by which group attachment to space occurs, and the way in which a sense of community is created and sustained. These mechanisms do not act in a vacuum, they act within the bounds of larger institutional activity and the conflicts that arise from that activity. The kinds of built space that exist in the city provide environmental objects that focus these conflicts and provide symbols of the groups in conflict.

While the results of this analysis are of theoretical interest, there are some practical applications and understandings that might be considered by planners and sociologists involved in community development. This analysis raises as many unsettling questions as it gives fruitful direction for community development. I have tried to be explicit that attachment to space, and the identification of community, occur in the context of social conflict. This is not the only way in which such attachment occurs, to be sure. Daily use of space, group definitions of space, cultural typologies of space, and other less conflictual processes have been documented by geographers (e.g., Lynch 1961; Tuan 1974; Gold and Burgess 1982). But in many instances, the integration of an in-group, and the creation of a feeling of community, are literally formed from the conflicts that arise between social groups. This is one of the seminal understandings of society that Durkheim provides us. So, if the goal of planning is to create some sense of community, how are planners to conceptualize their jobs in the midst of the kinds of social conflict that arises from development and re-development of urban space? Are they to be agents of one social group in that conflict, building "communities" for one group by excluding another? In creating "gated communities" for the rich, for example, are developers creating a spatial structure that integrates a community by social class? The gate and surrounding wall of such developments may define a "community" by excluding the outsider (lower social classes), and might indeed create a sense of community among the rich who are in basic conflict with the poor. But is that really what we desire in a "community"? Planning for "niche markets" begs a similar question. Given that we can create "communities" through spatial segregation of lifestyles, integrating some groups by exclusion of other groups, is that segregation necessarily good? Is the meaning of "community" simply segregation? These are issues that require serious thought on the part of those who would develop and redevelop urban space.

On another thoughtful note, Durkheim presents us with the idea that totemistic symbols are required if a sense of community is to be established. Especially in re-development of urban space, planners should be sensitive to the fact that inhabitants already have totemistic spaces, space that are symbolic of their community, spaces they do not want "redeveloped." Austin is just one example. City planning in the 1970s that included representatives of neighborhood and civic groups clearly showed that citizens wanted growth channeled away from areas that would degrade the central city creeks and Barton Springs. Yet the dictates of free market capitalism, and a city planning department intent on servicing new subdivisions, have nearly "developed" these central symbols of community to death. Indeed, it is this development that led to the creation of the SOS Coalition in the first place. Prior to their projects, planners and developers might be well served to make a thorough review of the inhabitants of the space to be developed, discovering meaningful spaces that already exist, and planning to enhance, rather than destroy, those spaces.

One idea might be built with an eye towards the geography that is already part of the larger ecosystem of the area. Barton Springs and the creeks of Austin provide obvious symbols of community because they fit the Hill Country environment into which Austin is built. Other places would have different environmental features, which could be used to create unique spaces within a development that represents the larger environment. As Barton Springs shows, space requires communal use in order for it to serve as community locus. But the case of Austin also shows that people will create their own totems through their institutional behavior. Thus, the planner and developer should not conceptualize themselves so much in the business of *building* totemic space as in the business of providing an environment in which community totems *can occur*. As the first step in this directions, perhaps new developments could apply the idea of "xeriscaping" to the planning of "community." Utilizing pre-existing geographic features, and retaining their uniqueness, would leave intact spaces that fit the surrounding environment, spaces that could more easily become meaningful places to residents. "Communiscaping"? "Xerimunity"? The idea would be to fit built space into the local geography so that people could define their communities by features that are representative of the larger environment.

I also think that the processes of integration, totemism, and sacred space might be fruitful analytic tools to use in further study of communities and their built environments. For example, how are ethnic and class relations affected by the increasingly segregated urban space we live in? Are groups becoming more conscious of their group identities as the rich move into walled compounds they call "gated communities," while the poor and minorities symbolize their concepts of themselves through the decorations of their space with what middle class society defines as "graffiti" (e.g., Cresswell 1992)? What applications might these processes have for the definitions of urban enclaves, both by sociologists who define enclaves institutionally, and non-academics who live in our Chinatowns and Little Havanas? Given the predominantly masculine symbolism of urban space, might there be spaces that are captured by women and given feminized meanings through gendered rituals, rituals that serve to create communities of women in a dominant masculine culture? These or similar types of studies could further refine the understandings of implicit religious processes in the relationship between built space, group attachment to that space, and community.

NOTES

1. For interesting cases of spaces used by communities to relate themselves to a larger cosmology, see Griaule and Dieterlen (1954), Seemen (1968), and Gesler (1993).
2. Since the initial writing of this paper, the coalition has been renamed the SOS Alliance. However, because the political election under analysis occured under this name, I will continue to refer to the group as the SOS Coalition.
3. As one reviewer so aptly put it, "Sometimes a swimming hole is just a swimming hole!"

REFERENCES

Bartkowski J., and S. Swearingen. (Forthcoming). "God Meets Gaia in Austin, Texas: A Casee Study of Environmentalism as Implicit Religion." *Review of Religious Research.*
Beauregard, R. 1995. "If Only the City could Speak: the Politics of Representation." In *Spatial Practices*, edited by H. Liggett and D. Perry. Thousand Oaks, CA: Sage.
Carter, E., J. Donald, and J. Squires. (eds). 1993. *Space and Place: Theories of Identity and Location.* London: Lawrence and Wishart.

Castells, M. 1983. *The City and the Grassroots: A Cross Cultural Theory of Urban Social Movements.* Berkely: University of California Press.

City of Austin. 1980. *Austin Tomorrow Comprehensive Plan.* Austin, TX: Department of Planning, City of Austin.

Cresswell, T. 1992. "The Crucial 'Where' of Graffiti: A Geographical Analysis of Reactions to Graffiti in New York." *Environment and Planning D: Society and Space* 10: 329-344.

Duncan, J. 1973. "Landscape Taste as a Symbol of Group Identity." *Geographic Review* 63(3): 334-355.

————. 1990. *The City as Text: the Politics of Landscape in the Kandyan Kingdom.* Cambridge, MA: Cambridge University Press.

Durkheim, E. 1951. *Suicide.* New York: Free Press.

————. 1965. *The Elementary Forms of Religious Life.* New York: Free Press.

Eliade, M. 1961. *The Sacred and the Profane: the Nature of Religion.* New York: Harcourt, Brace, Javanovitch.

Firey, W. 1945. "Sentiment and Symbolism as Ecological Variables." *American Sociological Quarterly* 10: 140-148.

Gans, H. 1962. *The Urban Villagers.* New York: The Free Press.

Gottdiener, M. 1985. *The Social Production of Urban Space* Austin: University of Texas Press.

Gottdiener, M., and A. Lagopoulos. 1986. *The City and the Sign.* New York: Columbia University Press.

Gottdiener, M., and J. Feagin. 1988. "The Paradigm Shift in Urban Sociology." *Urban Affairs Quarterly* 24(2): 163-187.

Griaule, M., and G. Dieterlen. 1954. "The Dogon of the French Sudan." In *African Worlds: Studies in the Cosmological ideas and Social Values of African Peoples,* edited by D. Forde. New York: Oxford University Press.

Gesler, M. 1993. "Therapeutic Landscapes: Theory and a Case Study of Epidauros, Greece." *Environment and Planning D: Society and Space* 11: 171-189.

Gold, J., and J. Burgess. 1982. *Valued Environments.* London: George Allen and Unwin.

Graber, L. 1976. *Wilderness as Sacred Space.* Washington, DC: American Association of Geographers.

Horizons Committee. 1976. *Austins Creeks.* Austin, TX: Austin Bicentenial Committee.

Howell, S., and S. Laska. 1992. "The Changing Face of the Environmental Coalition." *Environment and Behavior* 24(1): 134-144

Koch, O. H. 1928. *Master Plan for the City of Austin.* Dallas, TX: Koch and Fowler Co.

Kong, L. 1993. "Ideological Hegemony and the Political Symbolism of Religious Buildings in Singapore." *Environment and Planning D: Society and Space* 11(2): 147-170.

Lane, B. 1988. *Landscapes of the Sacred: Geography and Narrative in American Spirituality.* New York: Paulist Press.

Lees, A. 1985. *Cities Perceived: Urban Society in European and American Thought, 1820-1940.* Manchester: Manchester University Press.

Ley, D. 1983. *A Social Geography of the City*. New York: Harper and Row.

Lynch, K. 1960. *The Image of the City*. Cambridge: MIT Press.

Orum, A. 1987. *Power, Money, and the People*. Austin, TX: Texas Monthly Press.

————. 1991. "Apprehending the City: The View from Above, Behind, and Below." *Urban Affairs Quarterly* 26(4): 589-609.

Park, R., E. Burgess, and R. McKenzie. 1925. *The City*. Chicago: University of Chicago Press.

Relph, E. 1976. *Place and Placelessness*. London: Pion.

Rotenberg, R., and G. McDonogh. (eds.). 1993. *The Cultural Meaning of Urban Space*. Westport, CT: Bergin and Garvey.

Seeman, A. 1968. "Communities in the Salt Lake Basin." *Economic Geography* 14(3): 300-308.

Shields, R. 1991. *Places on the Margin: Alternative Geographies of Modernity*. New York: Routledge.

Schmitt, P. 1969. *Back to Nature: the Arcadian Myth in Urban America*. New York: Oxford University Press.

Snow, D., E. Rochford, S. Worden, and R. Benford. 1986. "Frame Alignment Processes, Micromobilization, and Movement Participation." *American Sociological Review* 51: 464-481.

Soja, E. 1980. "The Socio-Spatial Dialectic." *Annals of the Association of American Geographers* 70(2): 207-225.

Swearingen, S. (Forthcoming). "Environmental City? The Creation of Austin's Environmental Meaning." PhD Dissertation, University of Texas.

Tuan, Y. 1974. *Topophilia*. Englewood Cliffs, NJ: Prentice-Hall.

Warner, S. 1972. *The Urban Wilderness*. New York: Harper and Row.

Western, J. 1993. "Ambivalent Attachment To Place in London: Twelve Barbadan Families." *Environment and Planning D: Society and Space* 11: 147-170.

White, M. 1963. "The Philosopher and the Metropolis in America." In *Urban Life and Form*, edited by W. Hirsch. New York: Holt, Rihehart, and Winston.

Wilson, A. 1992. *The Culture of Nature: North American Landscape from Disney to the Exxon Valdez*. Cambridge: Blackwell.

Wirth, L. 1938. "Urbanism as a Way of Life." *American Journal of Sociology* 44: 3-24

Zukin, S. 1982. *Loft Living* . Baltimore: John Hopkins University Press.

ENVIRONMENTAL POLICIES AND COMMUNITY ACTIVISM:
THE TIMBER DEBATE IN OREGON

Kimberley D. Saliba

ABSTRACT

The timber conflict in the Pacific Northwest has had a significant impact on rural communities. Their historical dependency on the timber industry and federal timber revenues have made them particularly vulnerable to environmental policies that have limited logging on federal lands. Not only must we understand the changing economic structures of these communities but also how the relationship between environmentalists and timber workers have influenced these changes. With Curry County, Oregon, as a case study, I will use county histories, secondary economic analyses, and qualitative interviews, to show how activists on both sides of the timber debate have called for policies that will have far-reaching consequences for the environment and timber-dependent communities. Cooperative efforts may be the answer to achieving future community stability.

Research in Community Sociology, Volume 7, pages 171-200.
Copyright © 1997 by JAI Press Inc.
All rights of reproduction in any form reserved.
ISBN: 0-7623-0272-0

INTRODUCTION

The timber debate in the Pacific Northwest presents a battle of ideology and practicality, based on what people believe and how these beliefs are translated into public policy. Environmentalists claim that the nation's forests have been ravaged by the timber industry and have lobbied for increased environmental protection of these ecosystems for decades. Timber workers, on the other hand, argue that they know how to manage the forests and resent outside intervention, thus they have organized an increasingly sophisticated countermovement to challenge environmental legislation. Timber-dependent communities have been caught in the cross-fire. Admittedly, the economies of these communities have always been cyclical, but the economic hardships that many timber communities are facing in response to limited federal forest access and the consequent mill closures, job losses, and declining timber revenues are having significant effects on the communities' abilities to function. Both environmentalists and timber workers believe that their policies can help communities, but their policies are based on different assumptions, basically whether Nature should be valued for its ecological benefits or utilitarian services. In practical terms, these timber-dependent communities have tried to consider the economic ramifications of these differing environmental and timber ideologies and prepare for a future that may require significant change. Whether the forests represent complex ecosystems or board feet, the values of these disparate groups fuel a debate that will have long-lasting effects on these communities.

How communities change in response to economic decline and how people adapt to these changes have been the focus of a great deal of sociological research. Studies of resource-dependent communities, including those on social change (Machlis et al. 1990; Rowland 1993) and community stability (Lee 1987; Machlis and Force 1990), help us understand how the decline or loss of a resource industry can create social turmoil. Research on timber-dependent communities throughout the northwestern United States (Lee et al. 1990; Weeks 1990) and Canada (Byron 1977; Marchak 1983) have identified how vulnerable these communities are to changes in the timber industry. A history of overcutting, technological change, downsizing, and social conflicts have limited the extent to which these regions have ever truly enjoyed community stability. Given the ongoing timber battle, timber communities are facing new challenges that demand innovative adaptive skills, thus an area of community research that deserves further attention is the relationship between social movements and community empowerment.

The interactive relationship between the environmental and anti-environmental movements influences many different segments of society including social relations, political institutions, and local economies. The differing perspectives call for policies that determine to what extent forest resources can be used, leading to potential structural and cultural changes in timber-dependent communities. The degree to which community members respond to the activists, or even choose to get involved in the debate itself, is likely to be influenced by how extensive the effects of the timber policies are on the daily lives of the community. For example, federal forest policies have restricted access to public land that was once a source of timber revenues for counties. While government subsidies have masked the full impact of the revenue losses, the declining county funds affect all residents and could conceivably serve as a source of motivation to join the timber debate.

Using Curry County, Oregon, a rural community of 21,000 people on the southern Oregon Coast, as a case study, this paper explores the relationship between local grassroots environmental and timber activists and the effects this conflict has had on environmental policies and the subsequent decrease in timber revenue from former Oregon & California (O & C) Railroad lands, rising employment concerns, and losses in services. Whereas environmentalists argue that protecting the forests will bolster the economy by conserving timber resources for the long-term viability of the timber industry as well as maintaining the County's aesthetic appeal for tourism and the growing retirement community, timber workers believe that such drastic reductions in logging are not necessary and that a service industry will not be able to replace the timber industry. This debate has motivated many community members to take sides on which direction they want the County to take.

The Curry County government is particularly at risk because of its historical dependency on revenues from timber harvested on federal O & C land. The O & C land, located in 18 counties in Oregon, was to be used to build a railroad connecting Oregon and California. Because the railroad was not built, the land reverted back to the federal government in the early 1900s. Since that time a portion of the revenues from the timber cut on these lands was distributed to counties with O & C land. This money has served as a valuable source of funding for county governments who structured their budgets around the federally-distributed timber revenues. This land, however, is also home to the northern spotted owl. Federal restrictions of logging in endangered species habitat have drastically reduced the rate of timber harvest on all federal forest lands, including the O & C land, and the subsequent revenues available for county government operations. Given these losses, in addition to the well-publicized job losses in the timber industry, one would expect to find non-timber workers involved in the anti-environmental movement. One must ask then not just to what extent environmental policies have affected this timber-dependent community but also what role community members are playing in the timber debate.

To answer this question, I use data from my research on the relationship between two Curry County grassroots activists groups: the Kalmiopsis Audubon Society, representing the environmental movement, and the Oregon Project, dedicated to promoting timber issues. The dynamic interaction between the Kalmiopsis Audubon Society and the Oregon Project on the local level and through national networks calls for a greater understanding of how movements and countermovements influence each other's agendas and strategies, as well as the effects these movements have on communities. For this paper, I use secondary data from state and county histories of the O & C land, economic analyses of Oregon counties, community development surveys, and organizational material from the local timber and environmental groups. I also conducted qualitative interviews with seventy Curry County residents, including timber workers, environmentalists, concerned citizens, and government officials. I have reviewed the interview data to determine how people feel about the effect of environmental policies on the local economy and whether this serves as a motivating factor for activism. This paper presents the historical and economic data of the region to provide the structure within which the timber debate takes place and examines the environmental movement and countermovement with excerpts from interviews and county-developed surveys in order to clarify the cultural aspects of the debate through individual interpretations of how the battle affects their lives and their community.

THE CURRY COUNTY COMMUNITY

Curry County owes much of its character to its isolated location on the southern Oregon Coast. Only the hardiest of souls ventured this far down the coast in the 1800s to which the only access was by sea and a limited stagecoach road. Those rugged pioneers took what limited flat land they could find from the native people and set up their homesteads. Turning to the abundant natural resources around them, they worked as fishermen, loggers, miners, farmers, and ranchers. They took pride in their ability to survive in the wilderness and worked hard to tame the land.

These rural settlements created a culture based on an ideology well-known to frontier scholars such as Turner and Billington. Turner states that these frontier communities valued discovery, conquest, democracy, and personal development, "free from social and governmental restraint" (1947, p. 271). The frontier offered new dynamic opportunities for Americans and immigrants. Characteristics such as rugged individualism, ingenuity, and entrepreneurialism fortified the courageous men and women who moved out West. Billington attributes American optimism to the existence of the frontier. The "rags-to-riches" belief was most common on the frontier where "every man with skill and determination could make a fortune" (1966, p. 201). A dedication to growth, "manifest destiny," and faith in the future helped the pioneers persevere.

These characteristics were especially common in timber communities. Loggers achieved folk hero status with Paul Bunyan as a model. It was "those with timber sap in their blood who planted, grew, protected, harvested, and had an undiminished respect for the 'crop' [who formed] the backbone of the Northwest's economy" (Roberge 1973, p. 16). While the status of timber workers has diminished in response to the timber debate, the difficulty of the work and the necessity for the product continues to be a source of respect in some circles. One businesswoman stated in an interview, "Every once in a while you'll see a truck, a 3-log load. It's beautiful." Many descendents of the original frontier families still live in Curry County and many continue to live by the values of their forebears and want to maintain the heritage of their community.

While the isolated location of Curry County has contributed to the preservation of a unique microcosm of frontier beliefs which inform timber workers' self-identities, daily activities, and political efforts, being isolated has also contributed to the economic hardships of the region. Consequently, efforts have been made since the mid-1800s to improve access to western Oregon and California. While the Coastal and Siskiyou Ranges created some of the best temperate tree-growing regions in the world, the mountains also made it difficult to reach the natural resources that a growing nation desired. To remedy this problem, a plan was designed to build a railroad.

The O & C Land

To encourage development in the western frontier, the federal government commonly offered public land to the states and settlers for a minimal cost or for free. Given the limited access to resource-rich regions in Oregon and Northern California, proposals were made to build a railroad and developers turned to the federal government for land grants. In 1866, large tracts of land, totalling over 4,221,500 acres, were set aside to build a railroad from Portland, Oregon down the Willamette Valley and over the Siskiyou Mountains to connect to an existing line to Davis, California. There was a great deal of enthusiasm for the railroad and people looked forward to having a new means of transportation to expand commerce.

But instead of building the railroad, Southern Pacific and many others took advantage of the rising value of timber land by selling their land holdings to timber barons. The land fraud continued until President Theodore Roosevelt began an investigation in 1903, leading to the indictment of more than 1,000 people. While few were convicted, the Supreme Court determined that the sale of the land violated the purpose of the O & C Acts, which was to build a railroad. In 1916, Congress passed the Chamberlain-Ferris Act, thus reverting the land back to the federal government, allowing timber to be sold off the land, and providing a formula for the distribution of timber receipts between the state of Oregon, 18 O & C counties, and the federal government (Jones 1972). While the timber receipts were welcome, the loss in property taxes from the now public lands forced all 18 counties into economic straits.[1]

The region had to contend with financial ruin until the counties formed the Association of O & C Counties (AOCC).[2] They succeeded in passing the Stanfield Act in 1926, ensuring an appropriation of funds equal to the property taxes that would have been paid if the O & C lands had remained in private ownership, but further exacerbated their dependence by accepting the money in the form of a loan. After a number of other financial and policy conflicts, Congress then passed the McNary Act, as part of the O & C acts, in 1937, which abolished the tax equivalency guarantee but allowed for greater security in timber access and funds and emphasized the need for sustainable harvesting to ensure timber availability for future generations (Bureau of Governmental Research and Service 1981).

The 1937 O & C Land Act continues to serve as the basic guide for timber receipt distribution. The formula designated that the U.S. Treasury would receive 25 percent of the receipts, 25 percent of the timber revenues would go to the BLM and USFS for resource management, and the remaining 50 percent of the total receipts would be divided among the O & C counties for county operations (Jones 1972). The counties also receive United States Forest Service (USFS) receipts which are designated for schools and roads. Timber revenues rose significantly after World War II and continued to rise up through the late 1980s. The O & C counties felt secure in the continuation of these funds and designed county budgets around their receipt. In so doing, they became dependent on the O & C and USFS timber revenues for county operations. As an O & C County, with 57,600 acres of O & C land, the Curry County government also structured its budget around the timber receipts, thus intensifying the cooperative relationship between the County, the federal government, and the timber industry.

The Curry County community and the timber industry were not prepared for the emergence and success of the environmental movement. While the timber industry continued to log at a furious pace up through the 1980s, the local Kalmiopsis Audubon Society, which started in 1979, was actively sponsoring the designation of wilderness areas and the protection of endangered species. One environmentalist said that he first became concerned about the northern spotted owl in 1976. According to another member, this grassroots environmental organization was "the driving force" behind national legislation to protect forest ecosystems in Curry County, the Siskiyou National Forest, and around the Pacific Northwest. Local timber workers, beginning to organize in 1988, realized that they faced a powerful organized force when the northern spotted owl was listed as a threatened species under the Endangered Species Act in 1990, which resulted in the closure of much of the federal land that the timber industry depended on, including the O & C lands.

According to research conducted by the University of Washington's College of Forest Resources and Northwest Policy Center, the limitation of logging on the O & C lands and the consequent reduction in timber receipts will have significant social impacts as county budgets are stretched thin (Lee et al. 1991). Table 1 shows how the timber receipts rose and then fell in response to harvest levels on the O & C lands. The decline in harvest levels coincide with the listing of the northern spotted owl as endangered in 1990 and the Clinton Forest Plan enacted in 1993. The counties shown are classified as high O & C-payment counties and all are located in southwestern Oregon. The O & C receipts in all the counties experienced significant growth due to an increase in timber prices in the 1980s but then decreased significantly after judicial and legislative proceedings prohibited logging in critical endangered species habitat areas. The loss of these receipts has forced the O & C counties to reallocate their resources and reconsider the structure of their tax base. To aid the O & C counties through this unstable time, Congress passed the Omnibus Budget Reconciliation Act in 1993, under the Clinton Forest Plan, which created a safety net with special payments to be given to the counties through the year 2000. While the total O & C receipts for Oregon have declined from

Table 1. Schedule of O & C Payments to Oregon Counties, 1956 to 1996, ($1,000)

Year	Coos	Curry	Douglas	Jackson	Josephine
1956	700	360	2990	1867	1432
1960	956	491	4083	2549	1954
1965	1163	1057	4939	3090	2382
1970	1741	1081	7392	4624	3565
1975	2912	1801	12,362	7733	5961
1980	5153	3188	21,878	13,686	10,550
1985	3219	1992	13,666	8549	6587
1988	5905	3654	25,072	15,684	12,085
1990	5599	3464	23,772	14,871	11,458
1991	3790	2345	16,092	10,066	7757
1992	4917	3042	20,876	13,059	10,062
1993	3562	2204	15,125	9462	7290
1994	1629	1008	6917	4327	3334
1995	1618	1001	6871	4298	3312
1996	2270	1404	9638	6029	4645

Source: Bureau of Governmental Research and Service (1981); BLM Budget Justifications (1996).

approximately \$206,457,000 in 1990 to \$41,119,000 in 1995, the counties were paid \$79,246,000 in 1995 (Ehinger 1997). The receipts have been substantially below the payments to the counties since 1993. These special payments, however, will slowly decrease, with services declining along with them. The counties recognize that they eventually must find alternative funding, although efforts continue to be made to resume logging.

The history of the region's resource dependency and lack of economic alternatives have exacerbated the economic strain in Curry County. Curry County has been able to do little to reduce its dependency on the timber industry for jobs and revenues. Bray and Lee found that Curry County, in 1988 and 1989, had one of the highest payments in Oregon from federal forest lands, as a percentage of federal land ownership, and the highest payment, as a percentage of total county revenue (1991). In fact, federal forest receipts make up 66 percent of Curry County's total expenditures (Lee et al. 1991, p. 2). Given these significant percentages, the loss of these timber revenues are particularly difficult. One government official noted in an interview that, "It's a two-edge sword. The industry generates jobs and the economy and timber receipts from the O & C and the Forest Service pay for county government, schools, and roads." Therefore, the loss of timber jobs and receipts from the shut-down of the O & C lands creates an occupational and financial gap that the community has had a difficult time filling. The isolated location of the County makes it hard to attract alternative industries in order to diversify the economy. Even though the federal government is supplementing the revenues, there is widespread concern that harsher times are ahead.

This perceived hardship has increased the number of critics of the environmental movement. While some people recognize that this is a necessary economic transition, with many calling for increased protection of the natural environment in order to further develop the tourism and retirement industries, the "two-edge sword" provides a diverse base of disgruntled citizens, with timber workers fighting to protect their jobs and County residents and employees concerned about social services and jobs in the public sector. The Oregon Project has tried to use the O & C issue as evidence that environmentalists are hurting their community. Of particular note are the losses in County services. Everyone in Curry County is dependent on some form of county service. Due to the lack of financial resources, the local government offices had to reduce their hours and staff, roads are in disrepair, and school budgets are increasingly tight. The reductions in law enforcement, public education, health, and social services come at a time when there is an even greater demand for these services (Lee et al. 1991). The extremity of the budget constraints have not received significant media coverage, but those who are familiar with the County's dependence on federal support are found among the countermovement's cadre, such as local government officials.

The Association of Oregon & California Counties (AOCC) has joined the effort as the stewards of the O & C timber receipts. One Curry County and O & C official claimed in an AOCC press release, "Locking up virtually the entire O & C forest on the west side of Oregon is both unnecessary ecologically and contrary to federal law." In response to the Clinton Forest Plan, the AOCC argued that the Plan was both "illegal and immoral" because it did not consider the adverse social and psychological impacts on their communities (1993). The AOCC leader likened the situation to the "frog theory." He said that "if the water was boiling, the frog would jump out, but the water is heating up slowly, and like the frog, the community will be boiled before they know what hit them. It is a slow death." They feel that the federal government should take proactive steps to reduce the adverse effects on O & C county residents.

AOCC leaders have also tried to gain state control of the O & C land. Interviewees argue that local communities should own the land within their counties' borders, of which they will be "better stewards than the national government." The AOCC president stated that they would continue to use the O & C Acts' requirements that they use sustainable harvest methods and reforestation techniques, estimating that even though 45 billion board feet have been harvested since 1937, over 50 billion board feet remain on the O & C land, even more than existed in 1937. Local environmentalists, however, do not trust them. One woman predicts, "If the state gets the O & C land, it will generate a lot of short-term profits and revenue. They'll get their money and they'll be relieved. Then they won't make any effort to develop the tax base. They think it's great if the state gets the land but state forestry is eons behind federal land. We may argue with the USFS but they are knights in shining armor compared to the state." Oregon Project members disagree. They believe that local workers have a better understanding of how the land should be managed with such claims as, "We'll do it the best, on our own, better, and cheaper, if we are allowed to maintain the land to the best of our ability." This faction of the countermovement focuses much of their efforts on property rights issues and has united with national private property rights activists. They feel that the federal government has overstepped its bounds and must be held accountable for the hardships that federal legislation causes.

Job Availability in Curry County

The decline in the timber industry is the other side of the "double-edge sword." While there are many environmental benefits from protecting forest ecosystems including reductions in erosion, maintenance of watersheds, and preservation of species diversity, the prohibition of logging in endangered species habitats on federal land has not only contributed to the financial hardships of the O & C counties by limiting their timber receipts, it is also partially responsible for the increased loss of timber jobs. As one community-survey respondent stated, "Curry County is a great place to live, but a tough place to make a living." In addition to earlier losses due to overharvesting, automation, and international trade, timber workers argue that environmental laws have contributed to the downsizing of the timber industry. Similar to timber towns throughout the Northwestern United States and Canada, the former booming timber communities in Curry County now try to survive by servicing the needs of tourists and retirees.

Historically, timber jobs were readily available in the woods and there was "a mill up every crick." Steady employment attracted many people who wished to make their fortunes in the woods. The prolific resources and mild climate created a sense of optimism that "[Curry County] was the best place in the world." In fact, the population grew from 4,301 in 1940 to 21,000 in 1995 (County Records). Much of this growth is attributed to the timber "boom" in the 1950s. Timber families were respected members of their communities where they contributed both to the financial and social vitality of the region. They were influential in the media and politics, with state and federal policies further strengthening their economic positions. As the demand for timber increased many large and small logging operations and over 30 mills dotted the landscape up and down the southern coast. Timber workers could always find work, and the timber supply seemed inexhaustible. The apparent cornucopia of forests, however, began to diminish by the 1960s on private land which was not managed sustainably, in contrast to the requirements of the O & C lands. Consequently, the local timber companies had to turn to the federal government which owns over 60 percent of the land in the County. A former millworker admitted,

> Before it seemed like there was no end of trees, salmon, or rain. But now we're running out of trees and salmon, and until last year, rain. Before, there was no running out. It's a different world. It's a tougher world, financially. Everyone's feeling it. It's sad, inevitable. I look back... I asked in the 60s when we would run out. But it seemed a long way off in the future. Now that it's happened, everything feels poor. We used to have more money. I'm Chicken Little. I think the sky will fall. I worried about all these problems but I hoped they wouldn't happen.

But they have, and with a vengeance. Although timber companies now replant, environmentalists estimate that only 5 to 10 percent of old growth forests remain in the Pacific Northwest. Modern timber workers willingly admit that their ancestors had made mistakes and they claim that they learned how to be better land managers because of the environmental movement. As one mill worker said, "We would never go back to the way it was. Our forefathers screwed up." By the early 1970s, they were redefining their techniques based on environmental and timber management laws. The U.S. Forest Service's implementation of the Endangered Species Act in 1973 and the National Forest Management Act of 1976 further tightened the federal government's reins on the timber industry. The heavy cutting was not abated, however. The demand for wood remained high and timber workers were encouraged to harvest heavily through the 1980s. One environmentalist suggested that "the Reagan Administration facilitated the rapid harvest rates of the 1980s when eighty to ninety percent of the timber cut came from federal lands." This all came to an end in the late 1980s when a strong tide of environmental concern forced the timber industry to be accountable for their actions.

Environmental legislation such as the Endangered Species Act was well entrenched in the political arena before timber workers were fully aware of the effects it would have on their industry. The listing of the northern spotted owl in 1990 prohibited logging on federal land where owls are known to be nesting and similar limitations are in place to protect the marbled murrelet and several native fish and plant species. The Clinton Forest Plan has tried to balance the needs of the environment and local economies by classifying a variety of multiple use sites but few were satisfied with the compromise. Environmentalists, including Kalmiopsis Audubon Society members, continued to appeal timber sales and call for injunctions to close down further logging sites. While the 1994 "salvage rider" turned the tables by prohibiting appeals and exempting timber sales from environmental laws thus facilitating some logging, the overall loss of federal timberlands, increasing automation, and international competition have reduced the chance that employment in the timber industry will ever dominate the economy again.

Many companies have been unable to compete in the constricted market, forcing logging outfits and mills to close their doors. Smaller mills in Port Orford, Gold Beach, and Brookings, the largest towns in the County, began to close as they were unable to compete with larger mills for timber bids. Table 2 shows the mill closure rate for Oregon from 1980 to 1993. These statistics illustrate how quickly the industry has contracted. While harvesting increased in the 1970s and 1980s, inefficient mills were unable to compete. The increase in timber prices locked out many small timber companies from bidding on sales. Small logging contractors also had difficulties when they were unable to afford new technological changes. The estimated reduction

Table 2. Mill Closures in Oregon, 1980-1993

Year	Mills Closed	Jobs Lost
1980	11	1,321
1981	7	555
1982	13	1,452
1983	6	1,000
1984	14	1,258
1985	5	571
1986	2	116
1987	11	607
1988	12	715
1989	11	1,490
1990	28	2,379
1991	21	2,345
1992	21	2,722
1993	16	1,322
Total	178	17,853

Source: Ehinger and Flynn (1993).

of mills over the last 20 years in Curry County alone shows a drop from approximately 30 mills to three, with a handful of one-man operations. The last mill in Gold Beach closed in 1989, putting an additional three hundred people out of work. Environmentalists use such statistics to point out that many mills closed before the spotted owl issue, but there was a significant increase in mill closures in 1990, when the northern spotted owl was listed as an endangered species.[3] The mills that have survived are retooling and downsizing and are depending on their private timber reserves or innovative uses for timber that they used to consider scrap wood. One millworker noted that "If big companies don't tool down [for smaller logs], they go kaput." If they cannot afford to change their equipment, then they must continue to compete for the ever-dwindling supply of large timber, or old growth, a prospect that has little future.

Similarly, only the most efficient workers have been able to make it. A number of timber workers interviewed stated that the workers who are still in the industry are less likely to abuse alcohol and are "responsible family men" because employers can demand higher standards given the low supply of jobs. Timber workers had to adapt to survive, move to another timber region, or get out of the industry all together. As one logger's wife explained,

> It was hot. But then the spotted owl hit. The first year was traumatic. It went downhill quick and it's never gone back up. It's leveled but it will never be the same. There's been a lot of change. It's hard on the timber workers and the community. A lot of the town didn't know what to do. They didn't know what was going on. Loggers are in their own world.

Given the large number of skilled timber workers who remained and the small supply of timber, workers who were able to retain their timber jobs also have had to contend with lower incomes.

Granted, employment in the lumber and wood products industry in Curry County has always been cyclical. Residents recall many times when money was sparse. They always figured, however, that the next timber harvest would bring new financial infusions into the County. The employment statistics over the last few decades, however, make one wonder if the timber industry will ever be a source of economic prosperity again. The changes in the occupational structure of Curry County and the Pacific Northwest as a whole has left many despondent. One unemployed millworker believes that

Table 3.   Curry County Employment, 1972-1994

Year	Timber	Retail	Service
1972	1,500	700	400
1979	1,125	1,000	575
1988	1,100	1,280	830
1994	620	1,600	940

Source: Oregon Employment Department (1994); Curry County Commissioners Office.

"It's worse than Appalachia. In the 50s, 60s, and 70s, you could quit your job, go down the road, and, if you had the skills and were willing to work, get a new job." This freedom is long gone and many believe that "it's not over yet." Table 3 illustrates how occupational trends in Curry County have made a significant shift from employment in the timber industry to the retail and service sectors. In 1978, employment in the lumber and woods products industry in Curry County was approximately 1,500. In 1994, timber jobs were down to 620. It is not very surprising when timber workers ask, "Who's endangered?" and respond, "Timber workers." They find the threat to their livelihoods more crucial than the loss of endangered species, a position that environmentalists call "anthropocentric."

In addition, as the timber industry declines so do secondary industries who are dependent on the timber resources. For example, without the demand for equipment or repairs, saw shops are not able to survive. Carpenters and artists are also affected because the price of wood increases. The multiplier effect can be quite extreme, as evidenced by the economic conditions in Gold Beach. With the downsizing of the timber industry, the USFS lost employees, the mill closed, school enrollment declined, and many service industries have lost business including restaurants, grocery stores, and recreational facilities. As reviewed above, the County government also must contend with falling budgets due to the loss in O & C receipts. The loss in timber receipts, employment, and services affects everyone in the County thus potentially serving as a common bond for a diverse community.

A Community in Crisis

The changes in the timber industry have led to some significant changes in the standard of living in Curry County. This is particularly evident when one looks at the region over time. When the timber industry was booming, families were able to live comfortably in Curry

County. Unemployment rates were low and men were able to support their families. One businessman remarked, "With the increase in the cost of living, earning less, and more taxes, you can't afford anything now. With the mill here [in Port Orford] in the 50s and 60s, one person working could earn enough to buy a new house, a new car, your wife didn't have to work, and you could finance your kids' college. Now, you can't do any of that." The main group of people in the County with a stable income now appears to be retirees, many of whom move here from California. In contrast, the younger people in the community have few employment options.

The loss of social services and the lack of recreational opportunities and employment alternatives have led to an outmigration in young people. They recognize that the region offers very few occupational opportunities so many choose to leave. Those who stay often lack the education and income to maintain a living wage. Consequently, there has been a significant increase in juvenile delinquency and welfare dependency. A businesswoman noted that, "A lot of kids get into trouble around here. They don't have a lot of opportunities. But then they don't really have the money to get out and go to school either." Community officials are trying to meet the needs of these young people but declining funds limit their ability to provide the services necessary to improve the conditions.

The resulting social impacts from declining community stability resemble patterns in other areas of social upheaval. Job loss and financial constraints create significant stress that can contribute to community dysfunction. The lack of economic diversification and employment alternatives support Summers and Branch's claim that "many of the people left behind in rural areas find themselves in pockets of poverty that are plagued by economic stagnation and social decay" (1984, p. 143). Although County officials point out that it has been difficult to collect statistics, they believe that social problems have escalated in all timber-dependent communities, with incidents of alcoholism, drug use, domestic disturbances, and child and spousal abuse increasing as lives are disrupted. These social problems themselves can further contribute to a community's instability. Juvenile delinquency, substance abuse, and violence can weaken the bonds of trust and loyalty needed for a community to face their problems. Without resolution, a community may experience an outmigration of the very people they need to regain stability.

The combination of a desire to maintain their frontier heritage, the decline in timber receipts, the loss of timber jobs, the ripple effect throughout the community from the decrease in income, and the resulting community instability all serve as motivating factors for countermovement mobilization. Given that these factors affect a larger constituency than just timber workers, it is not surprising to find non-timber workers as members of the anti-environmental movement. It is surprising, however, that they make up a relatively small proportion of the group. The following section describes the environmental movement and how the countermovement emerged to challenge environmental efforts.

THE EMERGING COUNTERMOVEMENT

Curry County residents were slow to recognize the overwhelming significance the environmental movement would have on the timber industry and, consequently, the County. Besides the occasional "hippies" who came to the County to "get back to the land," residents had little contact with environmentalists and continued to harvest timber and maintain their traditional way of life in accordance with their frontier heritage. The educational system encouraged students to join the timber industry, the County government maintained their dependence on timber revenues to function, and the economy made little effort to diversify.

In contrast, the national environmental movement was making great strides in challenging the status quo. In line with the growing national environmental consciousness, the Kalmiopsis Audubon Society, a Curry County grassroots organization with 180 members, began in 1979, and a core group of activists continues to play a central role in the timber debate. Its members have been instrumental in designating wilderness areas, monitoring endangered species, and lobbying for environmental legislation to protect the forests of the Pacific Northwest. While aggressive logging in the 1980s obscured the effects of declining jobs in the timber industry, environmentalists were able to pass laws that limited timber access to environmentally-sensitive areas. In Curry County, environmental activists did not have to face any organized challengers until the late 1980s. Until then, local timber workers had been willing to compromise and improve their practices.

Then, an event occured which served as a catalyst for action. Oregon Project leaders claim that it was the conflict over the Silver Fire that made them conscious of their need to countermobilize. The Silver Fire broke out in the Siskiyou National Forest's Kalmiopsis Wilderness Area in the summer of 1987. Timber workers were surprised when their plans to salvage log the area were met with resistance from the Kalmiopsis Audubon Society and other environmentalists in Oregon. The U.S. Forest Service (USFS) determined that only minimal logging was allowed in the area, given its wilderness status. This event made timber workers realize that their ideological differences with environmentalists could not be bridged with compromise. They did not understand how some people could value environmental protection over economic prosperity. A retired millworker stated, "Use it, don't waste it, use all of it, replant it, and conserve it. Timber was put here to benefit man. It should be used for man." From such a position, with the help of the People of the West and in conjunction with the creation of the Oregon Lands Coalition, Curry County timber workers decided to create the Oregon Project in the fall of 1988. This group of over 350 timber workers and community supporters adopted the yellow ribbon, used to mark trees for harvest, as their symbol and "Oregon Project: Preserving Our Timber Heritage" as their slogan. They organized their first countermovement activity in 1988, the Silver Fire Round-Up, a rally to celebrate the timber industry and promote salvage logging.

In order to mobilize, the timber organization had to first identify its opponent. One might suspect that these workers would have an adversarial relationship with their employers and larger mills, who have benefitted from the rising prices due to the declining timber supply, but they believe that they are allies because they share a common goal in "getting the wood out." Timber workers throughout the Pacific Northwest quickly determined the source of their self-perceived victimization. As one independent logger stated,

> It's not loggers versus owls. It's loggers versus preservationists. Urban versus rural. Any resource industry is an ally. Fishermen were pitted against us a few years ago because logging has affected some streams but now they're more allies. And mining, and ranchers, and agriculture. In the paper, it said that it's two urban areas versus the rest of the state. It's liberal versus conservative.

The "enemy" became their most visible adversary: environmentalists, or "preservationists," who challenged the timber lifestyle and heritage. For example, they blamed the 1989 closure of the last mill in Gold Beach, which had employed 300 people, on the environmental movement and tried to monopolize on the fear that their industry was crumbling around them. Then, the northern spotted owl conflict exploded in March, 1989, when Judge Dwyer found a USFS forest management plan illegal and halted timber sales in spotted owl habitat, setting a precedent for future forest politics and leading to the owl's listing as threatened under the Endangered Species Act in June, 1990. The closure of further habitat areas gave the appearance of "shutting down the forest." The subsequent loss of jobs and timber revenue served as the final straw for many people who spent more time in the woods than they had in politics. The timber industry's greatest nemesis and the environmental movement's biggest coup became the Endangered Species Act (ESA).

They were limited, however, in their ability to effectively challenge the environmentalists. While some countermovements are able to develop from existing groups, and thus benefit from their organizational foundation and available resources, the informal social networks in the timber community offered little organizational or activist experience. Although Curry County is a member of the Association of Oregon and California Counties (AOCC) and the timber workers have representative organizations such as the Association of Oregon Loggers (AOL), the Oregon Lands Coalition (OLC), and the Northwest Forestry Association (NWFA), the timber workers in Curry County have no history of unionization and, of those interviewed, no one showed interest in having one. An environmentalist claimed, "[The mill] has broken every union. The timber industry would bust every union. Every union is being busted around the United States." The millworkers at the largest remaining mill, however, stated that they did not need a union because their employer "is a good man" and is responsive to their needs. While their lack of organization and experience hindered their initial ability to mobilize a countermovement, the dedication of local citizens to the protection of their community provided a ready source of grassroots activists. A movement/countermovement relationship was born.

It is important to understand the interactive relationships that develop between social movements and countermovements (Zald and

Useem 1987). Lo suggests that a countermovement must be "a social movement with its own mobilized membership, organization, and leadership" (1982, p. 119). The Oregon Project provides the central organization for countermobilization in Curry County. Most of those I interviewed commented that this is the first time that they have ever participated in a social movement. Some of their efforts include providing informational booths at fairs, writing letters to elected officials, sending members to lobby in Washington, D.C., and networking with other national "wise-use" groups. They also ask businesses to help the Oregon Project by giving money or having signs in their windows stating that they support the timber industry. A number of timber workers have checks stamped with "These are timber dollars" so that those who receive the check can understand that the money comes from the timber industry. Oregon Project members try to educate people on how they are all affected by the loss of the timber industry, not just timber workers themselves. These affiliations provide support for the timber movement beyond the frontlines of grassroots activism. Both the environmentalists in the Kalmiopsis Audubon Society and the Oregon Project members have become more focused on the state and national battles over resource use, but local protests at logging sites still occur occasionally. There is still a recognition that the local community must remain educated about the changes in the timber debate and the effects these changes can have on the community as a whole.

The Oregon Project's president is well known for his dedication to the timber cause and works hard to try and get people involved. He focuses much of his educational and recruiting efforts outside of the timber industry. In a 1994 newsletter, he implored his members to "take action...against our enemies." While the environmentalists I have met with want to help their communities, the Oregon Project tries to depict them as enemies "who do not care about people." In contrast, they try to portray themselves as the advocates of community stability, as shown with the Yellow Ribbon Motto: "Fighting to maintain the quality of life in your community through an adequate timber supply." Timber activists focus on how natural resource use contributes to the well-being of their rural communities in the present, whereas environmentalists argue that environmental protection will help communities and the timber industry in the long run.

The fact that the Oregon Project has 350 members in contrast to the Kalmiopsis Audubon's 180 members does suggest that there are more people concerned about the effects that environmental policies are having on Curry County and the Pacific Northwest in the short run. The participation of a few non-timber workers, such as teachers and local government officials in the Oregon Project signifies that other factors besides the loss of timber jobs appear to be at work to motivate people to mobilize. And, questions of community services, county rights, public land access, and economic development alternatives do intermingle with cries for environmental and job protection. There are not, however, as many non-timber workers involved in the countermovement as one would suspect. Even though several Oregon Project members I interviewed believe that they represent a large constituency in the community because they "speak for the needs of Curry County," the majority of their members continue to be loggers, millworkers, and log truck drivers. Frequent references to their frontier heritage serve as an overriding theme but relatively little effort has been made to expand their agenda beyond protecting the timber industry. Sociologist Robert Lee fears that the loss of this heritage may have significant impacts on the United States as a whole:

> Preserving and maintaining this nation's cultural diversity is as important to the survival of America as is maintaining biological diversity. What we are preserving in rural farming and timber communities is people, not abstractions or symbols, but real people who embody basic values which are fundamental to our nation's history and its tradition. The threat is not that we will lose a species or two. The threat is that we will lose the human spirit (Peterson 1993).

The leader of the Oregon Project suggested that they are not just fighting for the economic viability of the timber industry when he said, "It's not just a job. It's a whole way of life." But, we would find more non-timber people involved in the countermovement if they felt that their interests were also at stake.

Local environmentalists are part of this community as well but they see the community's history of resource exploitation as the main source of economic strife, because "without a healthy ecosystem there can be no industry to save." The environmentalists in Curry County are also affected by the loss of the timber revenues and county services but they would rather see the County government promote economic diversification than remain dependent on the timber industry. One man noted that the County is "tied to the O & C funds" but that "timber is not our future." Another Kalmiopsis Audubon Society member believes that environmentalists have the best interests of the community and timber industry in mind. She said, "Environmentalists and timber workers basically have the same goals—trying to hang onto jobs. The difference is that we are trying to protect the Earth too. We need to take [timber] as we can afford it, as we can regrow it, and try to keep everyone working." The differences in ideologies often override the common goals that both sides appear to share and in effect distance the debate from many community members.

One of the common goals is to have community stability, but it is likely that many people in the County are not even aware of how dependent they are on federal timber receipts and what risks they face in the future. Two government officials noted that the federal aid has helped mitigate but also mask the economic effects of the declining receipts. A USFS official believes that "They don't even realize that the money is coming from the government. They're close to losing 75% of their revenues. So, the money is coming from taxpayer's money. The effects in the County would be a lot worse without this. Maybe it's not a big deal but the figures look drastic to me." Although the AOCC and Oregon Project have tried to publicize the losses, the AOCC president notes that "they have not received a lot of media attention, and they won't until the train wreck comes." This lack of knowledge on the part of some community members is likely to limit the involvement of some people who might be more interested in the timber debate. The majority of individuals I met in the Oregon Project are aware of the loss in funds, given the education they've gained within their group, and want to resume harvesting timber on the O & C lands, but they have not made extensive efforts to publicize this information locally. A businesswoman made her awareness clear, however, when asked what she is concerned about. She responded, "Well, we havn't got no money. That's what they say. They lost the revenue from timber. I don't know what the government's going to do. The County is not prepared for the loss of revenue because of decreased timber." How the decreasing funds translate into cuts in services, how the County government adapts to these changes in the future, and how the media finally respond will all play a part in how the timber debate evolves.

Until the timber revenue issue receives more attention, the timber debate will continue to focus on the environment versus employment conflict. Many interviewed stated that they joined the countermovement because they were afraid that they were going to lose their jobs. They believe that "The environment doesn't put groceries on the table," although critics would argue otherwise. The bottom line for many members of the countermovement is trying to provide for their families. Potential job loss is a powerful motivation tool for mobilization. Local environmentalists, however, say that they do not want to hurt timber families. Nor do government officials. A USFS official agreed, "Lots of people are losing their jobs. It makes you feel bad. People say we are starving out their family. They blame it all on us because we don't care about the community or don't care about kids. It causes a lot of stress. All the reductions cause people to be pretty nervous...Our people really care about the land and the community. We try not to take things so personally." The timber conflict is an emotional battle that is fed by fear and frustration. Many people do not know what to do. In response, a timber wife argues, "For the sake of the community, [the government] should help the industry. If they don't take care of the industry, the community will die." Environmentalists counter such statements by saying that the community and industry could also "die" if the environment is not protected. As one environmentalist noted, "[Environmentalists and timber workers] are natural allies because we both want to preserve rural communities."

An interesting development in the timber debate is the way environmentalists have tried to incorporate economic issues into their arguments. They try to show how protecting the environment can help the community's economy and well-being. They recognize that they need public support and that many people are concerned about the economic ramifications of environmental policies. While environmentalists say, "Stumps don't lie," the conflict between ideology and practicality tends to play into the hands of their opponents. The Oregon Project has the emotional advantage because they can show how the immediate economic and social effects are related to environmental policies that limit employment and the funds available for County services. Curry County's lack of economic alternatives and high percentage of federal land tend to make the timber workers' positions more palatable to the community's working families, whereas environmentalists have found greater sympathy among artists, retirees, and businesses dependent on tourists.

Like any social movement, however, the Kalmiopsis Audubon Society and Oregon Project must contend with their inability to recruit everyone affected by the timber debate. Similar to Hibbard's findings in another timber-dependent Oregon town (1986), I have found that Curry County residents, particularly the "old-timers," are apathetic and, although they recognize the need for economic development, they resist change. Many people choose not to participate. Some feel like they cannot make a difference, others say that the timber conflict does not affect them, and many just do not want to expend the energy. Some who have been involved have lost their motivation. A logger's wife said, "It's a hard thing to do. It's very draining to be that involved in the fight. They're fighting for their lives. They just didn't think it was working so many people stopped being involved. It brought their spirits down." An independent logger believes that there are a number of reasons for limited involvement. He suggests that

> it is their home, family, they keep to their own little world. Less education plays a part. I don't know what it takes to get them motivated. Even if they all lost their jobs, our crew wouldn't get active. They'd find another job. County employees are even less involved even though they're affected too. It's people in general. I don't think there's anyway to motivate them. It's the 20-80 rule. 20 percent of the people do 80 percent of the work. On the other hand, the preservationist movement is well funded, and more educated. What motivates them? I guess they want to do good.

Many just hope that the future will work itself out. As another independent logger said, "We're just trying to survive. We study the options and just deal with it. You do what you have to do. We've been here forever. We've been able to survive on people we know. We just try to keep a low profile with minimal involvement. We don't have to go. As long as we can survive, then we're going to stay here. We're not gonna change the world. We just want the world to quit messing with us."

CONCLUSION

The relationship between the environmental and timber movements, however, will continue to "mess" with them because, as shown, the timber debate does have an impact on communities. These communities will have to adapt to the changes in the timber industry, which are brought on by movement and countermovement efforts to influence ideologies and policies. Whether people choose to empower themselves and get involved in the debate or not depends on a variety of factors including their dedication to the cause and the degree to which they believe a condition threatens their well-being. The task is to find a unifying force that can motivate people to sacrifice their time and energy. It is not an easy task and it certainly cannot be achieved if people are not aware of their common interests.

A potential source of common interest that could motivate people to get involved and work together is the loss of timber revenues which would create social changes that could affect all of the residents in Curry County. This issue has received relatively little attention but it is likely to play a significant role in the timber debate in the future. It is this common source of grievance that offers the largest constituency from which either side could recruit members, or from which the community itself could organize cooperative work groups. If social and countermovement leaders could focus on this common denominator they also might be able to reach across the gulf between their respective paradigms, and begin to devise strategies that meet some of their needs and the needs of the community.

The first step for the Kalmiopsis Audubon Society would be to gain a better understanding of the general economic concerns in the County. They could identify to what degree people are interested in protecting the environment and how they would be willing to compromise to regain some economic stability. For community members to believe that environmentalists care about humans, in addition to the environment, they would have to be more sensitive to the consequences of their policy proposals and offer alternatives to remedy some of the losses in timber revenues. The environmentalists could also create new alliances with groups who are represented less often but are affected by the loss in community services, such as poorer families. By trying to bridge differences, they may find that their mobilization efforts can become more effective. It is difficult to change people's ideologies, but an attempt at mediating practical concerns and limiting economic hardships could make community members more sympathetic to the environmental needs of their community.

The Curry County Oregon Project could also benefit from trying to understand why environmentalists are willing to sacrifice some short-term economic stability for long-term environmental and economic health. The Oregon Project generally represents the views of those who want to return to the "good ol' days" when they were free to log, fish, hunt, and build wherever and whenever they wanted. This alienates many people who do not want to return to the past but want to meet the needs of the future. The timber group would benefit from a revision of their agendas in order to incorporate some environmental and community service concerns. In effect, they could attract more supporters if they focused on how changes in the timber industry affect the community as a whole, not just timber workers. For example, given that many of the new residents are retirees, they may not be interested in employment issues. If their services, however, are threatened then they may become more sympathetic to timber issues. Educating the public on how the losses of the O & C timber revenues can affect their lives could tap into a large source of support that the Oregon Project has only begun to recognize. This does not mean, however, that the issue must contribute to further polarization. Instead of just using this issue as ammunition against the environmental movement, timber workers also have a responsibility for trying to find a balanced solution based on open communication and cooperation.

Focusing on community stability can serve as this unifying force. Given Curry County's state of flux, the economic and demographic changes have limited the shared histories and beliefs of its residents. The ideals of the newcomers, many of whom espouse environmental beliefs, conflict with the practical survival issues of timber-dependent families. The relationship between the environmental and timber movements thus not only has economic consequences for the community, but cultural impacts as well. The tensions that exist in this community and elsewhere in the Pacific Northwest due to the ideological conflicts between environmentalists and timber workers, as well as the newcomers and pioneer families, limit the efforts that could be made to develop economic alternatives and social policies. While not a new idea, it is important to reiterate the need for cooperative efforts in order to work through this difficult time of transition.

There are a few examples of people working together in Curry County on economic development and natural resource issues. In 1989, reports were developed by two groups, the Community Initiatives Program and the Curry County Strategic Assessment Task Force. These groups were organized to assess and provide alternatives for the County's economy. For example, the Task Force's mission was "to expand and diversify the Curry County economy in order to provide middle-income job opportunities for the current population and future generations while preserving the environment" (Bureau of Governmental Research and Service 1990, p. 2). While they were successful in identifying the problems and setting some goals, they have not been able to revive the economy. Another community development group now exists but they are still in the planning stages. There are also two groups who work on natural resource issues. These are the Salmon Trout Enhancement Program (STEP), which is trying to restore and maintain fish habitat, and the Watershed Councils, which have diverse memberships throughout the County working to assess and protect the County's watersheds. Given that watersheds involve forests as well as rivers, these groups have brought together a variety of concerned citizens including environmentalists, timber workers, fishermen, and biologists. These initial steps may create a foundation for further collaborative efforts and hopefully will provide a forum for communication across occupations and paradigms.

Other communities have tried to work together as well in order to develop strategies for resolving conflicts and strengthening economies. Under the Clinton Forest Plan, efforts were made to create Adaptive Management Areas which were charged with developing new management techniques, meeting economic objectives, and getting local people involved in the planning processes (Marshall 1993). Former opponents in Medford, Oregon, have found relative success in the cooperative Applegate Partnership as well. Curry County could benefit from using these other groups as models for developing cooperative organizations. These groups can effectively unify diverse contingencies and give them the opportunity to identify common goals and alternatives for achieving community stability.

Having a greater awareness of such interconnections is important for dialogue and compromise. Rather than exacerbating the animosity between the factions, finding common interests and developing shared solutions could go a long way in tearing down the walls that the timber conflict has created locally, state-wide, and nationally. Furthermore, promoting their common practical interests is likely to be more persuasive than focusing on ideological differences. Whereas not everyone feels strongly about environmental issues nor can relate to the region's timber heritage or unemployment concerns, they all depend on the County government for the maintenance of the community's infrastructure and services. Finding the balance between disparate interests requires finding a commonality and building new alliances in order to restore community stability. An environmental artist said, "It's a dead end scenario. Now it's just squabbling at the end of the game." It does not have to be. Even though this may be the end of an era, rather than seeing this as "the end of the game," it really is a new beginning for communities. As the timber debate evolves, what path communities take can be the start of a new era, with new opportunities.

With such changes it will be important to continue to observe the evolution of the timber debate through the interactive relationship between the environmental and timber movements. If and how environmentalists and timber workers resolve their conflicts will have significant impacts on rural communities. In addition, how community members respond is likely to influence the path that both the movements and communities take. Recognizing the potential consequences of the timber conflict, it would benefit the ·movement and countermovement activists and the communities in which they live if they could move beyond their differences to a greater awareness of their shared interests. Granted, the timber debate is far from over, as is the coming upheaval in the communities due to the loss of timber revenue. Therefore, researchers must remain in touch with the nerve sources of the communities they study in order to understand how such economic and social changes will affect the community as a whole. This debate is not just played out in the halls of Congress, but in the very lives of individuals who are trying to balance the needs of the environment, their local economies, and their communities.

NOTES

1.   Of historic interest, it was at this time that Curry, Josephine, and Jackson Counties, in the southwestern corner of Oregon, and Del Norte County, in northwestern California, decided to secede from the United States and form the "State of Jefferson." The start of World War I diminished interest in the separatist movement but it remains a source of public pride as indicated by such names as Jefferson Public Radio.

2.   For further details on the O & C lands, please see Bureau of Governmental Research and Service (1981).

3. This is not to imply that the media's unrealistic soundbite of "jobs versus owls," correctly reflects the movement/countermovement relationship. The timber debate is very complex and such simplifications only further exacerbate misunderstandings between the factions.

REFERENCES

Billington, R.A. 1966. *America's Frontier Heritage*. New York: Holt, Rinehart, and Winston.

Bray, M. and R.G. Lee. 1991. "Federal Forest Revenue Sharing with Local Governments in Washington, Oregon, and California." *The Northwest Environmental Journal* 7: 35-70.

Bureau of Governmental Research and Service. 1981. *The O&C Lands*. Eugene, OR: School of Community Service and Public Affairs, University of Oregon.

_____. 1990. *Curry County Strategic Assessment Task Force: Final Report*. Eugene, OR: University of Oregon.

Byron, R.N. 1978. "Community Stability and Forest Policy in British Columbia." *Canadian Journal of Forest Research*, 8: 61-66.

Curry County Records. 1996. *Curry County Demographics Report*.

Dodge, O. 1969. *Pioneer History of Coos and Curry Counties, OR: Heroic Deeds and Thrilling Adventures of the Early Settlers*. Coos-Curry Pioneer and Historical Association, Bandon, OR: Western World.

Ehinger, P.F. 1997. *O & C Receipt Report*. Eugene, OR: Paul F. Ehinger and Associates.

Ehinger, P.F., and R. Flynn. 1993. *Forest Products Industry Report on Mill Closures, Operations, and Other Related Information*. Eugene, OR: Paul F. Ehinger and Associates.

Hibbard, M. 1986. "Community Beliefs and the Failure of Community Economic Development." *Social Service Review* (June): 183-200.

Jones, R.B. 1972. "One by One." *The Source Magazine* (November-January) 1 (6-8, 9).

Lee, R.G. 1987. "Community Stability: Symbol or Social Reality?" Pp. 36-43 in *Community Stability in Forest-Based Economies*, edited by D.C. LeMaster and J.H. Beuter. Portland, OR: Timber Press.

Lee, R.G., D.R. Field, and W.R. Burch, Jr. (eds.). 1990. *Community and Forestry: Continuities in the Sociology of Natural Resources*. Boulder, CO: Westview Press.

Lee, R.G., P. Sommers, H. Birss, C. Nasser, and J. Zientek. 1991. *Social Impacts of Alternative Timber Harvest Reductions on Federal Lands in O and C Counties*. College of Forest Resources and Northwest Policy Center, University of Washington.

Lo, C.Y.H. 1982. "Countermovements and Conservative Movements in the Contemporary U.S." *Annual Review of Sociology* 8: 107-34.

Machlis, G.E., and J.E. Force. 1990. "Community Stability and Timber-Dependent Communities: Future Research." Pp. 95-106 in *Community and Forestry*, edited by R.G. Lee, D.R. Field, and W.R. Burch. Boulder, CO: Westview Press.

Machlis, G.E., J.E. Force, and R.G. Balice. 1990. "Timber, Minerals, and Social Change: An Exploratory Test of Two Resource-Dependent Communities." *Rural Sociology* 55(3): 411-424.

Marchak, P. 1983. *Green Gold: The Forest Industry in British Columbia.* Vancouver, B.C.: University of British Columbia Press.

Marshall, D.B. 1993. *The Clinton Forest Plan: A Wildlife-Based Critique.* Washington, DC: The Western Ancient Forest Campaign.

Roberge, E. 1973. *Timber Country.* Caldwell, ID: The Caxton Printers.

Robbins, W.G. 1987. "Lumber Production and Community Stability: A View from the Pacific Northwest." Pp. 12-21 in *Community Stability in Forest-Based Economies*, edited by D.C. LeMaster and J.H. Beuter. Portland, OR: Timber Press.

Rowland, M.J. 1993. "The Challenge of Change: Northwest Forests and Timber Towns." *Northwest Environmental Journal* 9(1): 20-23.

Summers, G.F., and K. Branch. 1984. "Economic Development and Community Social Change." *Annual Review of Sociology* 10: 141-166.

Turner, F.J. 1976. *The Frontier in American History.* Huntington, NY: R.E. Krieger Publishing Co.

Weeks, E.C. 1990. "Mill Closures in the Pacific Northwest: The Consequences of Economic Decline in Rural Industrial Communities." Pp. 125-139 in *Community and Forestry*, edited by R.G. Lee, D.R. Field, and W.R. Burch. Boulder, CO: Westview Press.

Zald, M.N., and B. Useem. 1987. "Movement and Countermovement Interaction: Mobilization, Tactics, and State Involvement." In *Social Movements in an Organizational Society*, edited by M.N. Zald and J.D. McCarthy. New Brunswick, NJ: Transaction Books.

PURSUING RURAL COMMUNITY DEVELOPMENT IN RESOURCE-DEPENDENT AREAS:

OBSTACLES AND OPPORTUNITIES

Richard S. Krannich and Brett Zollinger

ABSTRACT

This work focuses on a variety of challenges that confront resource-dependent communities in mounting the types of locally-initiated actions and resource mobilization episodes that comprise the core elements of community development. Focusing primarily on conditions and trends observed in rural resource-dependent places in the western United States, the discussion considers how varying patterns of resource-based economic activity can result in four different types of resource-dependent areas: sustained, cyclical, transitional, and declining. Theoretical concepts derived from an interactional field perspective of community development are employed in examining both obstacles and opportunities for the

Research in Community Sociology, Volume 7, pages 201-222.
ISBN: 0-7623-0272-0

emergence of locality-oriented interactions and collective action episodes in each of these resource dependency contexts. Recognition that resource-dependent places are not homogeneous provides an important point of departure both for understanding differential prospects for attaining community development outcomes and considering how planned interventions may enhance development potential.

INTRODUCTION

This paper examines some of the challenges confronting resource-dependent rural communities in North America, and evaluates the prospects for community development in such places. Consistent with the interactional approach to rural community development outlined by Kenneth Wilkinson (1991), the discussion focuses on the ways in which social, cultural and economic conditions in resource-dependent places influence the potential for local residents to engage in purposive, goal-oriented actions in pursuit of locality-relevant goals and needs. The capacity to engage in such actions is important in its own right, because the processes of interaction and resource mobilization can contribute directly to social well-being (Wilkinson 1979; 1991). Moreover, the ability of resource-dependent communities to act on their own behalf in response to changing patterns of resource demand, use, and management practices represents a critical factor in determining their adaptive capacity in the face of social and economic changes that in some instances threaten the very survival of long-established community structures and processes (FEMAT 1993; Little and Krannich 1989).

The discussion presented here is focused primarily on conditions and trends observed in resource-dependent areas in the western United States, where the senior author has spent much of the past two decades engaged in research on rural communities and the social and economic changes and development patterns affecting them. Traditionally, the social, economic and cultural conditions that characterize rural areas of the West have been closely linked to the region's natural resources. This is evident both from analyses that focus on the patterns of economic activity that characterize the region (see Hady and Ross 1990), and from the ways in which residents of rural places symbolically link themselves and their communities to the natural resources of the region. Frequent reference to places as "ranching communities," "mining communities," "logging communities," and so forth reveals the tendency among many rural communities in the region to exhibit development patterns and socioeconomic structures that reflect high levels of dependence on the availability and utilization of various land-based natural resources. However, in the 1990s rural communities throughout the American West are experiencing unprecedented transformations of the social, economic, and cultural landscapes that have characterized the region for most of the past century. As a result, there is a pressing need for increased understanding of and attention to the development trends, needs, and prospects confronting such places.

CONDITIONS AND TRENDS AFFECTING RESOURCE-DEPENDENT RURAL PLACES

Before addressing the obstacles to and opportunities for pursuing rural community development in resource dependent communities, it is necessary to consider some complexities that arise when attempting to understand such places. First, it is important to recognize that resource dependent communities do not comprise a homogenous category of rural places. Rather, they exhibit a wide range of social and economic conditions and trends—some are extremely dynamic, viable, growing places; others are characterized by uneven development patterns and cyclical periods of boom and bust; some have exhibited little change in economic and social conditions for many years; still others are in the throes of sustained and at times sharp decline. A variety of factors influence this variability, including: (1) the types of resources that are of concern (e.g., timber and other forest products, various mineral resources, energy resources such as coal, oil, and gas; land-based resources such as livestock grazing lands, etc.); (2) proximity to transportation networks and surrounding population centers; and (3) landscape-related and geographic features such as proximity to national parks or the presence of mountains, rivers, or other natural amenities.

It is also important to recognize that resource dependent communities are not static, but represent a "moving target" for those attempting to understand them. There are now considerably fewer resource-dependent rural areas in the United States than was the case only a few decades ago, and the number of such areas is likely to continue to decline in the future (see Hady and Ross 1990). Several factors are responsible for this trend. This is due in large part to the fact that the economies of many rural areas have become increasingly diverse as the result of growth in non-extractive industries such as manufacturing, government, and the service sectors (see Summers et al. 1976; Greider and Krannich 1984; Hady and Ross 1990). The new wave of rapid economic and demographic growth that has engulfed much of the West during the first half of the 1990s is being fueled by growth in government, services and manufacturing employment, with industries associated with retirement and recreation now dominating the economies of many high-growth areas (Gersh 1995). As a result, even in areas where resource-related industries have maintained relatively stable levels of activity, their relative importance in the overall mix of rural area employment has often declined (Power 1991; Rasker 1995). At the same time, in many areas there has been substantial erosion in the levels of resource-based employment and economic activity. This has occurred for a variety of reasons, including depletion of resources, shifts in market demand, reductions in labor requirements due to changes in production technologies, and restrictions on the utilization of some public-lands resources due to increased concerns about environmental damage and ecosystem sustainability (see FEMAT 1993). These factors have contributed to the virtual disappearance of resource-based economic activity in some areas that were traditionally resource dependent.

The erosion in levels of resource dependency across much of the rural landscape has led some observers to suggest that concerns about the potential for changing resource conditions and more restrictive resource management policies to impact the development prospects of such places are overstated, if not entirely misplaced (see Power 1996; Rasker 1995; Harris et al. 1996). The so-called "transformationist" argument (Carroll, personal communication) suggests that because resource dependency is no longer widespread across the rural landscape, the effects of policy decisions affecting traditional extractive uses, such as the dramatic reductions in allowable timber harvests from federal lands in the Pacific Northwest (FEMAT 1993), are unlikely to result in major problems of adaptation for most rural areas. Further, some who adopt this perspective argue that there is little reason to focus great attention or concern on those places which have remained resource dependent, because they must inevitably experience the same types of transformation to more diversified, non-extractive local economies. In short, this view holds that resource dependent communities are modern-day anachronisms—"social dinosaurs" that must either pass through the process of transition and economic diversification or face eventual extinction.

While there is no denying that many formerly resource-dependent places have experienced significant economic and social changes, this "transformationist" perspective is at best short-sighted, and at worst indicative of a disturbing level of insensitivity and cultural arrogance. There remain many places in rural America that still are and will continue to be heavily dependent on natural resource-based economic activities. Many of those places have only limited prospects for economic diversification, often because they are located in relatively inaccessible areas where most rural industries cannot operate and/ or are lacking in the kinds of amenity features that tend to draw growth associated with recreation and/or retirement (see Bunker 1989). The social and cultural fabric of these communities is tightly interwoven with resource-based economic activities, occupations, and lifeways (see Carroll 1995; Jorgensen 1984). The cultural traditions, social structures, and symbolic meanings and attachments that comprise the social fabric of local communities and contribute to the levels of social well-being experienced by local residents can be significantly disrupted when resource-based activities are threatened with collapse (Greider and Garkovich 1994).

In short, resource dependent rural communities continue to comprise a significant segment of the rural social and economic landscape in the West and in other parts of the United States. They represent a locus of concentration of persistent rural poverty in the United States (Humphrey et al. 1993), and in many ways represent one of the most important categories of places that have been "left behind" in contemporary rural America (see Wilkinson 1986a). For these reasons, they represent fertile ground for the "doing of rural community development."

TYPES OF RESOURCE DEPENDENT COMMUNITIES

The prospects for rural community development vary across types of community settings, and as noted earlier there is considerable variation in the social and economic conditions and characteristics of resource dependent communities. Recognition of this variability provides a point of departure for identifying several distinct kinds of resource dependent communities.

Sustained Development resource dependent places are characterized by relatively stable and enduring patterns of economic activity associated with natural resource production and use; often this relative stability emerges only after an initial development-phase boom associated with the construction of extractive and processing facilities. Examples of this type of development pattern would include communities such as Price, Utah or Rock Springs, Wyoming where large-scale coal mining and associated electric power generation have been dominant economic activities for a sustained period of time (in these cases, 20-30 years or more) and are projected to remain viable for at least several decades into the future. While the initial phase of boom growth may contribute to some social and economic disruptions (Freudenburg 1986; Krannich et al. 1985; Murdock and Leistritz 1982), such disturbances appear generally to dissipate over the longer term as economic and demographic stabilization occurs (Berry et al. 1990; Brown et al. 1989; Gold 1986; Greider et al. 1991).

Cyclical Development resource dependent places are characterized by periodic ebbs and flows in the level of economic activity associated with resource-based activities. Contemporary examples would include gold or other hard-rock mining areas like Beatty and Tonopah in southern Nevada, and petroleum resource extraction areas such Big Piney or Wamsutter in the Overthrust Belt region of southern and southwestern Wyoming. Such areas have experienced unstable and cyclical patterns of development over a number of years. This instability is in many instances linked closely to fluctuations in world resource markets and prices, with resulting ebbs and flows in the levels of resource extraction and processing. For example, high prices for petroleum products in the late 1970s and early 1980s contributed to dramatic increases in the levels of exploratory drilling and extraction, but by the mid-to-late 1980s declining prices resulted in a virtual collapse of exploration and well development activities in many petroleum-rich areas. Also, some areas where previous periods of boom had given way to bust as a result of declining resource reserves are now experiencing a resurgence of extractive activity and renewed economic and demographic growth due to the influence of new technologies that permit utilization of lower-grade, less accessible, and less productive resource deposits that could not be profitably accessed during earlier resource extraction eras. For example, many areas in the West where gold mining had collapsed a number of years ago are now experiencing major industrial mining developments associated with heap-leach mining technologies that allow extraction of microscopic gold particles from extremely low-grade ore deposits.

Transitional resource dependent places have traditionally been characterized by, and often continue to exhibit, significant levels of dependence on traditional resource-based economic activities. However, the economic and social character of these places is being substantially altered by a transition involving both long-term reductions in the degree of reliance on extractive activities and increasing levels of economic diversification, often involving alternative forms of resource-based economic activity. Examples would include places like Driggs, Idaho; Moab, Utah; and Winthrop, Washington—all places where retirement and recreation/tourism-based economic activities are gradually supplanting the long-term dominance of ranching, farming, mining, and/or timber production. During the 1990s many of these places have experienced unprecedented population growth as a result of amenity-oriented in-migration (see Johnson and Beale 1994).

Declining resource dependent places are characterized by a continued high level of reliance on traditional resource-based activities. However, in these places levels of employment and economic opportunity associated with those activities are in long-term decline, and there are no significant prospects for either a renewed surge of resource extraction or the emergence of alternative sources of employment and economic activity to take the place of losses in traditional resource-based industries. Examples would include remotely located logging and timber mill towns such as Eureka, Montana or Pierce, Idaho, where declining timber inventories and substantial reductions in Forest Service timber sales are contributing to a seemingly irreversible erosion of the areas' primary sources of economic activity.

OBSTACLES TO AND OPPORTUNITIES FOR RURAL COMMUNITY DEVELOPMENT

Sustained Development Resource-Dependent Communities

In places characterized by sustained, resource-based development patterns, a high level of resource dependency does not necessarily imply economic or social instability, at least in the near term. Despite the potential for longer-term vulnerability due to possible resource exhaustion or changes in resource-based technologies and industries (see Gramling and Freudenburg 1990, 1992), such places are often characterized by relatively high levels of aggregate personal income, substantial infrastructure and public services, and extensive organizational development during sustained periods of resource extraction and processing. The relative economic vitality of such places in comparison to many other places in the rural countryside often causes them to develop into service centers for surrounding rural area populations, contributing further to growth potential and some degree of economic diversification. For example, Price, Utah and Rock Springs, Wyoming have developed into important regional trade and service centers for surrounding small towns and rural, area populations, and as a result have been able to attract major retail and commercial service businesses that are seldom evident in less viable rural, area towns. Following initial periods of often rapid growth and then decline associated with the construction phase of development for large-scale extractive or processing facilities, these types of places also tend not to exhibit the sharp demographic fluctuations involving periods of rapid in-migration as well as out-migration that are so often observed in other types of resource-dependent places. As such, they tend to exhibit the requisite conditions that Wilkinson (1986b, p. 3) identified as essential for a community field to emerge or exist: a "local ecology" involving the presence of "collective organization through which residents of a small territory meet their daily needs," and "sufficient structures such as groups, firms, agencies, and facilities to meet all of the daily needs and to express all the major categories of the common interests of people." Locality-based social structures and organizations facilitate emergence or continued existence of a community field (Wilkinson 1991, pp. 88-90) as they serve as conduits for interactions that link together different subfields within the locale.

Sustained development resource-dependent places are character-ized by sufficient economic activity to allow residents the opportunity to establish relatively stable residence, which contributes to creation and persistence of local social structures and organizations. These requisite conditions allow for the emergence of locality-oriented interaction and collective action in pursuit of common goals. To the extent that a community field exists, both individual and social well-being are enhanced. Relative to other types of resource-dependent places (as well as many non-dependent rural communities), such places have many of the attributes associated with enhanced opportunities for the kind of community development that Wilkinson emphasized—purposeful actions by local residents that generate and strengthen the community field (see Wilkinson 1991, p. 91).

Cyclical Development Resource-Dependent Communities

Unlike the sustained development context, cyclical development resource dependent communities are confronted by substantial obstacles to attaining the levels of organizational structure and interactional ties among residents that are necessary for the emergence of collective community action. The "cycle of instability" observed in these places (see Krannich and Luloff 1991) makes it extremely difficult for the community to develop and sustain the kind of local ecology and organizational complexity needed to provide for the levels of social interaction opportunities needed to support collective action. During periods of economic and demographic decline associated with reduced levels of resource production, it often is difficult for such places to sustain even basic public service infrastructure, much less the array of social organizations needed to facilitate interactions. Instead there is a tendency in places like Beatty, Nevada or Wamsutter, Wyoming for the community and its residents to "get by" with only limited commercial or public services, heavy reliance on temporary housing and public infrastructure, and little if any development of new community organizations or other formal voluntary associations.

The departure of some residents displaced by reduced economic opportunities disrupts local social ties and relationships, and many of those who remain in the community during periods of decline are forced to focus their attention more closely on the challenges of meeting individual sustenance needs rather than participating in the community field (see Wilkinson 1991, Chap. 3). Under such circumstances, both individual and community well-being suffer. Alternatively, there is also evidence that economic decline may in some situations instigate collective action among remaining community members to either counteract or mitigate the change (Cottrell 1951; Krannich and Humphrey 1983; Humphrey and Wilkinson 1993). Such local collective action may involve purposeful community field strengthening—that is, what Wilkinson emphasized as the crux of community development. We are left in a bit of a quandary regarding the conditions under which local residents react to decline in ways that reduce the propensity for community development versus the conditions under which residents may act together to purposely pursue enhancement of the community field. Perhaps at minimum, there must be some generalized belief among community members that there are reasonable prospects for achievement of development outcomes before they will tend to engage in collective action. Such shared beliefs would seem less likely to exist when the community experiences a period of very sudden and precipitous decline, or when such decline is attributed to large-scale economic or political forces that are generally perceived as being beyond the scope of local influence.

Periods of growth can also create obstacles to community development in cyclical development resource dependent places. Prior experiences with cyclical instability can lead to doubts among community members about the prospects for sustainable economic and demographic expansion resulting from increased resource production. As a result, established local residents are often unwilling to commit either the time and effort or the fiscal resources needed to build local infrastructure and organizations to accommodate what are perceived to be temporary growth-related demands. The presence of many new in-migrants also creates an obstacle to community development, due in part to the fact that they may find it difficult to establish familiarity with others or to develop strong local attachments or commitments (see Greider and Krannich 1985; Berry et al. 1990; Krannich and Luloff 1991). Such conditions are especially likely to exist when the temporary nature of resource-related growth causes many new residents to anticipate that their tenure in the community will be relatively short. Also, social tensions and divisions between long-term residents and newcomers can further reduce the potential for the kinds of broad-based social involvement, openness of communication, and locality-based social participation that are necessary if community development is to occur.

With these obstacles in mind, what if any opportunities for rural community development might exist in such places? On balance, it would appear that the prospects for meaningful and sustainable community development responses are limited in such places. However, opportunities do exist. In some instances periods of growth induced by major resource developments can result in an infusion of planning, funding, and "bricks and mortar" infrastructure building as part of efforts to mitigate the adverse effects of extremely rapid growth. In these cases, the enhanced ability of the locality to meet some community service needs may allow some local residents to direct increased attention to activities that focus more on building of social structures and organizations. Local leadership capacity may also be enhanced if growth-induced pressures result in efforts on the part of established residents and officials to secure the kinds of training and information acquisition needed to effect improved community response. Also, the infusion of new residents during periods of growth can result in at least temporary increases in the number and availability of people with the knowledge and leadership skills that can help build community organization and action effort. To the extent that growth periods persist for more than a few months there is increased potential for such persons to become socially integrated and to develop the level of local involvement and identification needed to support their engagement in local action episodes.

Transitional Resource-Dependent Communities

In places where dependence on traditional resource-based activities is gradually giving way to different and generally more diversified economic activities, there are both significant obstacles and significant opportunities for accomplishing rural community development. Among the obstacles are a potential for reduced levels of economic well-being among at least a substantial segment of the local population. Some of those who are displaced by a loss of jobs in resource-based industries may find it extremely difficult to secure alternative employment due to age or skill requirements, or may find alternative employment to be highly inconsistent with the symbolic meanings and self-identities which often are associated with resource-based occupations (Carroll 1995). Also, in many instances the wage rates associated with recreation and tourism, retirement-related growth, and non-resource industrial developments are substantially lower than those for traditional resource-related activities, and many jobs in these industries are seasonal or part-time. These factors can result in high levels of unemployment and underemployment, the outmigration of some economically-displaced residents, and increased levels of concern about meeting basic sustenance needs among others who remain. All of these factors make it more difficult to sustain and build the levels of interaction, involvement, and commitment needed to pursue community development efforts.

In addition, transitional communities are likely to experience shifts in the composition of the local population as new residents move into the community in pursuit of employment opportunities and/or the community and environmental amenities that are often the cause of the economic transformation process. At least temporarily, the presence of substantial numbers of new residents can reduce the potential for broad-based collective action, if only because of the reduced levels of mutual familiarity that inevitably result (Freudenburg 1986). Moreover, new immigrants often bring with them values and preferences regarding community conditions that are in sharp contrast with those held by more traditional rural residents (Gersh 1995; Jobes 1995). At minimum this can reduce the potential for a collective sense of "common purpose" to emerge as a basis for cooperation and collective action among a cross-section of local residents. Often the differences that separate long-term residents from newcomers can give rise to tensions, hostilities and social conflicts. Many long-term residents of transitional rural towns in the West feel "under attack" in the face of changes associated with the influx of new residents from more urban settings; as Jobes (1995) points out, the "culture clash between locals and 'Californians' (who can be from anywhere) create constant tension and animosity." Such processes are evident in places like Moab, Utah and Driggs, Idaho, where long-term residents frequently express displeasure if not outright hostility regarding efforts by some newly arrived residents to influence established local decision making structures, to implement land use and planning ordinances, or to pursue election to public office. This is consistent with findings derived from research focusing on a transitional rural community in England, where longtime residents expressed high levels of discontent over what they perceived as the takeover of a traditional community social event by newcomers (Bell 1992). Obviously, such tensions can significantly undermine the prospects for community development processes to emerge and flourish.

At the same time, there are important opportunities for community development in transitional resource dependent rural places. In many cases, new residents bring to the community new ideas and entreprenurial and organizational experiences and skills that can enhance the ability of the community to establish effective ties with extralocal organizations and act on its own behalf (see Eastman and Krannich 1995). The growth of population and the infusion of new types of residents enhances the opportunity to establish new social organizations and associations that require a certain "critical mass" of like-minded persons that is often lacking in smaller, less dynamic rural places (see Krannich and Greider 1990). Finally, the prospects for economic and demographic growth and enhanced long-term community stability (albeit of a different form than that associated with resource-based traditions) may contribute to increased levels of optimism and enthusiasm regarding the future of the community. Active engagement in community affairs is far more likely to occur under conditions of optimism rather than the pessimism and even fatalism that often characterizes places confronted with persistent and seemingly irreversible stagnation or decline.

Declining Resource-Dependent Communities

This category is comprised of those places most often envisioned when the issue of resource dependency is raised. Such places, whether characterized by a gradual but persistent withering of resource-related opportunities or more dramatic "bust" effects associated with sudden resource depletion and facility closures, are the locus of depopulation, high levels of unemployment and underemployment, high levels of rural poverty, and a deterioration of infrastructure and social organizations needed to sustain the livelihoods and well-being of rural places and rural people (see Bunker 1989; Elo and Beale 1985; Nord 1994; Peluso et al. 1994).

These types of resource dependent communities are clearly among those rural places that have been "left behind" by the processes of technological change, global economic shifts, resource depletion, environmental damage, and changing resource management policies. Residents who struggle to remain in such places in the face of substantial hardship are often deeply committed to their community and to the lifestyles that they associate with traditional resource-based economic and social structures. However, the deep and seemingly irreversible downward spiral of life chances and sustenance structures in such places undermines the ability of residents to meet many of their daily needs within the context of the local ecological setting. In places like Eureka Montana or Pierce, Idaho where extremely high levels of employment and economic activity are based in the forest products industry, declining timber supplies and the looming threat of mill closure can stifle both economic development prospects and community action potential. In many such places the struggle for community survival is evidenced by vacant storefronts, "for sale" signs in homes, a downward trend in school enrollments, and declining membership and participation in churches, clubs, and other locality-based social organizations. Increased concerns about basic economic survival and the shredding of established social structures that results from the departure of residents who find it impossible to remain in the area contribute to an erosion of both formal and informal social structures that might otherwise provide opportunities for social interaction, mutual support, and collective response. The selective outmigration of many whose age, skills, and interests make them more able to secure opportunities elsewhere contributes to a deterioration of the human capital resources needed to channel local interaction into effective, goal-oriented community action. In such circumstances there is a high probability that despair, frustration, and a deepening sense of powerlessness will lead to a virtual collapse of the local social structures needed to pursue collective goals and needs.

At the same time, there is also some evidence to suggest that such conditions can give rise to individual and collective responses that may have socially corrosive consequences. As Padfield (1980) has suggested, residents of "dying communities" may engage in actions that have the effect of allowing them, at least temporarily, to "deny powerlessness" in an attempt to confront forces that, rightly or wrongly, are viewed as the source of their problems. Residents of declining resource dependent places are confronted with seemingly insurmountable threats to the sustainability and even the very survival of their communities and their traditional lifeways. It is therefore not surprising to observe that at times their reactions are characterized by deep-seated distrust of and hostility toward external agencies and authorities, and a tendency to search for ways to identify "villains" who can be blamed for the changes that threaten their individual and collective well-being. Currently this process of vilification is highly evident in the West, where various rural-based "local control," "home rule," "wise use," and "public lands reform" social movements have focused hostility and blame on federal land and resource management authorities whose resource management policies are considered to be major contributors to the decline of resource-based rural economies and communities. While the sense of "common predicament" (Sherif 1966) and identification of a common, external foe can contribute to a sense of collective purpose and solidarity that is consistent with the presence of community (see Gold 1985), the social structures and interactions that derive from such circumstances are inconsistent with the notions of community well-being and community development advanced by Wilkinson (1991). In the absence of realistic opportunities to either meet local needs for sustenance and infrastructure or to alter the forces of global economic, technological and social change that are at the root of decline in such places, the prospects for attaining the kinds of positive, locality-oriented actions that comprise Wilkinson's concept of community development would appear to be very slight.

SUMMARY AND CONCLUSIONS

As is true throughout rural America, the prospects for rural community development in many resource dependent rural places are not especially encouraging. Broad structural forces involving "factors at regional, national and international levels" (Wilkinson 1991, p. 100) constrain the rural development process in all rural settings, and nowhere are the impacts of such forces felt more deeply than in resource dependent areas. These forces in turn limit the potential for both the emergence of local, grass-roots efforts to improve local conditions and the probability that such efforts might succeed in attaining their goals.

However, it is important to recognize that resource dependency is a multifaceted phenomenon, and that development prospects vary across types of resource-dependent rural places. As is summarized in Table 1, the differing patterns of social and economic stability or change in the four types of resource-dependent places outlined here are associated with important distinctions in community development potential.

For sustained development places, the prospects for the kinds of collective social action and organization-building episodes that are central to community development are better than in many rural communities. Relatively abundant economic opportunities and infrastructural development contribute to a more stable context for

Table 1. Typology of Natural Resource-Based Communities and the Potential for Local Actions and Interactions Indicative of Community Development Processes

Type	Economic Characteristics	Obstacles to Community Development	Opportunities for Community Development
Sustained Economy	Stable patterns of natural resource extraction; economic and demographic stability over relatively long term	Influence of non-local social and economic forces that can limit local autonomy and discourage efforts at collective problem-solving (common to all settings)	Stable formal and informal organizations and stable social structures and processes enhance prospects for levels of involvement, commitment, and familiarity needed to support collective action
Cyclical Economy	Ebbs and flows of natural resource extraction; periods of rapid economic and demographic growth and decline	Unstable population as people move to community for jobs or out of community as economy declines, which reduces stability of interaction networks; value differences between newcomers and long-term residents create tensions that undermine collective action potential	Potential for mitigation in form of infrastructure funding or planned problem solving community forums; booms periods may increase the number of people with organization and leadership skills who could instigate collective action; dissatisfaction over instability may stimulate local efforts to pursue mitigation efforts and alternative development opportunities

216

Transitional Economy	Shift from natural resource extraction to a more diverse economic base; often recreation and/or retirement with their associated spin-offs	Decrease in natural resource extraction jobs and an increase in jobs inconsistent with long-time residents' skills and/or symbolic identities leads to outmigration; value differences between long-timers timers and newcomers can undermine collective action potential	Increase the number of people with organization and leadership skills who could instigate collective action; new businesses and infrastructure growth can contribute to increased optimism about community future and increased interest and motivation for pursuit of community enhancement
Declining Economy	Long-term diminishing production and employment in natural resource extraction; often due to depletion of resource and/or change in national/global markets	Sources of economic sustenance that maintain the population diminish; outmigration of residents displaced by economic changes undermines the stability of social organizations and interaction patterns necessary for collective action; alienation from and distrust of the larger society	Very restricted

217

the emergence and persistence of formal organizations and informal social structures that are key building blocks for community development. In such places relatively small investments in community development programs designed to stimulate and facilitate social interaction and organization-building have the potential to reap substantial benefits with respect to the emergence of development actions and enhanced community well-being.

Transitional resource dependent places also exhibit important opportunities associated with the infusion of renewed economic vigor and demographic changes that can bring new leadership, new ideas, and enhanced human capital resources. As such, the prospects for community development in such places are in some ways better than those of many other places scattered across the rural countryside. At the same time, there is a potential for some community residents to be displaced by the economic and social changes associated with the context of transition, and in many cases the tensions that emerge between established populations and new residents stand in the way of cooperative efforts to pursue locality-relevant needs and goals. In such settings, development policies and plans could effectively be targeted at providing retraining and support services for displaced individuals and facilitation of broad-participative and collaborative community self-assessment efforts designed to seek out common ground for collective action.

In contrast, for resource dependent places characterized either by decline or by cyclical instability, the prospects for meeting the daily needs of residents, building social structures needed for affiliation and interaction, and engaging in collective actions that could enhance social well-being appear to be limited at best. In the absence of economic and demographic stability these types of places often lack both the physical and organizational infrastructure needed to meet residents' needs for both service provision and affiliation. Further, the difficulties that confront residents of such places and the sense of hopelessness and alienation from the larger society that often emerges in response to extralocal forces of social and economic change provide little encouragement that local initiative and collective actions will result in meaningful improvements in well-being. While periodic infusions of new economic activity and new residents can provide some short-term improvements in those communities experiencing cyclical development patterns, such improvements are seldom enough to outweigh the difficulties associated with unpredictable growth patterns, economic displacement, and disruption of social structures needed to allow collective actions to emerge.

There are some prospects for externally-induced interventions that might help to improve the social capital and infrastructure conditions that help to restrict community development opportunities in resource-dependent areas characterized by instability or decline. Examples would include several recently-introduced federal initiatives to provide training programs and other resource infusions into communities affected by sharp shifts in federal resource management policies such as the reduced levels of timber harvest affecting large areas of the Pacific Northwest and the northern Rocky Mountain regions. Unfortunately, such programs represent little more than a drop in the bucket when evaluated in the context of the needs confronting resource dependent places. As Wilkinson (199, p. 101) observed, "As things stand, rural deficits in resources for meeting needs are a powerful barrier to community development and well-being."

For resource-dependent places, and for rural communities more generally, there is little evidence that a massive infusion of funding, training programs, leadership-building efforts, or other needs-oriented programs that could support development of the physical and social capital required for community development will be forthcoming in the foreseeable future. Although some programs do exist to enhance physical infrastructure, initiatives designed to generate the organizational structures and social infrastructure needed to stimulate and sustain local collective action are all but absent. If efforts to address the development needs of resource-dependent rural places are to succeed, they must include a focus on the interactional dimensions of community that are crucial for attainment of social well-being and sustainable community development outcomes.

ACKNOWLEDGMENT

This is a revision of a paper presented at the Kenneth P. Wilkinson Symposium on The Doing of Rural Community Development, Pennsylvania State University, University Park, PA, August 13-14, 1995; Utah Experiment Station Journal Paper No. 5076.

REFERENCES

Bell, M.M. 1992. "The Fruit of the Difference: The Rural-Urban Continuum as a System of Identity." *Rural Sociology* 57 (1): 65-82.

Berry, E.H., R.S. Krannich, and T. Greider. 1990. "A Longitudinal Analysis of Neighboring in Rapidly Changing Rural Places." *Journal of Rural Studies* 6(2): 175-186.

Brown, R.B., H.R. Geertsen, and R.S. Krannich. 1989. "Community Satisfaction and Social Integration in a Boom Town: A Longitudinal Analysis." *Rural Sociology* 54(4): 568-586.

Bunker, S.G. 1989. "Staples, Links and Poles in the Construction of Regional Development Theories." *Sociological Forum* 4: 589-610.

Carroll, M.S. 1995. *Community and the Northwestern Logger: Continuities and Changes in the Era of the Spotted Owl.* Boulder, CO: Westview Press.

Cottrell, W.F. 1951. "Death by Dieselization: A Case Study in the Reaction to Technological Change." *American Sociological Review* 16: 358-365.

Eastman, C., and R.S. Krannich. 1995. "Community Change and Persistence: The Case of El Cerrito, New Mexico." *Journal of the Community Development Society* 26(1): 41-51.

Elo, I.T., and C.L. Beale. 1985. *Natural Resources and Rural Poverty: An Overview.* Washington, D.C.: Resources for the Future.

FEMAT (Forest Ecosystem Management Assessment Team). 1993. "Forest Ecosystem Management: An Ecological, Economic and Social Assessment." *Appendix A of Draft Supplemental Environmental Impact Statement on Management of Habitat for Late Successional and Old Growth Forest Related Species Within the Range of the Northern Spotted Owl.* Portland, Oregon: USDA-Forest Service, Region 6.

Freudenburg, W.R. 1986. "The Density of Acquaintanceship: An Overlooked Variable in Community Research." *American Journal of Sociology* 92(1): 27-63.

Gersh, J. 1995. "The Rocky Mountain West at Risk." *The Western Planner* 16(3): 6-9.

Gold, R.L. 1985. *Ranching, Mining, and the Human Impact of Natural Resource Development.* New Brunswick, NJ: Transaction Books.

Gramling, R., and W.R. Freudenburg. 1990. "A Closer Look at 'Local Control': Communities, Commodities, and the Collapse of the Coast." *Rural Sociology* 55(4): 541-558.

———. 1992. "Opportunity-threat, Development, and Adaptation: Toward a Comprehensive Framework for Social Impact Assessment." *Rural Sociology* 57(2): 216-234.

Greider, T., and L. Garkovich. 1994. "Landscapes: The Social Construction of Nature and the Environment." *Rural Sociology* 59(1): 1-24.

Greider, T., and R. Krannich. 1984. "Changing Patterns of Sustenance Organization in Metropolitan and Nonmetropolitan Areas of the Rocky Mountain West, 1940 to 1980." *Growth and Change* 15(January): 41-49.

————. 1985. "Neighboring Patterns, Social Support and Rapid Growth: A Comparison Analysis from Three Western Communities." *Sociological Perspectives.* 28: 51-70.

Greider, T., R.S. Krannich, and E.H. Berry. 1990. "Local Identity, Solidarity, and Trust in Changing Rural Communities." *Sociological Focus* 24(4): 263-282.

Hady, T.F., and P.J. Ross. 1990. *An Update: The Diverse Social and Economic Structure of Nonmetropolitan America.* Washington, D.C.: U.S. Department of Agriculture, Economic Research Service Staff Report No. AGES 9036.

Harris, C., G. Brown, and B. McLaughlin. 1996. *An Assessment of the Social and Economic Characteristics of Communities in the Interior Columbia River Basin.* Walla Walla, WA: USDA-Forest Service, Interior Columbia Basin Ecosystem Management Project.

Humphrey, C.R., and K.P. Wilkinson. 1993. "Growth Promotion Activities in Rural Areas: Do They Make a Difference?" *Rural Sociology* 58(2): 175-189.

Jobes, P.C. 1995. "Migration in the West: A Gallatin Valley, Montana Case Study." *The Western Planner* 16(3): 10-13.

Johnson, K.M., and C.L. Beale. 1994. "The Recent Revival of Widespread Population Growth in Nonmetropolitan Areas of the United States." *Rural Sociology* 59(4): 655-667.

Jorgensen, J.G. 1984. "The Land is Cultural, So is a Commodity: The Locus of Differences Among Indians, Cowboys, Sod-Busters, and Environmentalists." *Journal of Environmental Ethics* 12(3): 1-21.

Krannich, R.S., and T. Greider. 1990. "Rapid Growth Effects on Rural Community Relations." Pp. 61-73 in *American Rural Communities,* edited by A.E. Luloff and L. Swanson. Boulder, CO: Westview Press.

Krannich, R.S., T. Greider, and R.L. Little. 1985. "Rapid Growth and Fear of Crime: A Four Community Comparison." *Rural Sociology* 50(2): 193-209.

Krannich, R.S., and C. Humphrey. 1983. "Local Mobilization and Community Growth: Toward an Assessment of the 'Growth Machine' Hypothesis." *Rural Sociology* 48(1): 60-81.

Krannich, R.S., and A.E. Luloff. 1991. "Problems of Resource Dependency in U.S. Rural Communities." Pp. 5-18 in *Progress in Rural Policy and Planning,* Vol. 1, edited by A. Gilg. New York: Belhaven Press.

Little, R.L., and R.S. Krannich. 1989. "A Model for Assessing the Social Impacts of Natural Resource Utilization on Resource-dependent Communities." *Impact Assessment Bulletin* 6(2): 21-35.

Murdock. S.H., and F.L. Leistritz. 1982. *Energy Development in the Western United States: Impact on Rural Areas.* New York: Praeger.

Nord, M. 1994. "Natural Resources and Persistent Rural Poverty: In Search of the Nexus." *Society and Natural Resources* 7(3): 23-38.

Padfield, H. 1980. "The Expendable Rural Community and the Denial of Powerlessness." Pp. 159-185 in *The Dying Community,* edited by A. Gallaher and H. Padfield. Albuquerque, NM: University of New Mexico Press.

Peluso, N.L., C.R. Humphrey, and L.P. Fortmann. 1994. "The Rock, the Beach and the Tidal Pool: People and Poverty in Natural Resource-dependent Areas." *Society and Natural Resources* 7(1): 23-38.

Power, T.M. 1991. "Wildland Preservation and the Economy of Utah." Paper prepared for Project 2000: Coalition for Utah's Future, Wilderness Task Force. Missoula, MT: University of Montana, Department of Economics.

Power, T.M. 1996. *Lost Landscapes and Failed Economies: The Search for a Value of Place.* Washington, D.C.: Island Press.

Rasker, R. 1995. *A New Home on the Range: Economic Realities in the Columbia River Basin.* Bozeman, MN: The Wilderness Society.

Sherif, M. 1966. *In Common Predicament: Social Psychology of Intergroup Conflict and Cooperation.* Boston: Houghton-Mifflin.

Summers, G., S. Evans, F. Clemente, E. Beck. and J. Minkoff. 1976. *Industrial Invasion of Nonmetropolitan America.* New York: Praeger.

Wilkinson, K.P. 1979. "Social Well-being and Community." *Journal of the Community Development Society* 10(1): 5-16.

_____. 1986a. "Communities Left Behind—Again." Pp. 341-346 in *New Dimensions in Rural Policy: Building Upon Our Heritage*, edited by Joint Economic Committee. Washington, D.C.: Congress of the United States.

_____. 1986b. "In Search of the Community in the Changing Countryside." *Rural Sociology* 51(1): 1-17.

_____. 1991. *The Community in Rural America.* New York: Greenwood Press.

FROM FUNCTIONAL TO SYMBOLIC LOCAL COMMUNITY:

A CASE STUDY OF A FOREST VILLAGE IN EASTERN FINLAND

Pertti Rannikko

ABSTRACT

This article concerns the dimensions of community and locality and the changes which occurred in them. In addition to the sociological concept of local community, I will use the basic geographical concepts of space, place and region as my points of departure. The subject of the case study is the ideal type of "death of the local community," that is, a small remote village which has lost its position in production and, as a result, ceases to be a functional community and a local social system. The article examines the development of the village from the viewpoint of the spatial division of labor, local institutions and local identity. The case study seeks to discover the current features of the community: In what ways do the village-related local phenomena

Research in Community Sociology, Volume 7, pages 223-246.
Copyright © 1997 by JAI Press Inc.
All rights of reproduction in any form reserved.
ISBN: 0-7623-0272-0

still exist? What, in fact, happens when a functional local community dies? Basic questions such as these were left unresolved when traditional local community studies reached an impasse in the 1970s, but they have now resurfaced in a new kind of locality study. Our case study shows that though the local community ceases to exist in one respect, its unity might remain strong in another. Though the village which is the subject of the study is long dead as a functional local community, a powerful symbolic community is left to remind us of the former status and identity of the region.

INTRODUCTION

The concept of local community has a long and contradictory history both in different fields of science and different research traditions. For decades local community studies had their own international "research style" (cf. Newby 1980, pp. 76-83; Maho 1982, p. 223): information gathered through interviews and participant observation was combined with statistical data concerning the population, and the life, customs, changes, and so forth, of the subject communities were described in detail.

In the 1960s and 1970s the traditional local community study entered a state of turmoil and started to languish. Modern societies were seen to be undergoing a homogenization, and the meaning of the local level as the determiner of the possibilities of life was being reduced. The study of a group of people living in a certain geographically-defined area was no longer considered to be important (see e.g., Stacey 1969, pp. 134-136; Bernard 1973, pp. 173-192). The concept of community was also found to be problematic due to the theoretical conflicts and the traditional ideological images connected to it. Romantic ideas of the community—the brotherly and close personal relations of rural villages and other communities—were especially shunned.

In the 1980s, however, local phenomena again began to interest social scientists. At first, they were not as interested in describing the local communities as in analyzing the processes on which the development of the localities was dependant (see e.g., Newby 1986; Bradley and Lowe 1984; Cooke 1989). They did not want to use the problematic concept of community but spoke instead about localities. The concept of locality, detached from the perspective of human life, was observed mainly on the basis of production relations. Gradually the emphasis moved from production-centric research to describing the customs, culture and subjective experiences of the inhabitants of the subject areas (cf. Duncan and Savage 1991; Jackson 1991). However, locality focused research encountered the same kinds of theoretical contradictions which formerly brought community studies to an impasse. To solve this impasse, more is needed than just abandoning the concept of community and replacing it with a new concept of locality. The various dimensions of the community should be outlined in greater detail and its diverse aspects studied (cf. Wilkinson 1986). This suggestion does not mean a return to the traditional approach of community study. The critical analysis of the traditional approach should be carried on further and be amended with those aspects which were left sketchy and unfinished.

In this article I will analyze the dimensions of community and locality, and the changes occurring in them, on the basis of the material provided by a small and remote Finnish forest village, Sivakka. Life and activity was at its liveliest in the 1950s, when there was a large amount of lumbering activity available around the village. Following the reduction and cessation of this activity, the social life of the village quickly withered. Through the Sivakka case study, I try to determine the present features of locality: What significance does the village and dwelling place have in people's lives? On which dimensions does the village-related locality or community still exist and on which has it died? What, in fact, happens when the economic base of a local community is said to die?

In addition to the sociological concept of local community I use the basic geographical concepts of space, place and region as my points of departure. These concepts help to clarify the key issues of locality studies, although a wealth of new concepts have been developed for the study of local phenomena (of these new concepts see e.g., Duncan and Ley 1993; Agnew 1987, pp. 26-28).

KEY CONCEPTS OF LOCALITY STUDIES

Local Community

The first word of the concept "local community" indicates a geographically-confined area. Studying the ideal type of "local community"—a small village, the extensiveness or limitedness of the area, at a given point in time is not a serious problem for local inhabitants, the villagers themselves. The outsider, however, may have problems recognizing the borders of the village. The second word of the concept, "community," indicates that there is social interaction which creates some kind of common ties between the people living in the area (Hillery 1955; Bell and Newby 1971, pp. 27-32). In sociology the concept of community has mainly been used, on the one hand, to refer to the social relations occurring in a certain geographical area (the interaction component) and, on the other hand, to emphasize membership in the group (the identification component). Attempts have also been made to conceptualize the same components of the community by speaking of a functional community and a symbolic community (Lehtonen 1990, pp. 23-29). A *functional community* is born as a result of concrete interaction and activity. A *symbolic community* binds people less to places and is manifested in consciousness and feeling. It can be cultural in origin, in which case it is a result of the interaction between people and customs. A symbolic community can also be ideological, in which case its reproduction is brought about by the ideological mechanisms.

The concept of community does not only depict the interaction processes of the people living in a given region, but also the social system. The region may have its own institutions (services, production, etc.) which form the local social system (Stacey 1969; Day and Murdoch 1993). The local system is usually part of the larger society, and its connections have continually intensified as a result of the increasing regional division of labor, the differentiation of society and other such changes. The change in the local social system is viewed in this article through an analysis of the changes which have taken place in different institutions, such as local services and voluntary associations.

Space and Place

The concepts included in local community studies may be explained by means of the concepts of space and place, which are familiar in geography. The former defines the examination related to the social division of labor and production; the latter considerations are associated with local sense and culture (cf. Johnston 1991, pp. 38-68; Beynon and Hudson 1993). In critical social geography, space is examined as the site of social processes, especially production. In this study the subject is some process (e.g., the change in the forest economy or the expansion of the welfare state) and its local concentration. Locality is then the context in which the concretization of the process is explicated (Newby 1986, pp. 213-214).

Among adherents to this social geographic tradition, the change of localities has often been investigated through the concept of the spatial division of labor (see Massey 1984). The economic differences between regions and localities are historically-relative and can change, in principle, as a result of two processes. First, through changes taking place in the geographical distribution of the requirements of production (e.g., relative distances change with the development of the transport and communication system). Second, through changing conditions of the production process itself (Massey 1979, pp. 234-235). Production processes change as a result of technological advance, which, in turn, is powered by the competition between individual sources of capital. The regional structure at any given time is a result of the forms taken by the spatial division of labor prevailing at various times. The production structure of a certain locality is thus constructed on several investment layers, each representing different phases of the wider (national and international) spatial division of labor.

While social geography seeks to link regions to politico-economic structures, human geography focuses on the examination of the regional relations and identity of individuals and communities. The region is, in this case, conceptualized as a subjectively perceived and experienced place (Entrikin 1991; Harper 1987). The key research themes involve the significances people attach to places; they are revealed to the researcher through the experiences, values, feelings and memories of the individual.

Many places also have their own identity, which is composed of the physical features and functions of the place and the significances connected to it (cf. Entrikin 1994). There are both personal significances and those common to a specific group connected to the place. Thus identity may be examined, on the one hand, as the relation of the individual to the place and, on the other, as a collective local identity. The local identity evolves as a result of long-term social practices. In this article I am not so interested in the relationship between individuals and place as in the local identity of the people living in a certain area.

Institutionalization and Deinstitutionalization of the Region

Geographers do not always differentiate between the concepts of place and region. Place, however, is more indicative of the significant world on the personal level, while region is more concerned with the communal and social analysis of space. The Finnish geographer, Anssi Paasi (1986, pp. 119-130; 1991, pp. 243-247), has created a theory of institutionalization of regions which is based on the notion that regions evolve as a result of human practice as a part of the regional system, exist for a time and then perhaps disappear. Such emergence and disappearance occurs all the time on different regional levels: on the local, regional, and national, as well as on broader regional levels. There are four stages in the institutionalization of the region which can be distinguished analytically. They can be simultaneous or their order may vary. The stages are (Paasi 1986, p. 121):

- *the development of territorial shape*, during which the region (a village, municipality, province, state, etc.) is outlined as an individual unit differing from other regions,
- *the formation of symbolic shape*, in which the signs and symbols characterizing the region (the name, etc.) evolve; on this basis the region is recognized and can be identified with,
- *the development of institutions*, at which time the institutions and social organisations connected to the region are established,
- *the establishment of the region*, when a certain region has a clear identity among the other regions of the regional system.

The roles of the region change and reproduce through social development. In the end the region may disappear totally from the regional system, in which case we may speak of the deinstitution-alization of the region (Riikonen 1995). This does not mean that some kind of vacuum takes the place of the negated region, but that the previous institutional structures are replaced by new practices related to the regional system. Some of the symbols and institutions of the region may also live on in the new situation as monuments to the earlier identity and status of the region.

The theorization of the deinstitutionalization of the region is closely related to the basic question of my research. It offers points of departure for considering what really happens when a village or local community dies. The institutionalization theory, however, offers no basis for the examination of the economic changes of the village. Those I analyze by means of the concept of the spatial division of labor.

STUDY MATERIAL

Sivakka, the subject of the study, is a village located in the municipality of Valtimo, in Finland's easternmost province, North Karelia (see Figure 1). Even in terms of sparsely-populated North Karelia, Valtimo is a remote municipality and Sivakka is, in turn, one of Valtimo's most outlying villages, over 20 kilometers from the municipal center. The settlement pattern of the region has been scattered hill settlement, in which the houses are located far from one another. The fields are scattered and filled with stones, so the production conditions are poor. From the beginning of the century to the 1960s the livelihood of the population was earned mainly from lumbering. In the 1960s the amount of lumbering in the region decreased rapidly, which led to the collapse of the village population. The decrease has continued with varying speed until the present day.

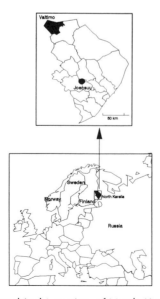

Figure 1. The Geographical Location of North-Karelia and Valtimo

Sivakka has been the subject of research at the University of Joensuu since 1973; a variety of research materials have been collected during this time. Sociologists, economists, folklorists, ethnologists, and historians have taken part in the multidisciplinary research groups. The core material for this article has been gathered during periods of fieldwork in 1983, 1988, and 1993. Free-form taped interviews as well as systematic questionnaires were completed by the villagers. The latter could be used to provide exact figures concerning the whole region and were a kind of population and household census, through which the housing conditions, and migration careers and occupations of the villagers were charted.

The free-form interviews involved the life-histories of the villagers as well as the village's past and present. When the 1993 interviews began the problem was defined and structure of this article had already been outlined, and I could therefore concentrate on gathering material for these purposes. I also re-analyzed my older interviews to serve the new research questions. In addition to the interview material I have also used written documentary material (mainly registries, index files of employment offices and articles from the local newspaper).

THE POSITION OF SIVAKKA IN
THE SPATIAL DIVISION OF LABOR

A Lumberman-Smallholder Village

Though the first inhabitants of Sivakkavaara arrived as early as the mid-seventeenth century, the population did not rise over some 30 or 40 until the last years of the nineteenth century. Nature dictated the terms of living in a natural economy. A poor crop might cause epidemics and death from starvation, so the increase in population was very irregular. The population in the region did not start to grow steadily until the turn of the century, and thereafter growth continued to be steady until the end of the 1950s. This phase of rapid population growth was connected to the initiation and generalization of lumbering. It formed the economic base of Sivakka from the beginning of the century to the 1960s. Lumbering was clearly the main occupation and the chief source of livelihood; small-scale agriculture and cattle-raising were clearly secondary. Agriculture alone could hardly provide a sufficient income in the region, since farms contained only a few hectares of cultivated land.

The men of Sivakka were more lumbermen than small farmers. Cattle-raising was women's work and practiced more for domestic use than for trade. Lumbering, as a profession, stabilized at the beginning of the twentieth century, particularly in those regions where the state and the forest companies owned large areas of forest (Rannikko 1995, pp. 110-111; Alapuro 1979). The majority of the extensive forests in the Sivakkavaara area are owned by the state, so the main employer in the region was the National Board of Forestry. The timber companies also owned thousands of hectares of land, so they too operated large logging camps in the area around the village.[1]

Outlying regions like Sivakka had many natural preconditions for the expanding forest industry: large forest resources, waterways providing ready float routes and the possibilities of local transport in winter. The growth of lumbering strictly followed the change of seasons and the success of different stages was crucially dependant on the natural conditions. In the early days of the logging camps only heavy logs were cut and work was done only in the winter. When the forest had enough snow and the swamps had frozen, a teamster gathered a group which included himself, the horse and two or three men to fell the trees. The winter logging camps usually lasted until March or April. After a few weeks' break, log floating began; its purpose was to transport the logs from the headwaters to the main float routes during the spring floods. From the 1920s onwards more and more smaller wood was taken as cordwood. This prolonged the annual lumbering period since the making of cordwood started as early as August and a large part of the bark was removed in the spring.

In the early days the lumbermen had to take care of their housing themselves, so they often lived in nearby houses or in poorly-maintained temporary lodgings. The Barracks Law of 1928 forced the employers to build or procure lodgings which fulfilled given requirements. The barracks then started to become the centers of the logging sites, around which the work was organized. The foremen used them as offices and lived there during the logging periods.

The barracks were built and left empty as the work progressed. The largest barracks, and the people scrambling around them, formed a substantial community with their own shops and matrons, and so forth. The small farms of the region made money by selling milk, butter, meat, potatoes and other foodstuffs to the barracks. The permanent residents of villages like Sivakka played their own roles in the spatial division of labor in the forest sector. They offered a "well-organized system of way-stations for the forces of industry; it would have been difficult or even impossible for industry to move on in the wilderness without it" (Pälsi 1923, p. 196). The permanent residents of the region were also a cheap and useful labor reserve for the expanding logging work.

The logging sites also brought forest workers to Sivakka from other places, however, chiefly from eastern Finland. Many lumbermen set up families with Sivakka girls and remained in the area permanently. Thus the percentage of lumbermen-smallholders living in the area permanently grew and that of the casual lumbermen gradually started to decrease.

The Local Level Loses its Place in the Organization of Lumbering

In Finland logging remained labor-intensive and was based on physical work up until the 1950s. At the time it was economical to scatter the labor force to live in the forests. The small farms fed the lumbermen and insured their livelihood when the forest industry did not need them (Rannikko 1995, pp. 110-112). As a result of intensified international competition, the forest industry and National Board of Forestry interest in rationalizing logging increased in the 1950s and especially in the 1960s (Raumolin 1985). The logging process underwent a rapid transformation: creek floating was replaced by truck transport; in local transport, first agricultural and then forest tractors replaced horses; power saws replaced hand saws and developed quickly; bark was removed in factories. Other technical innovations included extensive clear cutting, forest cultivation, intensive treatment of the land, chemical fertilizers as well as coppice control, and so forth.

In addition to the adoption of new methods, the problems of logging had to be viewed from totally new starting points. What had previously been strong was now weak. Where the winter snow had once made local timber transport by horse possible, it now became a problem for mechanical transport. Earlier, the lumbermen-smallholders working on farms during the slack season in the forest had guaranteed a regular labor reserve for the logging. Now the desire was to replace these seasonal "amateurs" by a trained professional.

The lumbermen-smallholders were replaced in the late 1960s and early 1970s by permanent lumbermen who were employed year-round (Oksa and Rannikko 1988, pp. 227-228). Lumbering was separated from farm work as a distinct profession, and more and more lumbermen started to move to apartment and row-houses in population centers.

Lumbering almost came to a complete halt in Sivakka in the early 1970s. In 1970, when the crisis was at its height, over 20 villagers were still employed in lumbering for at least three months of the year. Thereafter, only 3-5 persons had significant earned income from the forest. Since the 1970s the housing and transport of lumbermen has been organized in Valtimo from the municipal center, where a row-house was built for the National Board of Forestry. With the new logging technology, it was more economical to concentrate the labor force into small centers where it was easy to provide transportation to the logging site in the mornings (Rannikko 1995, pp. 112-114; Oksa 1993). Nowadays, stands marked for cutting are cut in a month or two, unlike the several winters it previously took. The short life and mobility of these logging camps has, in turn, made it uneconomical to build and use barracks. Sivakka, like other outlying villages, lost its position in the organization of lumbering. Forests are still cut in the area, but the labor is brought from elsewhere. The cessation of logging has been so complete that in the autumn of 1993 no one from Sivakka was employed in lumbering. A local level like Sivakka no longer has any importance in the organization of lumbering.

Income and Population Structure After the Cessation of Lumbering

The mechanization of logging, and the disappearance of the lumberman-smallholder occupation, occurred in a very short period of time. The speed of the change is seen in the population of the land register villages of Sivakkavaara and Koiravaara (see Figure 2).[2] In the 1950s the population of the area was still growing, but in the early 1960s the population dropped rapidly. The decrease in population reached its peak in the 1970s, after which the decrease has been slower.

In 1983 there were 23 inhabited houses in Sivakkavaara, in 1993 there were 21. However, the population in 10 years has been reduced by one-third. This is a result of the fact that over one-half of all

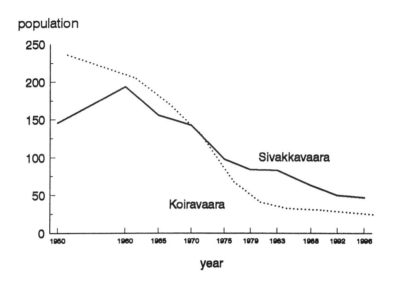

Source: Valtimo registries.
Figure 2.   The Population of the Land Register Villages of
Sivakkavaara and Koiravaara in 1950-1996

households are one-person households. Even though the village has
not actually been deserted, that is, no houses have been left empty,
the population has still decreased and the age structure has become
more and more top-heavy. In 1993 half of the women and one-third
of the men were over 60 years old. There were only two children
under 10.

   In 1993 only two people in Sivakkavaara had continuous year-
round work that guaranteed their living. The size of the working
population was, however, somewhat larger in 1993 than in 1983 (see
Table 1).[3] Most of their work is either temporary or longer-term but
part-time. The employment of the people of Sivakkavaara can be
characterized as "permanently temporary," and the line between their
being employed or unemployed is indistinct.

   The employment pattern of the people of Sivakkavaara resembles
that of the lumbermen-smallholders, which had long slack seasons
between periods of logging and floating. At that time the lumbermen
worked on their farms in slack seasons. Nowadays almost no one

Table 1. The Population Structure of Sivakkavaara in 1983, 1988 and 1993

	1983	1988	1993
Children under school age	7	3	1
Schoolchildren and students	12	5	6
Pensioners	21	26	20
Working population	9	7	12
Unemployed	16	4	6
Housewives or otherwise at home	8	7	2
Total inhabitants	73	52	47

engages in agriculture on their farms, but the upkeep of the household is very time-consuming (chopping firewood, looking after the vegetable garden and the potato field, picking berries, etc.). There is no shortage of things to do even in times of unemployment, except perhaps in winter. Many people in Sivakkavaara do unpaid socially-useful work. One charts old forests, another chops firewood for the elderly woman next door, a third collects local folk traditions, a fourth takes care of the landscape.

The importance of taking care of one's own affairs and going out into nature can also be seen in the fact that a few men of the baby-boom years have recently returned to the village. In 1983 the typical inhabitant of Sivakkavaara was an elderly woman who lived alone in her cottage and whose children had moved to different parts of the country. During the last 10 years, many such women have moved to the municipal center; and one of their sons has replaced them. When work ran out in the cities of Southern Finland the sons returned to their native villages, where living on a small income is easier than in the apartment houses of the cities. In many cases a divorce preceded the move.

Since the village was poor to start with, the effects of the economic depression of the 1990s were not as strong in Sivakka as they were in the rest of Finland. While the rest of the country has become poorer, the relative position of Sivakka has improved. In recent years the labor markets in Finland, as a whole, have moved towards the "permanently temporary" situation that Sivakka has experienced for the entire century. Adapting to temporary employment is easier in small villages like Sivakka than in cities, where earning one's living and the entire lifestyle are influenced by wage labor.

Unemployment benefits have, to some extent, become a sort of civil salary in the countryside because there are useful and interesting things to do there. The simplest way of promoting and expanding this kind of useful work would be to pay a "civil salary." It would increase the people's possibilities to decide for themselves what they will do and how to use their time.

THE FORMATION AND LOSS OF LOCAL INSTITUTIONS

Services

Basic services have been important local institutions in Finnish country villages. Most often, attention is usually given to the school. The Sivakkavaara school district was established in 1930, and its borders have subsequently been very important in shaping the regional borders of the village of Sivakka. The significance of the school was not limited only to education, but played a key role in the social life of the village. The teachers directed various programs and hobby groups and were, for example, the founders of the village sports club.

As the population grew and the outlying villages were modernized, an increasing number of services continued to come to Sivakka. At its height the village had several shops. At some time or another the post office, bus lines, and so forth, appeared in the village. A belief in the future and the improved quality of life was strong in Sivakkavaara and the surrounding hills in the late 1940s and the 1950s. The inhabitants actively worked for better services and road projects by gathering petitions, sending delegations and writing to newspapers. At the turn of the 1940s and 1950s there were even plans for a new school district. They were never carried out, but the municipality built a dormitory in Sivakkavaara, where pupils from the remote areas were housed.

After the cessation of lumbering and the rapid decrease in the population, the position of Sivakka as a functional community started to diminish. While in 1960 about 400 people lived in Sivakkavaara and the hills surrounding it (Koiravaara), today there are only 65 people living there (see Figure 2 and note 2). On the basis of such a small number of people, services and activities can no longer be organized.

Considering the speed with which the population of Sivakka plummeted, basic services were maintained in the region for a long time, until the 1980s. In 1960, there were 78 pupils in the school;

in 1970 there were still 40; but in 1979 there were only six. The Sivakkavaara school was closed in 1982, and the children of the village have since attended the lower stage of comprehensive school in Ylä-Valtimo, 15 kilometers away. They attend the upper stage in the municipal center of Valtimo. The home village is no longer the same type of growth community for the young as it was for the baby-boom generation in their time. The smaller the age groups have become, the greater the need to direct their free-time activities outside the village.

The last shop shut down in the mid-1980s. At about the same time the Sivakkavaara voting district was terminated. The post office had already shut down. The mobile shop stopped visiting the village a few years ago. The nearest shops are over 20 kilometers away in the municipal center. The mobile library, however, still stops in the village. For years the nearest bus stop was ten kilometers away, but nowadays a bus stops in the village on school days. There is regular taxi service between Sivakka and the municipal center a couple of times a week. Another indication that services have to be sought elsewhere is that the taxi is the only local service now available in Sivakka.

The Life-span of the Association Activities

The beginning of lumbering in the Sivakka region meant quite an upheaval in the life of the village. The backwoods village still partially existing in a wilderness culture became a meeting place for logging workers from all over Finland. The world penetrated the village community, bringing new ways of life and new attitudes. While the lumbermen in many places adopted radical ideas, the logging regions of Eastern Finland became strong left-wing bastions. In Sivakka, the lumbermen's identity and the centuries-old tradition of resistance of the unrefined culture were combined to form a unique local identity, which emphasized the juxtaposition of the official society and prevailing culture (Knuuttila 1989).

The structure of associations in Sivakka has clearly been related to the lumberman's consciousness of the region. There was a branch of the Lumbermen's and Floaters' Union in the village, but no farmers' association. The role of religion has been scarce, and there have been no active local religious bodies. Among the political movements, only the leftist parties have have branches there; the Social Democratic Party had already established a branch between the wars. Political activity increased after the war. The Sivakkavaara Democratic Association was founded after the legalization of communist activity. For a long time in the Sivakkavaara voting district, the People's Democrats got over half of the votes.[4] Both the Social Democratic and the People's Democratic Associations had open-air dance floors in Sivakka. In 1949 a sports club, Sivakan Syöksy, which became part of the Worker's Sports Association (Työväen Urheiluliitto), was founded in the area.

The life-span of association activity followed that of lumbering and the population. The prosperity after the wars was short. Sivakan Syöksy ceased operations in 1964. Political activity lessened and gradually died away. The open-air dance floors have been in ruin for two decades. Together with the fall of employment and the population, association activity in Sivakka also collapsed. At the same time, the clear political identity of Sivakka crumbled. In the general elections of 1983, nearly half of the voters opted for the populist Finnish Rural Party.

During the last ten years the village action committee and the hunting and fishing association have been active in Sivakka. The village action committee of Sivakka was established in 1983 (for Finnish village activity, see Rouhinen 1981; Oksa 1992, pp. 995-996). Village activity was quite brisk in the early years, primarily in respect to organizing gatherings and protesting against the closing down of the services in the village. For many years, however, there has been little activity and meetings have also been held sporadically. In 1994, the village committee of the neighboring village of Ylä-Valtimo proposed that the two village committees be combined since, for instance, the villages are part of the same school district. The proposal was not warmly received in Sivakka, whose residents wanted to preserve their own village committee.

The task of the Sivakkan Erä-Veikot hunting association and fishing association has been to organize hobbies related to the natural resources of the area. Going out into nature, picking berries, hunting and fishing are an essential part of the way of life which the people of Sivakka have internalized from childhood. Interest in these hobbies has been maintained to this day, so the organizational work they require has continued. Though other aspects of "Sivakkaness" may lessen, nature and the landscape will become more important ingredients in it (cf. Oksa and Rannikko 1996).

Emphasizing the Role of the Municipality Center

As jobs, services and communal association activity have been terminated in Sivakka, the meaning of the village in the everyday life of people has diminished. The village is no longer the level at which activities are organized. Services are now available only in the municipality center of Valtimo, where nearly all municipal services are nowadays clustered. Instead of being active in village clubs and associations, the residents are now active in associations which function throughout the municipality but are concentrated in the municipal center. According to our interviews, the people of Sivakka hardly take part in such activities, but nearly everyone visits the municipal center at least once a week to shop or to take care of other business.

The emphasized role of the municipal center is a result not only of the continuing drop in the population of the outlying villages; there are also institutional changes involved. A particularly important phase was the expansion of the welfare state in the 1970s and 1980s. At that time major reforms were introduced to health care, social services and the school system, which brought a greatly increased number of new services and jobs to the rural municipalities (for details see Pyy and Rannikko 1995). These new services (health centers, daycare centers, vocational schools, etc.) have been, almost without exception, located in the municipal centers. They have become influential service and residential centers and dominate the social life of the whole municipality.

Many public services involve caring work, which women formerly did without pay at home and within the immediate community. The reduction in traditional social relations, and the transfer of these tasks to the public sector has, by no means, severed the local ties of the people, but has meant a modernization of these ties (cf. Cox and Mair 1988, pp. 312-313). A new fabric of social relations, services and other everyday routines has been woven together around dwelling places and workplaces.

SOCIAL AND SYMBOLIC COMMUNALITY

Mutual Relations

The transfer of jobs and services away from the village and its immediate surroundings has meant an increase in mobility. The significance of the immediate dwelling area and neighbors in people's lives has diminished (cf. Jussaume 1992). Since 1973, in every round of interviews we have been told that visiting and just popping in to see neighbours has lessened. Most people say that their most regular associations are with relatives. As many people from Sivakka have moved to the municipal center or farther afield, contacts with friends and relatives are directed more and more beyond the village. Even though meeting neighbours has become less common, the people of Sivakka are still very aware of the news of the village and the affairs of their neighbors. Nowadays communication and exchange of information are done mostly by telephone.

For its inhabitants Sivakka no longer functions as a network of social relations through which they link themselves to the larger society. A few men living alone, especially remigrants, are an exception to this general trend. To them, spending time with their mates is an essential part of the everyday routine. This group calls itself the "second village committee." Along with fishing, hunting and beer drinking they help elderly people by chopping firewood. Even though there are conflicting attitudes in the village towards the second village committee, it serves as a kind of safety net into which a person can drop after returning from the outside world during times of crisis. The life-histories of others are known, and people treated cruelly by the world can get in touch with themselves and encounter fewer problems.

Local Identity

From the standpoint of shaping regional identity, the derivation of the names describing the region—their content and meaning—is important. Sivakkavaara appeared as a village name as early as the seventeenth century, when the first houses in the area were marked in the land register. In the general parcelling of land in the mid-nineteenth century, the region was divided for redistribution into two land register villages, Sivakkavaara and Koiravaara. The land register village of Koiravaara was larger in both area and population than Sivakkavaara until 1960. It consisted of several hill settlements, some kilometers apart from one another, which surrounded Sivakkavaara. One of these inhabited hills was called Koiravaara, and among the others were Lusikkavaara, Kuoppavaara and Tikku. Colloquially, these hill settlements were referred to by their own names, and thus Koiravaara by no means meant the entire land register village, but only one hill settlement.

When speaking of the people of Sivakka, the inhabitants of the surrounding hills were usually included. The establishment of the Sivakkavaara school confirmed this interpretation, because the school district included Koiravaara and Lusikkavaara as well as Kuoppavaara and Tikku. Sivakka, or Sivakkavaara, often occurred as the village name in the names of the associations of the area: Sivakan Syöksy, the Democratic Association of Sivakkavaara, Sivakan Erä-Veikot and the Sivakka village action committee. Since all the surrounding hills except Koiravaara were totally deserted in the 1960s and 1970s, the people living in the region have considered themselves to be Sivakkans.

The village of Sivakka is nowadays an entity with a clear identity, and there is nothing indistinct about its name and borders. A certain local patriotism, a pride in one's own village, is part of being a Sivakkan. When speaking of people, it is important to note whether a person is from Sivakka or not. The unity of the people of Sivakka against outside quarters and threats is an essential element of the village's rich story tradition (Knuuttila 1989).

There is still interest in the region's story tradition in Sivakka. The baby-boomers also know these stories and they have different ways of treasuring them. For example, the second village action committee uses stories to flavour their meetings and social life, and incidents and new stories spring up around them. The men like to tell a story about the time they took tape recorders to the school attic to record the ghost sounds which someone said he had heard there.

Despite the enormous economic and population changes, or perhaps because of them the local identity has remained strong in Sivakka. It is a symbolic communality which expresses itself, in consciousness and feelings, as a sense of belonging. In Sivakka, the basis for this community is the past, in the practices and interactions of the period when the village flourished. When it ceases to have a functional basis, it may easily take on chauvinistic qualities which limit and hinder cooperation with outsiders. The wish of the people of Sivakka to keep their village committee independent despite the shortage of activity is indicative of the difficulties in cooperation.

Another example of the rise of local patriotism was the villagers' way of reacting to the Lake Sivakkajärvi fishing tourism project in 1988. A Valtimo restaurateur's plan to stock the lake and bring tourists in to fish was rejected in the old local way, by circulating a petition. In the petition the villagers declared their wish to preserve the lake both as a peaceful wilderness lake and for their own use. The petition was signed by 47 villagers, all but two households and the four villagers who had negotiated the project with the restaurateur. At a meeting held at the village school to discuss the project, only one of the signatories was present: the head of the village committee to hand over the petition.

CONCLUSIONS

The development of Sivakka has been studied above from the viewpoints of the social division of labor, local institutions and local identity. Like many other remote villages in Eastern Finland, Sivakka occupied an important position in the spatial division of labor of the forest sector from the beginning of the century to the 1960s. The village formed its own local social system, a local community which flourished in the years after the war throughout the 1950s. The village had the most important local institutions of the country village at the time, the school and services as well as associations. There was a functional and practical interaction between the people living in the region, and that created a sense of community and local identity.

The change in the nature of lumbering, however, led to the displacement of Sivakka's regional role. As the lumbermen-smallholders living on their small farms disappeared from the lumbering sites, Sivakka very quickly lost its place in the spatial division of labor in the forest sector. The population of the village collapsed, and thus the village no longer had the base for organizing services and association activity. Nowadays, they are organized in the municipal center, where the services and social participation are concentrated.

Nearly all the local institutions have vanished in Sivakka. The village has lost its role as a part of the regional system; the deinstitutionalization process has advanced a long way. The new institutional structures are located in the municipal center. Sivakka is no longer a functional local community. Many symbols of Sivakka, however, live on and remind us that the symbolic community is still strong in the village. The people of Sivakka have wanted to keep their village action committee, not so much for functional needs but as a sign of the existence of the village.

Sivakka exists in the collective traditions of the people who live and have lived in the village. It is evident in their consciousness and feelings. The experiences of the past and the living story tradition preserve the local identity which some of the villagers consciously seek to carry on. However, in the future, the identity of Sivakka will be based more on the relationship of individuals to place than on collective significance. As the significance of functional and social aspects dwindles, nature and the landscape will become more and more important.

Naturally, my case study does not, and does not even try, to refute the argument that the local factor has great importance in the lives of people. Their local bonds, however, keep on changing. At the same time, old local communities die and new bonds are created to replace them. The death of a local community is a multi-dimensional process. The existence of the local community may cease on one dimension, but still remain strong on another. The subject of my case study has been a kind of ideal type of death of the local community; in other words, a small remote village which first lost its productive position and then died as a functional community and a social system. A strong symbolic community instead remains to tell of the former position and identity of the region. The dimensions of community may also disappear in a different order. For example, in a section of town gaining large numbers of new inhabitants in a short period of time, the symbolic community may disappear faster than the functional local community (cf. Riikonen 1995).

ACKNOWLEDGMENT

I would like to thank Tonja Goldblatt for the English translation, and Jukka Oksa and two anonymous reviewers for their helpful comments.

NOTES

1. The land-ownership situation in North Karelia differs remarkably from the Finnish norm. In Finland the largest ownership group is the private sector (especially farmers). The state and company-owned forests are concentrated in Eastern and Northern Finland, while those in the southern and western portions of the country are privately-owned.

2. The population of the land register village of Sivakkavaara is limited to a rather small area, but the land register village of Koiravaara extends to a very large area composed of the hills surrounding Sivakkavaara. In speaking of the inhabitants of Sivakka, the people of the surrounding hills are usually included; the main part of Koiravaara used to be part of the Sivakka school district. When I speak of Sivakka in this article, I mean this larger area, including the school district, Sivakkavaara refers to the smaller area. This differentiation is necessary mainly because the actual systematic material, on the basis of which exact numerical data can be presented, has been gathered from this smaller area.

3. The 1993 data is based solely on interviews conducted in the village. In 1983 and 1988 index files of employment offices were also used. The total amount of unemployed persons could therefore be somewhat higher in 1993 than the table indicates.

4. The People's Democrats (SKDL) were a post-war communist-led political umbrella organization. Communism in Finland has traditionally been championed by two rather different groups: the working class of the large industrial centers (industrial communism) and the smallholder-lumberjack family variety (backwoods communism) of Eastern and Northern Finland (Allardt 1964, pp. 112-131). The People's Democrats, Social Democrats and Center Party were the largest parties in Finland until the 1970s.

REFERENCES

Agnew, J.A. 1987. *Place and Politics*. The Geographical Mediation of State and Society. Boston: Allen and Unwin.

Alapuro, R. 1979. "Internal Colonialism and the Regional Party System in Eastern Finland." *Ethnic and Racial Studies* 2: 341-359.

Allardt, E. 1964. "Patterns of Class Conflict and Working Class Consciousness in Finnish Politics." Pp. 97-131 in *Cleavages, Ideologies and Party Systems*, edited by E. Allardt and Y. Littunen. Helsinki: The Westermarck Society.

Bell, C., and H. Newby. 1971. *Community Studies*. London: George Allen and Unwin.

Bernard, J. 1973. *The Sociology of Community*. Glenview, IL: Scott, Foresman and Company.

Beynon, H., and R. Hudson. 1993. "Place and Space in Contemporary Europe: Some Lessons and Reflections." *Antipode* 25: 177-190.

Bradley, T., and P. Lowe. (eds.). 1984. *Locality and Rurality*. Norwich: Geo Books.

Cooke, P. (ed.). 1989. *Localities. The Changing Face of Urban Britain*. London: Unwin Hyman.

Cox, K.R., and A. Mair. 1988. "Locality and Community in the Politics of Local Economic Development." *Annals of the Association of American Geographers* 78: 307-325.

Day, G., and J. Murdoch. 1993. "Locality and Community: Coming to Terms with Place." *The Sociological Review* 41: 82-111.

Duncan, J., and D. Ley. (eds.). 1993. *Place/culture/representation*. London and New York: Routledge.

Duncan, S., and M. Savage. 1991. "New Perspectives on the Locality Debate." *Environment and Planning A* 23: 155-164.

Entrikin, J.N. 1991. *The Betweenness of Place: Towards a Geography of Modernity.* London: Macmillan.

_____. 1994. "Place and Region." *Progress in Human Geography*18: 227-233.

Harper, S. 1987. "A Humanistic Approach to the Study of Rural Populations." *Journal of Rural Studies* 3: 309-319.

Hillery, G.A., Jr. 1955. "Definitions of Community: Areas of Agreement." *Rural Sociology* 20: 111-123.

Jackson, P. 1991. "Mapping Meanings: A Cultural Critique of Locality Studies." *Environment and Planning A* 23: 215-228.

Johnston, R.J. 1991. *A Question of Place: Exploring the Practice of Human Geography.* Oxford, UK and Cambridge, MA: Blackwell.

Jussaume, R.A. 1992. "The Demise of 'Little Communities' in Rural Japan." Pp. 215-230 in *Research in Community Sociology*, vol. 2, edited by D.A. Chekki. Greenwich, CT: JAI Press.

Knuuttila, S. 1989. "What the People of Sivakka Tell about Themselves: A Research Experiment in Folk History." Pp. 111-126 in *Studia Fennica*, vol. 33, edited by A.-L. Siikala. Helsinki: Suomalaisen Kirjallisuuden seura.

Lehtonen, H. 1990. *Yhteisö* (Community). Tampere: Vastapaino.

Maho, J. 1982. "Study and Restudy of a Village." Pp. 223-234 in *Theories and Methods in Rural Community Studies*, edited by H. Mendras and J. Mihailescu. Oxford: Pergamon Press.

Massey, D. 1979. "In What Sense a Regional Problem?" *Regional Studies* 13: 233-243.

_____. 1984. *Spatial Divisions of labor.* London: Macmillan.

Newby, H. 1980. "Trend Report: Rural Sociology." *Current Sociology* 28: 1-141.

_____. 1986. "Locality and Rurality: The Restructuring of Rural Social Relations." *Regional Studies* 20: 209-215.

Oksa, J. 1992. "Regional and Local Responses to Restructuring in Peripheral Rural Areas in Finland." *Urban Studies* 29: 991-1002.

_____. 1993. "The Benign Encounter: The Great Move and the Role of the State in Finnish Forests." Pp. 114-141 in *Who Will Save the Forests?*, edited by T. Banuri and F.A. Marglin. London and New Jersey: Zed Books.

Oksa, J., and P. Rannikko. 1988. "The Social Consequences of the Differentiation of Agriculture and Forestry. A Case Study of Two Villages in Finnish Forest Periphery." *Acta Sociologica* 31: 217-229.

_____. 1996. "The Changing Meanings of Rurality Challenge Rural Policies." *Maaseudun uusi aika*, (Finnish Journal of Rural Research and Policy) 3 (English Supplement): 3-14.

Paasi, A. 1986. "The Institutionalization of Regions: A Theoretical Framework for Understanding the Emergence of Regions and the Constitution of Regional Identity." *Fennia* 164: 105-146.

_____. 1991. "Deconstructing Regions: Notes on the Scales of Spatial Life." *Environment and Planning A* 23: 239-256.

Pyy, I., and P. Rannikko. 1995. "Welfare State at the Crossroads: The Case of Remote Rural Areas in Finland." Pp. 97-109 in *NordREFO*, vol. 3, edited by K. Aasbrenn. Stockholm: Nordiska institutet för regionalpolitisk forskning.

Pälsi, S. 1923. *Tukkimetsistä ja uittopuroilta* (From Logging Camps to Floating Creek). Helsinki: Otava.

Rannikko, P. 1995. "Restructuring of Forestry and Forest Villages in Eastern Finland." Pp. 109-118 in *The Peasant State*, edited by L. Granberg and J. Nikula. Rovaniemi: University of Lapland Publications in the Social Sciences.

Raumolin, J. 1985. "The Impact of Forest Sector on Economic Development in Finland and Eastern Canada." *Fennia* 163: 395-437.

Riikonen, H. 1995. "Sukupolvet ja alueellinen muutos (English Summary: The generations and regional transformation)." *Terra*, Journal of the Geographical Society of Finland 107: 88-100.

Rouhinen, S. 1981. "A New Movement in Search of New Foundation for the Development of the Countryside: The Finnish Action-oriented Village Study and 1300 Village Committees." *Acta Sociologica* 24: 265-278.

Stacey, M. 1969. "The Myth of Community Studies." *British Journal of Sociology* 20: 134-147.

Wilkinson, K.P. 1986. "In Search of the Community in the Changing Countryside." *Rural Sociology* 51: 1-17.

PART IV

BUILT ENVIRONMENT AND CITIZEN INITIATIVES

DO CITIZEN INITIATIVES AFFECT GROWTH?

THE CASE OF FIVE SAN DIEGO SUBURBS

Richard Hogan

ABSTRACT

Census and Construction reports from five contiguous San Diego suburbs suggest that speculative growth and overbuilding during the 1980s inspired citizen-initiated growth control measures that proposed annual limits on new housing units in three of the five cities. Interviews with officials and extended observation of the planning process suggest that each city attempted to accomodate growth control within the limits of state demands for affordable housing and its ability to entice large development projects. The effects of citizen initiative, state demands, and vacant land that might entice developers jointly explain the type of growth control adopted and the subsequent pattern of growth. The effects of growth limits, which were adopted in two cities, and alternative plans for controlling growth are considered in conclusion.

Research in Community Sociology, Volume 7, pages 249-275.
Copyright © 1997 by JAI Press Inc.
All rights of reproduction in any form reserved.
ISBN: 0-7623-0272-0

Recent studies of growth control offer contradictory evidence on both the cause and consequence of suburban growth control measures. Donovan and Neiman (1992), in a survey of Southern California cities, find that the percent of the population employed as professionals and the growth rate, 1970-1980, are the best predictors of municipal growth control measures (p. 330). Using a national sample, however, Logan and Zhou (1990) find no effects of growth (1960-1970), education, or home ownership in predicting growth limits or moratoriums.

More important, Logan and Zhou (1989) find no effect of growth control ordinances, reported in their 1973 survey of suburban cities, in predicting 1980 population (after controlling for 1970 population and a set of other variables), although they find that the use of environmental impact statements predicted higher median rents and that environmental zoning (including open space zoning) predicted a decreasing percentage of black residents (pp. 465-467). Thus while exclusionary zoning might be viewed as effective in protecting the interests of wealthy whites (Jackson 1985, p. 241; Plotkin 1987, pp. 73-74, 227-249), it is not clear that even the wealthy white suburbanites can stop the growth machine (Molotch 1976).

Logan and Zhou (1989, pp. 468-469) suggest, however, that growth control might be effective if the citizen initiative is not preempted by the developers. They offer a brief analysis of a few cases where they suggest "that growth control measures [were] not intended to control growth" (p. 468) and offer the "challenge to study growth politics with a finer grain of detail" (p. 469).

Specifically, Logan and Zhou (1989) identify three San Diego County suburbs where citizen initiatives that would have placed limits (caps) on new housing permits were challenged by growth control measures initiated by local government, or by developers in collaboration with local government. Unlike the citizen initiatives, at least some of these growth control measures would allow growth to continue so long as developers provide the infrastructure—sewage, water, parks, schools, and even special tax districts. Logan and Zhou (1989) report that the citizen initiative passed in all three cities, but in two of these three cases the government sponsored proposition received more votes, so the citizen initiative was preempted by the city (Logan and Zhou 1989, p. 468).

Clearly, these citizen initiatives were "preempted" (Gamson 1990),[1] but the critical questions are, "Why?" and "So What?" Why do suburban cities develop growth control initiatives? Why do cities preempt these initiatives? Do citizen versus council initiatives have different effects? And, most important, how do growth control initiatives affect future growth?

The contradictory evidence on these issues reflects, in part, the limits of survey data in capturing the complexity of geographic and historical differences in the economic and political context within which growth and growth control occur (Donovan and Neiman 1992, pp. 332-333; Fishel 1995, pp. 249-251). As Logan and Zhou (1989) suggest, we need more detailed case studies, but we also need some basis for generalizing from the specific case to the larger population of suburban cities. In analyzing growth and growth control, the peculiarity of the sunbelt (Molotch and Logan 1984, pp. 489-490), the West Coast (Logan and Zhou 1990, p. 126), and California, in particular (Fishel 1995, p. 225) require explanation. Similarly, differences between growth and growth control in the 1970s and in the 1980s (Logan and Zhou 1990, pp. 118-119) also require explanation.

Quite apart from the problem of generalizing across time and place, however, it is equally important to distinguish citizen initiated and council initiated growth control and to distinguish both from regional or State initiatives, which also impinge upon the planning process. In California, for example, regional planning complicates the simple distinction between "citizen" and "growth machine" interests. As Plotkin (1987) has argued, the "exclusionary" interests of "citizens" is, at times, opposed not simply by developers but by "inclusionary" State and federal interests. In the case of growth control, a major opposing interest is the regional and state planning officials, who are demanding that each city provide its "regional" share of affordable housing, based on the availability of vacant land and jobs and the projected growth in new housing (SANDAG 1990). In this case it may not be the "growth machine" but the "welfare state" that is inspiring local governments to preempt citizen growth control initiatives.

Finally, the "growth machine" perspective (Molotch 1976; Molotch and Logan 1984) tends to view growth as more or less uniform, rather than distinguishing efforts to attract industry, which, in turn, fosters growth (Perrucci 1994) from purely speculative growth, particularly in the development of large-scale "planned communities." This latter form of speculative growth seems to characterize the 1980s, particularly in Southern California.

This speculative growth is cyclical, however. Surplus capital is diverted from the production of goods and services in search of short-term profits, but speculation generates new accumulation crises, thus yielding cycles of boom and bust (Harvey 1976, pp. 289-290), which are evident between 1970 and 1990, particularly in Southern California.

Ultimately then, in order to evaluate the flurry of growth control initiatives in Southern California in the late 1980s and to evaluate their effect on subsequent growth, it is necessary to move beyond surveys of suburban cities. Specifically, it is necessary to locate growth and growth control in cycles of economic boom and bust and cycles of political opportunity, which include not only economic but political challenges to the authority of city planning departments (Tarrow 1994; McAdam 1982). In a more detailed analysis, it is possible to distinguish the inclusionary versus exclusionary demands on city planners and the extent to which a "growth control" or "growth machine" coalition is established. It is, in fact, possible to distinguish varieties of growth and no-growth that represent different constellations of constituent, government, and developer cooperation in what Rudel (1989) has characterized as "tri-lateral" negotiation.

The following analysis combines data from government documents and from a five-month nonparticipant observation study (in 1992) in a more detailed analysis of growth control and growth in five contiguous suburban cities in San Diego County. San Diego County was selected because county voters approved a regional growth control planning referendum in 1988, which suggests popular support for growth control. These particular cities were selected because they are contiguous suburbs in the region that experienced the highest rate of growth between 1970 and 1980. They provide a particularly appropriate set of cases for comparative analysis, because three of the cities faced citizen initiated growth control measures in the late 1980s, and two of these were pre-empted by council initiated alternatives.

In this more detailed analysis of growth control in San Diego suburbs, the problem of preemption, which Logan and Zhou (1989) suggest, is a clear and present danger but not an inevitablility. In only one of three cases analyzed here was the citizen initiative preempted by a ordinance that did not impose building caps. In all six cities, however, there were efforts to deal with the contradictory demands of growth control and affordable housing and the contradictory interests of regional planning authorities, local residents, and developers.

Based on these tentative conclusions, some practical policy alternatives for dealing with growth will be considered in closing, in the hope of inspiring debate on the relative merits of conservative, liberal, and radical alternatives in efforts to control growth. First, however, we shall turn to the speculative growth in housing units, 1970-1990, and the construction of San Diego suburbs in that period. The speculative growth in this period, particularly in Southern California, explains why growth control initiatives emerged in San Diego County. Then we can take a closer look at five contiguous suburbs in the most rapidly growing region of the county, to understand why citizen initiatives did not emerge in two of these cities and what, if any, effect these initiatives had on subsequent growth. Finally then we can consider in more detail how the contradictory demands of constituents and regional planning officials and the ability to entice developers explains how and why one city developed an elaborate alternative to growth control.

GROWTH AND GROWTH CONTROL IN CALIFORNIA

In analyses of growth control, urban planners, sociologists, economists, and lawyers review comparable literatures, evaluate similar evidence, and offer contradictory conclusions. Part of the problem is that the evidence suggests contradictory conclusions. Baldasarre and Protash (1982) in a 1978 survey of Northern California city planners found that population growth, proportion of homes that are owner occupied, and occupational status of residents predicted growth control policies. Donovan and Neiman, in a 1988 survey of Southern California suburbs found significant effects of population growth, 1970-1980, but no effect of estimated growth 1986-1989. They found effects of occupation but not of income or home ownership. Logan and Zhou (1990), however, in their 1973 survey, based on a national sample, found no effects of growth (1960-1970) and no consistent effects of socio-economic status. Apparently, growth between 1970 and 1980 (but not 1960-1970 or 1986-1989) inspired growth control, but only in California cities. In Northern California, in the 1970s, growth control was more likely in "exclusive" suburbs. By the late 1980s, however, in Southern California, growth control measures were adopted even in less exclusive suburbs.

Fishel (1995) offers a explanation for these seemingly contradictory findings. He argues that in the 1970s the California Supreme Court facilitated growth control in ways that other states did not (pp. 218-232), which resulted in the "explosion" of California housing prices in the 1970s (pp. 232-234) and, ultimately, the "ubiquity" of growth control ordinances in the 1980s (pp. 248-249). Consequently, the lack of growth effects in Logan and Zhou's (1990) data might be due to the national sample they use and the time period that they study. This might, in fact, explain the "West Coast" effect that Logan and Zhou (1990, p. 126) report and the diminishing effects of demographic variables in predicting growth control, in California, between 1978 and 1988.

In short, the California courts, beginning in the late 1960s, consistently ruled against the developer and in favor of the citizens. This allowed more resourceful cities, beginning in the 1970s, to successfully impose growth control, despite the resistance of developers, or even city governments. By 1980, the success of growth control initiatives, particularly in Northern California, produced snowball effects (Fishel 1995, pp. 248-249), as the cost of initiating growth control fell (after pioneers developed successful campaigns that could be imitated) while the threat of uncontrolled growth increased (as developers sought new locations, in cities with vacant land and limited restrictions on new development).

Fishel (1995, pp. 232-248) discounts the effects of population growth, the citizen initiative, and even Proposition 13 (the tax revolt) in fueling the speculative rise in California housing prices and the emergence of growth control. Instead, he focuses attention on the anti-developer stance of the California courts. He also discounts the notion of a speculative "bubble" because of the sustained rise in housing prices between 1970 and 1988, except during the recession of 1982 (pp. 244-245). In this regard, while he provides a useful corrective in bringing the state back in, he also tends to minimize the influence of the developer in the speculative growth of California real estate.

Between 1970 and 1990 financial and real estate interests were speculating in the future value of California land, seeking approval for new land uses, particularly large-scale planned communities, which would increase the market value of the land. The speculative nature of this enterprise is clear in the negotiations for master plan approval. As one developer explained, in a personal interview, "[T]he owners never intended to build [so] they didn't care about dropping the number of units." They just wanted approval so that they could reap windfall profits when selling the land, which they have since done.

The speculation in land-use futures followed a pattern of boom and bust cycles that became increasing protracted and severe, especially in Southern California. As seen in Table 1, which displays percent change in Gross Domestic Product from 1970-1991 in California and the United States, the biggest, most sustained boom was in the mid 1980s (from around 1983 through 1988). During the Reagan years, de-regulation, the "sage brush rebellion," the "new" federalism, and the legacy of the 1978 tax revolt facilitated speculation in California real estate. Then, the combined effects of the savings and loan crash (Calavita and Pontell 1992) and the economic depression marked the end of the long cycle of boom and bust. Consequently, although growth control movements emerged in the 1970s, the major burst of growth control initiatives, particularly in Southern California, was in the mid to late eighties (Donovan and Neiman 1992, pp. 325-326), at the height of the boom.

Clearly, cities that developed growth control in the late 1980s were more effective in halting growth, first, because the boom years of 1983-1988 were (more or less) behind them and, second, because the

Table 1.   Percent Increase in California and U.S. Gross Domestic Product, 1971-1991

Year	% Change		Year	% Change	
	Calif.	*U.S.*		*Calif.*	*U.S.*
1970			1981	2.0%	0.8%
1971	1.2%	1.6%	1982	0.3%	-3.1%
1972	8.3%	4.0%	1983	4.6%	2.6%
1973	4.2%	4.2%	1984	7.7%	5.3%
1974	1.1%	-1.5%	1985	5.4%	2.3%
1975	1.9%	-1.8%	1986	5.2%	2.0%
1976	5.5%	3.9	1987	5.1%	2.2%
1977	4.3%	3.5%	1988	4.5%	3.0%
1978	5.5%	3.7%	1989	3.8%	1.6%
1979	3.6%	1.4%	1990	2.4%	0.2%
1980	1.6%	-1.7%	1991	-2.0%	-1.8%

Note: Early figures were transformed intò 1987 dollars using conversion ratios from Statistical Abstract of the United States (1994, p. 451), which provides national figures.

Source: California Almanac (1991, p. 268); Survey of Current Business (1994).

combined effects of the savings and loan crash and the economic depression of the early nineties would slow growth in any case, even without growth control.

Nevertheless, there were significant regional differences in the political economy of growth, 1970-1990. As Table 1 indicates, the California economy follows the national trend, in general, between 1970 and 1991, but the boom is much more dramatic. After 1973, California GDP grows at a more rapid rate than national GDP, particularly in the 1980s. Then, in 1991, the California economy crashes, posting its first decline in GDP since the 1960s and actually surpassing (although only modestly) the national rate of decline.

As Fishel (1995, pp. 250-251) explains, California continued to grow in the 1980s, despite high housing costs, because of the abundance of vacant land, the booming economy, and the expectation that housing values would continue to rise. Once the economy crashed, however, and housing prices declined in the 1990s, the recession was protracted in California.

What distinguishes California, however, is not just the intensity of economic boom and bust cycles, but the corresponding cycles of political opportunity and grassroots political challenges. Fishel (1995) focuses on the facilitating influence of the courts, but the challenges to local government included both citizen and state demands. Growth control, particularly in Southern California was a latecomer, which benefitted from earlier challenges that expanded political opportunities between 1970 and 1990 (on cycles of opportunity, see McAdam 1982; Tarrow 1994). Statewide citizen initiatives produced the California Coastal Act of 1972 and the Tax Revolt of 1978 (Lo 1990). Local citizen initiatives, along with the threat of initiative or recall, produced a variety of growth control ordinances, especially in the 1980s in Southern California (Donovan and Neiman 1992).

The tax revolt, in particular, created serious problems for city planners who lacked the funds to develop public services and who faced a constituency (both locally and nationally) that was hostile to the needs of government officials. As one planning director reported, in a personal interview,

> Proposition 13 [the tax revolt] had major effects, particularly in bedroom communities.... For the next four to five years cities looked for creative solutions. Developers were required to pay more fees.

The solution to fiscal crisis and constitutent hostility was to mobilize the support of the development interests, using environmental regulation to collect "more fees" (or to demand mitigation) that the city might use in lieu of property tax revenues. The consequence was increasing dependence on developers, particularly large national and international development companies that could afford to pay the cost of developing in the post-tax-revolt era.

> There were in the 1980s small guys [developers] but most now are large firms [who employ people] with three-piece suits and UCLA degrees. After Proposition 13 the small guys disappeared as the cost went up.

The mobilization of developer support after the tax revolt fueled the building boom of the 1980s, which, in turn, generated a new grassroots political challenge—growth control. The planning director (quoted above) explains the boom-bust cycle as follows.

> Between 1981 and 1983 our motto was "our job is to facilitate quality development." That changed amid citizen threats to throw out the [city] council. Growth control was adopted. [Before growth control] there were bulldozers everywhere and no parks. [In response to citizen concerns] Council's attitude changes, so staff must change.

Southern California in the late 1980s was the ideal location for growth control. The building boom of the 1970s provided "worst-case-scenarios" (like the "Inland Empire" (Highway 163) corridor between Riverside and San Diego) to illustrate the dangers of uncontrolled growth. The experience of pioneers, like the city of Petaluma, in the 1970s, provided models for emerging no-growth movements, and the 1980s provided a particularly conducive environment, as cities could imitate each other in what appeared to be a wave of popular support for growth control (on learning and imitation, see Cohn and Conell 1995).

In this regard, Fishel (1995) offers an important contribution, in indicating how California courts facilitated growth control. He fails, however, to consider growth control in the context of affordable housing (which he treats in a separate chapter, which focuses on New Jersey courts). California courts, while protecting the exclusionary interests of growth control and environmental regulation, were also defending the inclusionary interests of affordable housing. Thus the

court defended the contradictory (exclusionary and inclusionary—
see Plotkin 1987) interests that challenged local government,
particularly in the 1980s and especially in San Diego.

At the same time that California cities faced the threat of citizen
recall and initiative measures, demanding growth control, they also
faced increasing pressure from regional and State officials to provide
affordable housing. The California Department of Housing and
Community Development published guidelines in 1977 and required
that all cities comply by October of 1981 in revising the housing
elements of their General Plans to incorporate their regional share
of affordable housing (SANDAG 1990, p. 208).

The City of San Diego was among the California cities that fell
short of its regional share of affordable housing. Then, in 1985, the
State Appelate Court decided that San Diego City could not approve
a permit for a planned residential community until the city could
indicate substantial progress in efforts to "conserve and improve the
condition of existing housing stock" (McCutcheon et al. 1989, pp.
19-20). After this decision, California cities, and San Diego County
cities, in particular, struggled to provide their share of affordable
housing, even as citizen anti-growth interests were mobilizing.

Between the 1985 lawsuit and the 1988 county-wide referendum
on regional growth control planning, San Diego cities faced the
contradictory demands of constituents demanding growth control
and regional planning officials demanding affordable housing. The
five San Diego suburban cities analyzed below responded to these
demands by attempting to preempt, coopt, and mobilize constituents
in elaborate public relations and planning efforts, including efforts
to revise the city's General Plan for development (in three of the five
cities). These General Plan revisions, which are still continuing in at
least one of these cities, have, perhaps more than anything else,
extended the housing construction depression, as the cities hesitate
to approve new projects (or even old projects) while negotiations on
a new plan for development continue.

In sum, the following analysis will suggest that citizen initiated
growth control was a response to speculative over-building in the
1980s. In San Diego County, most suburban cities adopted some
version of growth control in the 1980s. In fact, the County initiated
the development of a regional growth control plan, after voters
approved a government inititated referendum in November of 1988.
How cities responded, however, was determined, to a large extent,

by the contradictory demands of constituents versus regional planning officials and by the willingness of private developers to subsidize municipal planning efforts. Specifically, elaborate alternatives to growth limits were adopted only when cities faced the following situation. First, constituents demanded severe limits on future growth. Second, State and regional planning authorities demanded a substantial number of new affordable housing units. Third, private development companies were willing to pay the cost of providing creative solutions to the contradictory demands of residents and regional planning officials.

CREATING SAN DIEGO SUBURBS, 1970-1980

The five San Diego suburban cities, which will be the focus of this analysis, are, in varying degrees, the ideal site for a successful growth control movement. They are, in varying degrees, "middle class" suburbs, where residents (if not landowners) are more concerned with life and work than with speculation in the future value of their land (Molotch 1976, p. 328), but that was not true in 1970. In fact, development created the suburbs, just as it created the exurban area (near the University) as a middle class residential and commercial district.

Between 1960 and 1970, exurban development at the northern edge of San Diego City, just inland from a quaint coastal residential and commercial settlement (called "La Jolla"), was fostered by the cooperative efforts of public and private interests. Since the development was not part of the quaint coastal settlement and was part of the vacant land that was legally part of San Diego City, this expansion into the exurbs was "legally" negotiated (much as Rudel 1989 would suggest) without much apparent controversy.

Once a major highway system (Highways 5, 805, and 52) was built through this section of the county (see Feagin 1988, on federal subsidies for development) the "legal" development of exurban lands continued. The rate of growth was declining, however, as exurban areas offered fewer possibilities for windfall profits and as legal constraints on coastal and wetlands development increased. After 1970, with new residential development and increased environmental regulation, exurban development and the expansion of the highway system was much more problematic and much more likely to involve federal, state, county, and city authorities, as well as grassroots opposition to widening the highway or adding units to an increasingly populated area.

Once these exurban regions were developed, however, and the highway system was expanded to provide "rapid" transit throughout the county, that which had been considered rural was then within the reach of "suburban" development. Consequently, between 1970 and 1980, the "pull" of undeveloped land and the "push" of declining opportunities in exurban areas inspired speculation in the future development of rural areas that might become suburban ("if you build it they will come"). The "suburban" cities selected for analysis became, in varying degrees, middle class suburbs between 1970 and 1980. They are located in that part of the county that experienced the most dramatic rate of growth at the height of the speculative growth boom and the grassroots political movements.

As seen in Table 2, San Diego County was not significantly different from the state, as a whole, in growth (1960-1970) or socio-economic status of residents in 1970. Only two of the five cities selected for analysis had populations over 25,000 in 1970 (cities 1 and 4 in Table 2), but both cities were growing rapidly—at two to four times the county average. These were not, however, particularly wealthy communities. They reported, in general, lower median family income and median value of owner-occupied housing. They were relatively suburban, however, reporting average or slightly higher rates of owner-occupied dwellings. Even city 3, which had a population of less than 15,000 in 1970, reported comparable median income and reported housing values that were only moderately above the county figures. Only city 5, the smallest and fastest growing city, reported substantially higher housing prices than the county as a whole in 1970.

By 1980, four of the five cities (cities 1-4) had populations over 25,000. The county and all four cities far exceeded statewide rates of population and new housing growth, and their rate of housing growth far exceeded their rate of population growth. Between 1970 and 1980, City 3 became a wealthy suburb, with median income and housing value far exceeding the county figures. Meanwhile, City 5, although not particularly wealthy, was the fastest growing bedroom community in the county. Population more than tripled in the 1970s and owner-occupied homes constituted 76 percent of all occupied units (in 1980).

Table 2. Population and Housing Growth, and Socio-economic Status in California, San Diego County, and Five Suburbs, 1970-1992

	CA	CO	City 1	City 2	City 3	City 4	City 5
1970							
Pop. (60-70)	27%	31%	62%	45%**	62%**	125%	87%**
Housing (60-70)	30%	34%	68%	64%**	63%**	128%	(NA)
Owner-occupied	55%	57%	57%	67%**	53%**	62%	67%**
Median value*	$23	$22	$20	$21**	$25**	$21	$28**
Median Income*	$11	$10	$8	(NA)	$10**	$09	(NA)
1980							
Pop. (70-80)	19%	37%	89%	45%	138%	75%	349%
Housing (70-80)	33%	60%	124%	73%	198%	100%	346%
Owner-occupied	56%	55%	55%	59%	64%	55%	76%
Median value*	$84	$91	$75	$83	$123	$83	$89
Median Income*	$22	$20	$17	$18	$26	$18	$18**
% College Grad	20%	21%	14%	15%	26%	14%	(NA)
1990							
Pop.(80-92)	31%	40%	82%	112%	81%	.76%	141%
Housing (80-90)	21%	31%	56%	83%	77%	55%	122%
Median Income*	$41	$40	$37	$35	$51	$38	$35
% College Grad	23%	25%	19%	18%	36%	18%	15%

Notes: * All dollar values are in thousands of dollars.

** These figures, not reported in County and City Databooks, are from SANDAG 1970 and 1987 reports.

Source: County and City Databooks (1972, 1983, 1994).

Although the county and most of the cities experienced an incredible building boom in the 1970s, a few distinctive patterns of growth deserve attention. Unlike cities 1 and 3, city 4 experienced a declining rate of growth in housing and, particularly, in population in the 1970s. City 4 continued to grow, but its rate of growth peaked in the 1960s. A similarly deviant yet distinctive pattern is evident in city 5. Unlike the other four cities, in city 5, housing units did not increase more rapidly than population, although both increased dramatically, in the 1970s. Finally, city 2 is the only city that experienced increasing rates of population and housing growth in the 1980s. Even there, however, population increased more rapidly than housing units in the 1980s, indicating, as in the other cities, that the speculative frenzy of overbuilding diminished in the 1980s.

GROWTH PLANNING AND POLITICS
IN FIVE SUBURBAN CITIES

In 1986 and 1987, three of these San Diego suburban cities (cities 1-3) were challenged by citizen-initiated growth control measures. Only city 4, whose growth rates peaked in the 1960s, and city 5, where housing growth did not outpace population growth in the 1970s, did not face citizen-initiatives on growth control in the local elections of 1986 (cities 1 and 3) and 1987 (city 2). Thus it appears that citizen initiatives emerged in those cities that were experiencing speculative growth at the height of the building boom, specifically, in cities 1-3.

How did the cities respond to the challenge of citizen initiated growth control? All three attempted to preempt the citizen initiative, but, in city 1, the citizen initiative out-polled the council alternative. Thus city 1 now has an ordinance restricting new housing unit approvals to 800 units per year. In city 2, the council preempted the citizen initiative but imposed an even more stringent cap on new units—only 500 per year.

Only city 3 managed to preempt the citizen initiative, which demanded building caps, with a facility management program that would permit growth and, at the same time, insure that the developer provided the public facilities (including schools and special tax districts that are not covered by Proposition 13 limitations). Former city planning officials (who now work as consultants) explained (in a personal interview in the form of a group discussion) the process as follows.

> The city turned to the developers...[in desperation]. Growth control was essentially a developer project. The assumption by developers was [that] here is a plan we can live with.

The planning director of city 4, which did not face a citizen growth control initiative, also wanted to establish a facility management program and bemoans the fact that he can't get the developers to cooperate on a similar plan for his city.

> We're trying to entice them...[but] it is difficult because the city is almost (about two-thirds) built out. We can't get the big developers to put in the infrastructure.

Thus city 4, where growth peaked in the 1960s, could not entice developers to fund city planning, despite efforts to provide incentives for redevelopment in targeted "economic incentive zones," incorporated into the General Plan revision of 1990.

In city 5 there was no growth control initiative, although the council did declare a temporary moratorium on the approval of new multi-family units, and, as we shall see, negotiated with regional planning authorities and interested developers in a plan for controlled growth, which is part of its General Plan revision.

The critical question, however, is, "So What?" Did any of these growth control initiatives affect subsequent growth? Table 3 suggests that they did, but that the effects were not uniform.

Table 3 provides comparative data on new housing approvals in these five cities, 1982-1995, with new approvals presented as the percent of total units in place in 1980, which indicates, crudely, rates of new approvals, as opposed to the actual number of units, which tends to be much larger in the larger cities. The data reported in Table 3

Table 3.   New Housing Units Authorized in Five Contiguous San Diego County Suburban Cities, 1982-1995, Expressed as Percent of Existing Housing Units in 1980 (Numbers Indicated in Parentheses)

| | citizen initiative | | | no initiative | |
| | success | preemption | | | |
year	city 1	city 2	city 3	city 4	city 5
1980	32,733	14,962	15,352	27,153	6,508
1982	1.6%	0.7%	2.7%	1.0%	0.9%
1983	3.8%	5.8%	8.4%	2.8%	4.0%
1984	6.7%	6.4%	12.4%	8.2%	9.0%
1985	8.2%	14.6%	15.9%	10.7%	8.5%
1986	7.8%	11.8%	20.3%	11.7%	28.3%
1987	14.5%	19.2%	4.2%	7.3%	8.9%
1988	5.2%	13.1%	2.8%	6.0%	9.9%
1989	9.0%	6.2%	2.3%	2.6%	12.2%
1990	3.1%	2.7%	3.5%	1.4%	7.0%
1991	4.3%	2.2%	0.9%	0.8%	6.2%
1992	1.6%	2.2%	0.3%	0.8%	4.8%
1993	1.6%	0.7%	0.8%	0.9%	5.8%
1994	2.0%	0.7%	1.9%	0.8%	5.4%
1995	1.5%	1.4%	4.0%	1.4%	6.2%

Source: U.S. Construction Reports, Series C-40

are from U.S. Construction Reports (Series C-40), which report "New Privately Owned Housing Units Authorized in Permit-Issuing Places." These data provide the best indication of what city planning departments are doing and how that is affected by economic and political constraints, such as growth control.

All five cities experienced a sharp rise in housing approvals in 1983 and a decline in the early 1990s, although smaller cities (city 2, 3, and, especially, 5) tend to report higher rates of growth. It appears that new approvals declined whether there was a growth control initiative or not, however, and, among growth control initiative cities, the difference between citizen initiative (city 1) and preempted growth control (cities 2 and 3) does not appear to be important. Among growth control initiative cities, however, there appears to be a difference between cities that imposed annual growth limits (cities 1 and 2) and those that did not (city 3).

In city 1, the citizen initiative passed and was supposed to limit approvals to 800 per year, effective May 1987, but that goal was not achieved until 1992. Part of the problem in this city was that developers were suing for damages resulting from the ordinance, which complicated implementation efforts. City 2 preempted the citizen initiative but imposed a cap of 500 units per year, in March of 1987, which was achieved in 1990. This city also attempted to develop an infrastructure or facilities plan, but that was still in the planning stage in 1990. In any case, although both of these cities were slow in implementing the new approval limits, it appears now that they are well below the limits, and there are no indications that new approvals are likely to exceed the growth control limits.

In the other preempted growth control city, city 3, annual limits were not imposed, but new development was tied to an elaborate plan to provide the infrastructure required to sustain additional development, effective November 1987. In this city, with the complicated alternative to limits on new approvals, we see the most immediate and dramatic decline in new approvals (in 1987) but also the clearest evidence of recovery, beginning in 1993 and continuing into 1995. Of the three cities that faced citizen initiatives, only City 3 has shown any sign of recovery from the depths of the 1992 depression.

Recovery in Cities 4 and 5 (which were not challenged by citizen initiatives) is less clear. City 4 experienced a less dramatic boom and a more dramatic decline, particularly in the 1990s. Here, the planning director is attempting to entice developers but, so far, with limited success. City 5 experienced the most dramatic boom, in 1986, and seems to have established a new baseline for annual approvals, which is considerably higher than the pre-boom baseline. Even without citizen initiated growth control, this suburban city seems to have established a new standard, approving approximately 300 new units per year (about 400 in 1995).

City 1 failed to preempt the citizen initiative, while city 2 preempted the citizens but imposed building caps in any case. City 4, as the planning director explained (above), has attempted to entice to developers into a facilities management program, so far without success. Thus only city 3 was effective in preempting building caps and only city 5 has been able to sustain growth.

What distinguishes these two cities is not the perspecuity of their city planning directors but the magnitude of the crisis that inspired "creative" solutions and the ability of the city to entice developers to pay the cost of these alternatives to building caps. Table 4 reports vacant land and "regional share" of housing (and affordable housing) allocated to each city in the 1990 Regional Housing Needs Assessment. As indicated in Table 4, cities 3 and 5 are significantly less "built out" than their neighbors, particularly city 2. Since both vacant land and growth rates are used to calculate regional shares, both of these cities have significantly higher new housing obligations than the neighboring communities. Since city 3 has become a wealthy suburb, the burden of affordable housing is even greater than in city 5, where housing is already relatively affordable.

Table 4. Percent of Total Acres Vacant in 1990, Percent of 1990 Housing Units to be Added as "Regional Share," 1991-1996, and Percent of These Units to be Guaranteed "Affordable" for San Diego County and Five Contiguous Suburbs

	County	City 1	City 2	City 3	City 4	City 5
Vacant	60%	36%	23%	48%	35%	53%
Share	11%	15%	14%	23%	16%	25%
Afford	20%	13%	12%	18%	13%	14%

Source: SANDAG, Regional Housing Needs Assessment (1990).

Clearly, both city 3 and city 5 had sufficient vacant land to entice big developers into a creative solution to the "growth control versus affordable housing" problem. Nevertheless, the problems and the solutions were qualitatively different in these two communities. City 5 did not face a citizen initiative and was thus less desperate in efforts to meet affordable housing goals, particularly since housing was less expensive than in city 3. City 5 had a more serious problem, however, as a bedroom community attempting to cope with the tax revolt. Thus the solution for city 5 was to entice industrial capital (actually, a medical-industrial complex) which might provide a tax base and an employment base to sustain further residential gworth.

A regional planning official, in a personal interview, explained the situation in city 5 as follows:

> The problem with development in progress [is that] developers already have vested development rights. In [city 5], that was not the case. The developers cooperated because they didn't have vested development rights. They negotiated a solution. We told the city that they need to develop a policy. They could declare a moratorium and put all on hold or could work with one developer and see if we could work out a policy. Now we are working with three developers. Developers are getting development agreements (vested rights) and are conditioned to build affordable housing.

Unlike city 5, city 3 had an industrial base and was becoming an increasingly expensive place to live, but it had already committed to a number of large development projects, including a thousand acre country club, hotel, and upscale residential development project and a larger but basically similar project that was already well under way. While city 2, which was almost 80 percent developed, could afford to adopt building caps, city 3 could not. The potential legal threats were clear. San Diego City had already lost a suit challenging its efforts to provide affordable housing. On the other hand, as city 1 developers demonstrated so effectively, developers could sue city 3 for failure to honor master plan approvals. Nevertheless, unlike cities 1 and 4, city 3 could entice big developers who claimed over four thousand acres of municipal property to invest in creative solutions that would allow for future development.

ACCOMODATING CONTRADICTORY INTERESTS

City 3, the suburban city that managed to preempt citizen-initiated growth control by "enticing" developers to provide the infrastructure, is now actively involved in efforts to mobilize constituents. The city is, in fact, in the process of revising its General Plan through a lengthly process that involves citizen advisory committees and public "workshops" where committee proposals are presented and discussed.

A consultant who is the facilitator for one of the citizen advisory committees explained, in a personal interview, the city's strategy.

> [The city] wanted to represent all the interests—Audubon society, regulatory agencies, landowners...Other people came. All were treated the same. If the idea is to build a consensus, even if there are bomb-throwers it is better to have them on the inside....

> Local environmentalists are noisy constituents who get placed on committees. There are [in fact] two distinct points of view that are overlapping in this city— [1] environmental issues are important: preservation, and [2] growth is bad.

There is an anti-developer coalition of environmental and no-growth constituents, including representatives from the Audubon Society and various citizen organizations that have rallied in opposition to developers. Members of this coalition are routinely appointed to citizen advisory committees and are frequently involved in public discussion of zoning commission and city council decisions. They are very much involved in the General Plan update.

The city has been struggling to accomodate these constituents' concerns and to develop a new basis for a return to legal formalism, which is, essentially, the goal of the General Plan update. The planning director, at a breakfast meeting for interested parties, explained the strategy as follows.

> The General Plan update is comprehensive....Why are we updating?...The technical stuff is out of date. Plus, there have been changes in perspective on development. We need to incorporate the growth management plan...We need to take the whole package to the voters to make sure of approval for the direction we plan to take in the future...so that we can preempt challenges once development commences.

There is no doubt in the planning director's mind that development will recommence.

> The pendulum swings. In the 1980s staff facilitated growth. That has slowed based on citizen concerns [but] it is now swinging back to facilitate, helping out [but] not compromising on standards.

In fact, the proposals for habitat conservation, open space, hiking trails, and affordable housing, which are major components of the General Plan update, require that development recommence. A developer whose project was to provide the base for a citywide habitat conservation plan (with land offered as mitigation for habitat destruction) explained this quite clearly to the "habitat conservation" citizen advisory committee. "Without allowing development," he asserted, "there is no money for preserves." The same may be said for open space and trails,[2] and dependence on the developer is even greater in the proposal to provide affordable housing.

The affordable housing goals in the updated Housing Element of the General Plan are to be met by requiring that 15 percent of all new housing units be affordable for low or very low income households. Without development the city will not be able to comply with state mandates for providing its share of affordable housing. Thus the planning director in this suburban city must facilitate development to meet the requirements of state law and, as already noted, to implement the proposals of the citizen advisory committees for habitat conservation, open space, and a citywide trail system.

In fact, much of the recovery in this city can be attributed to a single large developer who has successfully negotiated to provide what appears to be all of the new affordable housing units in the city—a total of 344 apartments. In exchange, the developer is allowed to complete the 1,000 acre luxury community that has been stalled due to a variety of environmental and other concerns that are being incorporated in the General Plan update. In fact, the developer will be allowed to sell more than half of the apartments to other developers, who prefer to pay fees in lieu of building affordable housing.

Thus one might conclude that city 3 successfully preempted the growth control initiative by mobilizing the support of the developers, and has since mobilized constituents, who have been granted the privileges of membership in the process of revising the General Plan. Now that the citizen plans for open space, hiking trails, and habitat conservation, and the legally mandated plans for affordable housing have been developed, the city is, once again, attempting to mobilize the support of developers, who will pay the cost of implementing the revised General Plan.

DISCUSSION

This analysis suggests that growth control initiatives were a response to growth, but that the context and nature of growth specifies the effects. Citizen initiated growth control measures were more likely in cities where population and housing growth peaked in the 1980s, at the height of speculative overbuilding. These data also suggest that not just growth but speculative growth predicts citizen initiated growth control. Cities that were overbuilding (where housing units grew more rapidly than population) were more likely to face citizen initiatives.

The case studies also suggest that citizen initiatives, even when preempted by city council alternatives, do affect the type of growth control that is ultimately adopted. In all three of the cities that faced citizen initiatives, the citizens demanded building caps (annual limits), which were implemented in two of these three cases. Cities that did not face citizen initiatives did not, in either case, impose caps, suggesting that while citizens may want caps, city councils generally do not.

Annual data on new housing approvals, 1982-1995, indicate, however, that whether council or citizen initiated, annual limits (caps) on new approvals seem to be effective in the medium run, at the cost of continued growth in the short run. Elaborate alternatives to annual limits seem to produce more dramatic short-term effects but also appear to be less effective in controlling growth in the long term. No limits, as might be expected, tends to produce sustained growth, but only if the city is able to entice developers.

It appears, however, that efforts to preempt building caps with elaborate alternatives that require developers to cooperate in "facility management" plans are, at least partly, inspired by demands of state and regional authorities and limited by the capacity to entice large development companies to pay the substantial cost of such creative alternatives to building caps. Specifically, data from the San Diego Regional Housing Needs Assessment of 1990 indicates that it was those cities with substantial vacant land and corespondingly substantial obligations to provide their "regional share" of new housing units, in general, and "affordable" housing units, in particular, that were most inspired to adopt alternatives to building caps.

Cities whose "regional share" of new, affordable housing (as determined by regional planning authorites and prescribed by state law) is substantial will be inspired to develop alternatives to building caps in order to meet their obligations. If they fail to meet state guidelines, they are liable for civil suit and might, in fact, be prohibited from issuing any new building permits (or undertaking any projects) until they meet their obligations. Thus cities facing the most serious problems in efforts to accomodate the contradictory demands of exclusionary citizen demands for building caps and inclusionary State demands for affordable housing are likely to be inspired to search for creative alternatives.

Their ability to find such alternatives and to effectively preempt citizen demands is limited, on the one hand, by the mobilization of grassroots support for building caps and, on the other hand, by their ability to entice big developers to cooperate in developing and implementing the extremely costly alternative of "facilities management." Cities with large tracts of vacant land will be more successful in this regard, because the cost of "facilities management" can be absorbed more easily by large-scale developers. For big projects, the start-up cost of developing a program can be spread across a large number of units, so that costs can be passed on to the consumer, particularly in a booming market.

PRACTICAL POLICY IMPLICATIONS

This tale of five cities has provided the much needed detail that aggregate survey data generally conceal. All five cities faced the challenge of contradictory demands for growth control (or habitat conservation) and affordable housing. A regional planning officer explained, in a personal interview,

> Between 1980 and 1985 we sat down with each jurisdiction and looked at their General Plans. All but a couple were adequate through 1990. We have since concluded, however, that between 1996 and 2001 there would be four to seven jurisdictions with greater population and housing growth than their General Plan allowed....Cities are caught between city council support for growth control and state requirements for affordable housing.

The five cities analyzed here responded to the crisis in different ways. City 1 attempted to preempt the citizen growth initiative but failed and was then sued by developers who had already received preliminary approval for new development. It took some time for the city to resolve its problems with the developers, but the city has now become a slow growth suburb. City 2 was successful in pre-empting the citizen initiative, but adopted a council-sponsored initiative that insured, in the long run, slow growth.

The data reported in Table 3 suggest that in both of these cities caps on new development effectively reduced the rate of growth. In city 3, where an elaborate alternative to caps was developed and a major General Plan revision undertaken, new housing approvals dropped dramatically and remained low through the economic depression of 1992. In this city, however, it appears that perseverance will be rewarded. At least one of the major developers is being allowed to complete his project, now that he has agreed to provide the city's affordable housing stock.

The two cities that did not face citizen initatives have also attempted to negotiate some combination of facilities management and growth control with developers, but city 4 has been frustrated by the lack of big developer interest in his city (which is largely—about two-thirds—built out). City 5, which did not face a citizen growth control initiative, but did declare a temporary moratorium on apartments, has been negotiating with developers, using regional planning authorities to facilitate efforts to broker a mutually satisfactory plan for controlled growth that includes habitat conservation and affordable housing.

Thus, based on the experience of these five San Diego suburbs, it appears that citizen initiatives for growth control were a response to speculative over-building in the 1980s. City councils attempted to preempt these initiatives by providing alternatives (or supplements) to building caps that would facilitate efforts to meet affordable housing goals and to accomodate developers whose projects had already received at least preliminary approval. Cities with substantial vacant lands are, it appears, most stongly opposed to building caps. In this analysis, the only city that adopted caps in the council initiative (City 2) was more than 75 percent built out.

Nevertheless, the problem of preemption appears to be less threatening than Logan and Zhou (1989) have suggested. The only city that was able to preempt the citizen initiative with an elaborate alternative to caps was City 3, which faced not only the citizen initiative, but a substantial commitment to build affordable housing, substantial tracts of vacant land, and large development projects that had already received at least preliminary approval.

Furthermore, it is not clear that council initiated growth control measures were necessarily less effective in controlling growth. Whether imposed by citizens or adopted by council, it appears that caps effectively reduce growth in the medium run. Elaborate alternatives have more drastic, immediate effects, but they may, ultimately, provide a basis for continued growth. In this case, "facility management" alternatives to building caps might, in fact, be "measures not intended to control growth" (Logan and Zhou 1989, p. 48), but it does appear that this the exception rather than the rule.

Finally, cities without citizen growth control initiatives do not necessarily sustain growth. As seen in city 4, growth is predicated on the ability to attract developers who are willing to provide the affordable housing and to provide the infrastructure (or public utilities). Cities without vast tracts of undeveloped land are less successful in this regard.

So, what conclusions might we draw from this tale of five cities? What type of growth control might be most effective, assuming that its proponents can effectively pressure local government for growth control measures? It really depends on what constituents want and what they are willing to pay for.

If one is willing to sacrifice public services, affordable housing, habitat conservation, and the "big picture" planning of the more progressive cities, building caps may be the answer. Alternatively, facilities and infrastructure management programs (if the developers can be enticed) might provide the basis for a progressive planning vision at the cost of increasing local planners' dependence on the private sector. Perhaps, the former (caps) are the solution for cities that are already "built out," while the later is the preferred solution for cities with large tracts of vacant land—that can be developed and preserved with the help of the developers.

A third possibility, of course, is to do nothing. Given the political climate and the clear and present danger of growth control, the city is likely to develop some sort of plan for regulating growth, even if local residents are not mobilized in opposition to growth. Ultimately, speculative growth resolves itself, at least temporarily, in economic depression, even if there are no new legal constraints. This might be the best choice for rapidly growing suburbs, where local government is already having problems dealing with uncontrolled growth and doesn't really need a citizen initiative to further complicate an already complex planning problem.

The problem with doing nothing is that Californians have done too much already. The tax revolt was a critical factor in producing speculative growth (for an alternative view, see Fishel 1995). More than anything else, the tax revolt created local government's dependence on the developer and the creative solution of using environmental legislation to extract fees and concessions from developers, who might pay the cost of providing public services. Of course, there are many Americans today who believe that schools and other public services should be provided by the private sector. Others (Altshuler et al. 1993), believe that "regulation for revenue" is, at least, preferrable to building caps. It really depends on how much you like capitalism versus republicanism, and many Americans seem to prefer the efficiency of market constraints to the efficacy of "too many Thursday night meetings."

The liberal solution is simple—citizens should pay the cost of providing public services. Fishel (1995) thinks that local governments should be required to pay for regulatory takings and blames the California courts for refusing to protect "normal" use of property. Since raising taxes appears to be illusionary at the present time, however, at least in California, perhaps we might consider a more modest proposal. City governments could condemn all the property within their jurisdications and place bonds in escrow to cover the market value of the land. Then the city could proceed to abolish property rights that do not include specifically sanctioned usuage rights. The guarantee of usuage rights would secure the homeowners' rights to sell or keep but not the speculators' rights to hold land in anticipation of windfall profits when new uses are approved. Simply stated, you couldn't own land that you were not allowed to use.

Lest this seem a utopian dream, one should expect that usage rights without proprietary rights would create even more hotly contested zoning disputes, but that seems a fair exchange for the benefits of exiling the speculator. Of course, the other cost is that the city must pay the price of developing land-use plans and preserving open space, protecting habitat, building affordable housing, schools, or whatever. If citizens prefer to fund public services through the surplus profits of international speculation, then they should, perhaps, do nothing.

ACKNOWLEDGMENT

Comments and suggestions from Robert Perrucci, the anonymous reviewers, and members of the Sorrento seminar were particularly helpful in this endeavor.

NOTES

1. "Pre-empted" growth control, in both cities, refers to a citizen initiative that was defeated by a council-initiated growth control measure, regardless of the type of measure (building caps versus infrastructure/facility plans) adopted.

2. The advisory committee proposed a special bond issue to fund the open space/trail system, but when a developer asked the committee who would pay for the trail system, he was told, jokingly, that he would.

REFERENCES

Altshuler, A.A., J.A. Gomez-Ibanez, and A.M. Howitt. 1993. *Regulation for Revenue: The Political Economy of Land Development Extractions.* Washington, D.C.: Brookings Institute.

Baldasarre, M., and W. Potash. 1982. "Growth Controls, Population Growth and Community Satisfaction." *American Sociological Review* 48: 339-346.

California Almanac. 1991. Fifth Edition, edited by James S. Fay. Santa Barbara, CA: Pacific Data Resources.

Calavita, K., and H.N. Pontell. 1992. "The Savings and Loan Crisis." Pp. 233-258 in *Corporate and Governmental Deviance*, edited by M.D. Ermann and R.J. Lundman. New Yoek: Oxford University Press.

Cohn, S., and C. Conell. 1995. "Learning From Other People's Actions: Environmental Variation and Diffusion in French Coal Mining Strikes, 1890-1935." *American Journal of Sociology* 101: 366-403.

Donovan, T., and M. Neiman. 1992. "Community Social Status, Suburban Growth, and Local Government Restrictions on Residential Development." *Urban Affairs Quarterly* 28(2): 323-336.

Feagin, J.R. 1988. *Free Enterprise City: Houston in Political-Economic Perspective.* New Brunswick, NJ: Rutgers University Press.

Fishel, W.A. 1995. *Regulatory Takings: Law, Economics, and Politics.* Cambridge MA: Harvard University Press.

Gamson, W.A. 1990. *The Strategy of Social Protest*, 2nd Ed. Belmont CA: Wadsworth Publishing Co.

Harvey, D. 1976. "Labor, Capital, and Class Struggle around the Built Environment in Advanced Capitalist Societies." *Politics and Society* 6: 265-296.

Jackson, K.T. 1985. *Crabgrass Frontier: The Suburbanization of the United States.* NY: Oxford University Press.

Lo, C.Y.H. 1990. *Small Property Versus Big Government: The Social Origins of the Property Tax Revolt.* Berkeley: University California Press.

Logan, J.R., and M. Zhou. 1989. "Do Suburban Growth Controls Control Growth?" *American Sociological Review* 54: 461-471.

————. 1990. "The Adoption of Growth Controls in Suburban Communities." *Social Science Quarterly* 71: 118-129.

McAdam, D. 1982. *Political Process and the Development of Black Insurgency, 1930-1970.* Chicago: University of Chicago Press.

McCutchen, Doyle, Brown, and Enersen, Attorneys at Law, 1989. "Shaping Future Developments in a Slow-Growth Era: A McCutchen Land Use Seminar," Winter. San Franciso, CA.

Molotch, H. 1976. "The City as a Growth Machine." *American Journal of Sociology* 82: 309-332.

Molotch, H. and J.R. Logan. 1984. "Tensions in the Growth Machine: Overcoming Resistance to Value-Free Development" *Social Problems* 31: 483-499.

Perrucci, R. 1994. "Embedded Corporatism: Auto Transplants, the Local State, and Community Politics in the Midwest Corridor." *Sociological Quarterly* 35: 487-505.

Plotkin, S. 1987. *Keep Out: The Struggle for Land Use Control.* Berkeley: University California Press.

Rudel, T.K. 1989. *Situations and Strategies in American Land-Use Planning.* New York: Cambridge University Press.

San Diego Association of Governments. (SANDAG). 1970. "1970 Census Subregional Area Data Tables and Computer Maps." Unpublished, available through U.C.S.D. Library, Government Documents.

————. 1987. "Household Income Report." San Diego, CA: SourcePoint.

————. 1990. "Regional Housing Needs Statement, San Diego Region." San Diego, CA.

"Statistical Abstract of the United States." 1994. U.S. Department of Commerce, Bureau of the Census.

Survey of Current Business. 1994. "Gross State Product, 1977-91," by Richard M. Beemiller and Ann E. Dunbar. 74(8, August): 80-97.

Tarrow, S. 1994. *Power in Movement: Social Movements, Collective Action and Politics.* New York: Cambridge University Press.

U.S. Construction Reports, Series C-40. 1968-1995. U.S. Department of Commerce, Bureau of the Census.

PART V

PERCEPTIONS OF GLOBAL ENVIRONMENT

THE CHANGING STATUS OF GLOBAL WARMING AS A SOCIAL PROBLEM:

COMPETING FACTORS IN TWO PUBLIC ARENAS

Jerry Williams and R. Scott Frey

ABSTRACT

Despite scientific consensus that a gradual increase in the mean global temperature during the latter part of this century can be linked to human activity, global warming has received limited attention as a social problem. This paper examines the changing status of global warming as a social problem over the last ten years. An extended version of Higartner and Bosk's (1988) public arenas model of social problem construction is used to analyze how social problems compete for public attention. A content analysis of *UPI* wire reports and *Science* articles suggests that the status of global warming as a social problem is linked to its dramatic potential in the media, real world events such as climatic extremes, the complexity of the problem, the viability of proposed solutions, the economic cost of remediation,

Research in Community Sociology, Volume 7, pages 279-299.
Copyright © 1997 by JAI Press Inc.
All rights of reproduction in any form reserved.
ISBN: 0-7623-0272-0

and existing political realities. It is argued that these factors determined the ability of global warming to compete for attention with other social problems in the public arenas of discourse.

INTRODUCTION

Over the last ten years global climate change has come to be defined as an important social problem. Scientists have predicted that with an average increase in temperature of 0.8-3.5 degrees Celsius (1.4-6.3 degrees Fahrenheit) brought about by rising greenhouse gases in the atmosphere, the impact upon global weather patterns, ocean currents, mean sea level, and the subsequent human costs could be overwhelming (Anderson 1994, p. 553; Flavin 1996). However, as pointed out by Hilgartner and Bosk (1988, p. 54), objective conditions do not by themselves determine the extent of public interest in any social problem (environmental or otherwise) or the amount of media coverage it will receive at the community, national, or regional levels. Rather, social problems must compete for attention in the limited space provided by various public arenas (Hilgartner and Bosk 1988). This paper examines the varied public interest in global warming over the last ten years in terms of six factors that have helped or hindered its ability to compete in these public arenas of discourse. These factors include the dramatic potential of global warming as a social problem, real world events such as climatic extremes, the complexity of the problem, the viability of proposed solutions, the economic impact of remediation, and existing political realities. The content of media reports from two arenas of public discourse are examined to illustrate these six factors: United Press International wire reports for the period 1984 to 1994 and short articles appearing in *Science* between 1986 and 1994.

Other analysts have sought to examine the variability of global warming as a social problem over time. Mazur and Lee (1993), for example, looked at the quantity of coverage of various global environmental problems including global warming for the period from 1978 to 1992. They differentiate between the "substantive content of a story, which should be intelligible to a careful reader or viewer," and the simple image that most readers or listeners actually absorb from a story (Mazur and Lee 1993, p. 683). Their analysis, however, addresses only the quantity of coverage and pays little attention to the substantive content. Such an analysis misses some important issues. For example, the changing nature of the debate over time, including the extent of counter claim activity arising in response to the original claims. Additionally, by focusing on the quantity of media reports, the analysis is largely descriptive, thus not addressing the competition for attention in the public arenas or the unique characteristics of global warming that may govern this competition.

In contrast to the quantity of coverage approach taken by Mazur and Lee (1993), Ungar (1992) sought to understand the substantive issues involved in the development of global warming as a social problem by reviewing articles from various technical and popular media sources. He identified the record heat of 1988 as the major force behind increased public concern with global warming. Or, as Ungar (1992, p. 488) notes: "the greenhouse effect became a celebrity social problem because it piggybacked on real events." Although record heat may indeed have been an important factor in the ability of global warming to compete for public attention, it is not the only factor. A broader understanding of these factors is important if we are to understand the temporal variation of public interest in global warming.

The current analysis, then, moves beyond these two analyses by systematically exploring not only the quantity of media coverage, but the substantive content of these reports and the factors that have contributed to the ability of global warming to compete in the arenas of public discourse. In the first section of this paper, we present a constructionist model based upon the public arenas model of Hilgartner and Bosk (1988). The actual procedures used are then discussed. In the final sections, we examine the six competitive factors in terms of how well they explain the varied interest in global warming over the ten-year period studied.

THEORETICAL CONSIDERATIONS

The discussion of global warming as a social problem has been approached in a rather precarious way. This precariousness stems from the dual nature of global warming as both a natural phenomenon and a human caused social problem. While global warming appears to be a natural process whereby carbon dioxide, nitrous oxide, methane, and CFCs increase in the atmosphere thus trapping heat in the atmosphere (Price 1991, p. 315), a significant share of the increase in greenhouse gases seems to be related to human activity (Kerr 1995, p. 1667). As stated by Price (1990, p. 316): "the principle cause for increasing concentrations of the infared-absorbing gases (or 'greenhouse gases') are found not in natural processes, but in human activities." Such activities include the burning of fossil fuels, the raising of livestock, rice farming, forest clearing activities, leaking refrigerators, and the manufacture of electrical components. The scientist interested in understanding the implications of global warming is then faced with the problem of approaching a natural phenomenon as concurrently a natural happening and as a condition brought about by human activity. Further, a discussion of global warming is also complicated by theoretical considerations common to any discussion of social problems. Specifically, what is a social problem and how does it become identified as a problem? There are two perspectives: the realist perspective and the constructionist perspective (Thomason 1982).

Realism

A realist approach to social problems asserts that social problems are "real," objective phenomenon with "real" impacts. The task for the researcher, then, is to discover what the problem is and to educate the public about possible dangers and potential remedies. This approach to social problem development is implied by what Jonathan Weiner (1990, p. 58) called a "slow eureka" about global warming. He states

> We have known about this thing (global warming) a very long time, but we have understood it a very short time. From Arrhenius on, people simply did not know what they were looking at. Nor was there any single moment when everyone cried Eureka! There was only what one student of the greenhouse calls the evolution of an awareness (Weiner 1990, p. 58).

Realism pervades our discussion of environmental problems because such a view of reality is the modus operandi of scientific thinking, the major claims-maker to the identification of social problems. Scientists, therefore, often see their roles as discoverers of what is real; that is, of "real," objective phenomenon. The realist approach to environmental social problems is further described by Taylor and Buttel (1992, p. 405) in the following terms:

> We know we have environmental problems because, in short, science documents the existing situation and ever tightens its prediction of future changes. Accordingly, science supplies the knowledge needed to stimulate and guide social-political action.

The realist perspective has an important shortcoming in its ability to describe the variable interest in global warming. More precisely, the realist perspective is inadequate because it ignores the complex manner in which individuals negotiate and construct their experiences of the natural and social worlds. Social constructionists have pointed out that our experience of the world is always done in terms of what we already know. To experience a tree, for example, is to experience it as "like" other trees; that is, we typify or categorize experience in terms of previously held conceptual categories. Alfred Schutz (1962) has pointed out that the origin of these conceptual categories stem from our individual biographies, historical circumstances, and cultural background. Kempton (1991, p. 334) has demonstrated that one's perception of global warming is, indeed, strongly connected to other environmental problems (conceptual categories) such as stratospheric ozone depletion, tropospheric air pollution, photosynthesis, and seasonal geographic temperature variation. Therefore, if we are to understand the varied interest in global warming as a social problem, we must use a model of social problems that is sensitive to this ongoing construction of reality. Various "constructionist" models of social problems have sought to address precisely this problem.

Constructionism

Constructionist models of social problems suggest that all social and natural problems are constructions, that our understanding of any problem is perhaps only one of many interpretations of reality (Spector and Kitsuse 1977). "Scientific knowledge should not be regarded as a representation of nature, but rather as a socially constructed interpretation with an already socially constructed natural technical object of inquiry" (Bird 1987, p. 255). Constructionism has a potentially important drawback; it often leads to a relativistic perspective where no claim to reality is privileged. Speed (1991, p. 396) states that constructionists hold the view that "what we know is determined by our ideas, so that our view of reality is only that, a view, something constructed in our heads, invented by us. We can never know reality, we can only have views of reality. In a nutshell, our ideas determine what we know."

Such a position is inadequate because it does not distinguish between what an experience "is" and our experience of it. What we experience is not only a function of what we think about an object or phenomenon, but also what the object or phenomenon "is." Global warming as a social problem, then, is both a social construction and some sort of objective reality. It is constructed in respect to our experience and definition of it, and yet it exists in some way independent of our definitions. If this distinction is not made, constructionist models of social problems have a tendency to become relativistic; that is, to accept no claim to reality as better than any other (see, e.g., Douglas and Wildavsky 1982). This position seems untenable in respect to global warming when the scale of what is at stake is considered.

Three constructionist models of social problems have been widely used: the normative model, the value conflict model, and the public arenas model (Hilgartner and Bosk 1988; Spector and Kitsuse 1977). Spector and Kitsuse suggest (1977), however, that even though the normative and value conflict models account for the construction of social problems according to social and cultural definitions, they fail to address the processes that account for the variation in status of a social problem over time. In response to this criticism they formulate a natural history model. The Spector and Kitsuse natural history model, however, is largely descriptive and therefore not truly a constructionist model. Social problems are seen to progress through four stages: claims-making, legitimation by official organizations or institutions, reemergence of the original claims by the original group because of a dissatisfaction with the institutional process, and finally, a rejection of the institutional response by the original claims-making group (Spector and Kitsuse 1977, p. 130). Importantly, in no way does the model account for the constructedness of our experience of the natural world.

Dunlap (1992, pp. 90-91) presents a similar model of social problems that he calls a "natural decline model" in an analysis of public opinion trends in environmental concern. Originally articulated by Anthony Downs (1972), the model suggests that social problems move through a five stage cycle: the pre-problem stage, the alarmed discovery and euphoric enthusiasm stage, a realization of the cost of progress stage, a gradual decline in public interest stage, and a post problem stage where the problem is replaced as the center of public concern by a new problem (Dunlap 1992, p. 90).

While natural history/natural decline models appear to describe the general history of social problem development, they are quite limited because they are descriptive, not explanatory. Spector and Kitsuse (1977, pp. 130-159) point out that natural history models do not account for the complicated processes that cause changes in the course of a social problem over time. Hilgartner and Bosk (1988, pp. 54-55) also criticize natural history models, suggesting that they are inadequate because many social problems can be seen to exist in more than one stage at a time, often moving from one stage to another and then back again. Hansen (1991, p. 447), in a similar way, also criticizes natural history models as they apply to environmental social problems because they "gloss over the interactive nature of meaning construction among and between institutions in society."

In response to these shortcomings, Hilgartner and Bosk (1988) formulate a public arenas model of social problems. They argue that a more accurate model of social problems should account for the competitive process by which all social problems must vie for status in public arenas. They describe social problems not as "objective and identifiable" entities, but rather as collective definitions (Hilgartner and Bosk 1988, p. 53). In its constructionist orientation the public arenas model suggests that social problems are recognized as social problems through acts of social definition. For them, all social problems are first articulated by "claims-makers" who attempt to define reality in a particular way in relation to others who are attempting to do the same. Competition is, therefore, central to the public arenas model and begins in this first stage when definitions of the problem are selected. Competition continues in the limited space available in "public arenas of discourse" when social problems compete with other social problem formulations for public attention (Hilgartner and Bosk 1988, p. 55). This competition stems from the limited space available in these public arenas. Further, according to Hilgartner and Bosk, all social problems in the public arenas compete according to five "principles of selection" (Hilgartner and Bosk 1988, p. 72). These principles or factors include the dramatic potential of the problem, prexisting culture themes or preoccupations, political biases, carrying capacity of the public arena, and the institutional rhythm (timing) of the specific arena in question (Hilgartner and Bosk 1988, p. 72).

In the case of global warming, it seems quite clear that other factors should be considered. Ungar (1992) began the process of extending the public arenas model in his discussion of global warming, finding an additional competitive factor to be important: real world events. He provides evidence that the record heat of the summer of 1988 allowed global warming to attain "celebrity" in a way not possible before. Real world events, then, provided a competitive advantage in the public arenas for social problem status. It seems reasonable, then, that a public arenas model seeking to describe the varied interest in global warming must include the effect of these real world events.

Three other competitive factors are thought to be important in accounting for the variation in concern with global warming over the last ten years. First, Wilmoth and Ball (1995) have argued (in an application of the public arenas model to overpopulation) that a social issue must be packaged with a solution in order for it to compete in public arenas. They state

> ...we argue that a social problem is a collective definition of a social phenomenon as bad. Merely identifying a badness, however, does not make a social problem worthy of public attention: In order to compete for attention in the various public arenas, a plan of action is needed (Wilmoth and Ball 1995, p. 320).

Second, the complexity of the potential social problem also seems quite important in terms of how well a social problem can compete for public attention. Global warming may indeed be hampered in this competition for just this reason as its basic features are not part of everyday concern. Rather, much of the conversation about global warming is of a scientific nature not easily available to lay people. Less complicated issues are, perhaps, better able to compete in the public arenas of discourse.

Third, it also seems appropriate to consider the cost of implementing a program of remediation upon the ability of global warming to compete in the public arenas. Dunlap (1992, pp. 90-91), for example, suggests that interest in environmental problems, as well as social problems in general, start to decline when their cost of remediation is considered.

To summarize, the constructionist model of social problems used in this analysis is based on Hilgartner and Bosk's (1988) public arenas model. An attempt was made to describe the factors that have enabled global warming to compete in the limited space found in the public arenas of discourse. These factors include the dramatic potential of global warming as a social problem, real climatic events, the complexity of the issue, the viability of a proposed solution, the economic impact of remediation, and existing political realities.

DATA AND METHOD

Two media sources were examined: the popular arena as represented by the abstracts of 533 United Press International (*UPI*) wire reports indexed on the Lexis/Nexis data base for the years 1984 to 1994, and the scientific arena as represented by a series of 83 short articles appearing in *Science* from 1986 to 1994. Both media sources were chosen because each represents a distinct discourse and audience. They are also concise and written to express one major theme, for example, to illustrate a scientific claim or to cover a specific piece of governmental legislation. Weber (1990, p. 23) suggests that this is important when analyzing whole texts for themes because such concision allows for more reliable coding.

In an effort to understand the competitive factors that have advantaged or disadvantaged global warming in the arenas of public discourse, we categorized each of the articles and wire service reports into one of six substantive categories. These categories emerged from an intensive assessment of the underlying content of the articles and reports. Categories included claims, counter claims, neutral, political realities, solutions, and the economic impact of remediation. These categories are described in Table 1 below.

ANALYSIS AND DISCUSSION

Temporal Variation in Concern with Global Warming

While scientists have been discussing the possibility of global warming since at least 1906 (Weiner 1990, p. 57), media coverage of the issue appears to have not been widespread until about 1986 (see Figures 1 and 2). Further, data reported in Figures 3 and 4

Table 1.Coding Categories

Claims	Global warming presented as a real and significant problem.
Counter Claims	Global warming described as an insignificant or nonexistent problem, or to articles which questioned previously stated claims.
Neutral	Articles concerned with the science of global warming making no claims or counter claims about the status of global warming. (Found exclusively in *Science* typically technical, scientific articles.)
Political Realities	Articles describing political activity related to global warming including reports about political summits or meetings, or any other coverage of national or international political responses to global warming not specifically aimed at proposed solutions.
Solutions	Articles that describe potential solutions or remedies to either the accumulation of greenhouse gases or provide ways to reduce existing concentration of those gases.
Economic Impact of Remediation	Articles that refer to the potential economic cost of addressing global warming, for example, of cutting carbon dioxide emissions.

and 4 indicate that the majority of articles and wire reports written between 1984 and 1987 were of a claims-making nature; that is, they sought to bring global warming to public attention by articulating a new conceptual category: "global warming" that had not been recognized before. Indeed, the period between 1984 and 1987 amounted to a "honeymoon period" for global warming problem development and was relatively free of counter claims activity. During this stage of formulation, claims-makers sought to "package" global warming in terms of other, previously identified problems. It was during this time that public concerns about global climate change were first engaged with a discussion of the so called "nuclear winter" (Sagan, Erlich, Kennedy, and Roberts 1984; Ungar 1992, p. 487). The hypothesized devastation of the planet under such a scenario was easily linked to human activity and led the way for a new conceptual category that included the idea of human caused global climate change. Similarly, the asteroid theory of dinosaur extinction also became widely disseminated during this period, therefore helping to create a global climate change conceptual category.

The close identification of global warming with other problems and previously existing conceptual categories illustrates that any experience, including any new experience, is always a function of what we already know. Schutz and Luckmann (1973, p. 229) observe

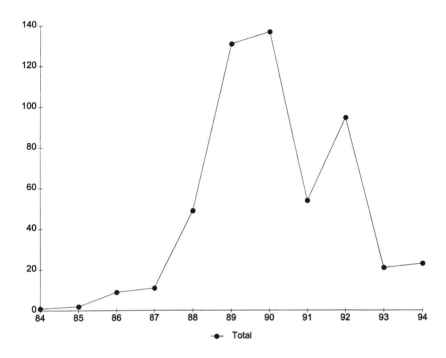

Figure 1. Annual Number of United Press International (UPI)
Wire Reports on Global Warming between 1984 and 1994.

"on the other hand, there is a form of familiarity in which objects, persons, properties, events are not grasped as the 'same,' but as 'similarly' determined, previously experienced objects, persons, properties, or events, whereby the relevance structures predominate in the current situation do not demand any transformations transcending this 'similarity'." That is, global warming was first conceptualized as "like" nuclear winter or the change in climate caused by a large prehistoric asteroid.

Kempton (1991, p. 334) suggests that "new information on global warming is being filled into four prior concepts: stratospheric ozone depletion, tropospheric (near surface) air pollution, plant photosynthesis, and seasonal geographic temperature variation." His analysis of public understanding of global warming quite convincingly demonstrates that each of these categories are indeed linked to global warming often to the extent that false conclusions are made. A 1988 *UPI* wire report illustrates these assertions.

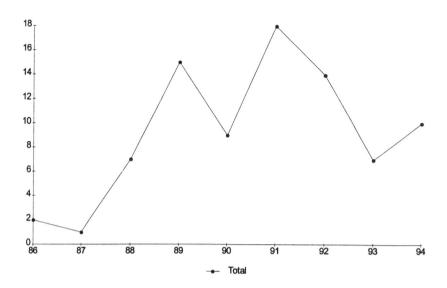

Figure 2.   Annual Number of Articles on
Global Warming in *Science* between 1986 and 1994.

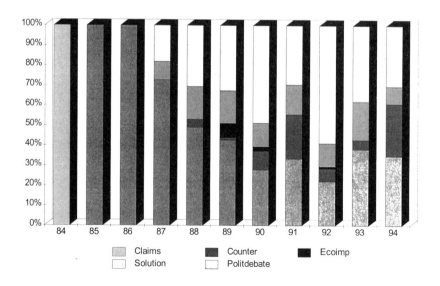

Figure 3.   Percent of Annual Number of United Press International
(UPI) Wire Reports on Global Warming by Category, 1984-1994.

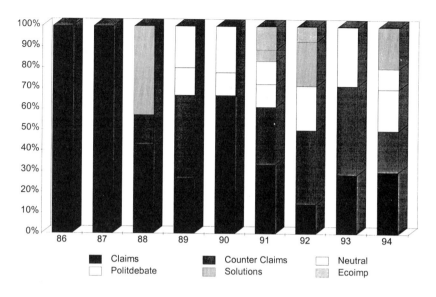

Figure 4. Percent of Annual Number of Articles on Global Warming in *Science* by Category, 1986-1994.

Reporting on a prediction of increased solar activity the writer suggests that the "sun steps up formation of ozone in the Earth's upper atmosphere. That action should temporarily moderate the "greenhouse effect," a global warming trend caused by depletion of the protective ozone layer by the burning of fossil fuels, farming and other human enterprises" (Kolberg 1988). Here, ozone depletion is incorrectly linked to the greenhouse effect, a previously identified environmental problem.

Global warming, then, was first identified as a potential social problem between 1984 and 1987 and was brought to awareness, at least in part, by its connection to previously existing conceptual categories such as nuclear winter, dinosaur extinction, and ozone depletion. Further, during this formulation period claims-making activity was by far the most prevalent form of discourse and was relatively unencumbered by counter claim activity. In the following years, however, global warming came upon rather serious competition in the public arenas of discourse therefore dramatically changing the nature of the debate. We now turn to a discussion of the factors that both helped and hindered this competition in the years following 1987.

Competitive Forces

Hilgartner and Bosk (1988, p. 55) suggest that the public arenas of discourse are not an unlimited resource; rather, these arenas are subject to the limits of public attention. They state "...we focus on competition: We assume that public attention is a scarce resource, allocated through competition in a system of public arenas." In regard to global warming six factors seem to have been important in this competition: the dramatic potential of global warming as a social problem, real world events, the complexity of the issues involved, the viability of a proposed solution, the economic cost of remediation, and the existing political realities.

Positive Forces

Two of the six factors appear to have had a positive influence on the ability of global warming to compete in the arenas of public discourse: the dramatic potential of global warming as a social problem and real world events. The dramatic potential of global warming is closely linked to the devastating projections of its impact. The potential extent of human and nonhuman misery involved with global climate change indeed seems to have initially helped global warming in the competition for public attention. Such predictions include population displacement due to rising sea levels and widespread drought and resulting crop failures. The scale of these potential problems alone provided sufficient drama to the public, political, and scientific debate. This dramatic potential is illustrated by James Hansen's testimony before Congress in May of 1989. With "99% confidence" he concluded the recent warm spell in North America was due to global climate change (Kerr 1989, p. 1042). His testimony was carried by both national and international news and became embroiled in controversy when the Bush administration was accused of trying to persuade Hansen to soften his claims in order to make them seem more uncertain (Newman 1989).

Real world events also seem to have had a positive impact on the ability of global warming to compete in the public arenas of discourse. Ungar (1992, p. 483) suggests that "environmental social problems resemble the nuclear threat in that both require 'real-world' events that unleash authentic social scares for claims-making activities to command concerted attention in public arenas." Further, he argues that the record heat of 1988 was indeed just such an event. This analysis suggests that the record heat of 1988 and 1989 may have had a positive impact upon the ability of global warming to compete in the public arenas. The number of *UPI* wire reports reached their highest point in 1989 and 1990 (see Figure 1). *Science* coverage reached a peak in nearly the same years, 1989 and 1991, with a momentary decline in 1990 (see Figure 2).

Real world events, then, seem to have had a positive influence on the ability of global warming to compete in the public arenas of discourse. It is worth noting, however, that while real world events have the potential for positively influencing the status of global warming as a social problem, they also have the potential for doing the reverse. The end of the North American drought in the early part of the 1990s is concurrent with a downturn in media coverage of global warming issues. The very lowest levels of coverage in *UPI* after 1985 occur in the years 1993 and 1994.

Negative Forces

Four additional factors seem to have limited the ability of global warming to compete in the arenas of public discourse. These factors include the complexity of the issue, the viability of a proposed solution, the economic impact of remediation, and existing political biases.

Global warming can be seen as a very complex social problem because of the complexity of the scientific claims involved, and the intricate processes required to accurately model global climate change. This complexity not only fosters debate within the scientific community but also within the political and public realms. The complexity may impede the ability of global warming to compete in the arenas of public discourse in two ways. First, coverage in the media, in particular the popular media, usually involves a very low level of technical sophistication. Therefore, it is likely that more complicated issues are less likely to be given much attention. Global warming, then, is automatically disadvantaged in the public arenas of discourse because its major premises are only understandable in technical terms. Second, complicated scientific issues are by nature subject to deconstruction. Taylor and Buttel (1992, pp. 405-406) suggest that "Science-centered environmentalism is, however, vulnerable to deconstruction. Environmental problems, almost by definition, involve multiple, interacting causes, allowing scientists to question the definitions and procedures of other scientists, promote alternative explanations and cast doubt on the certainty of predictions." In this regard, the often rancorous scientific debate about global warming may itself inhibit the competitive status of global warming in the arenas of public discourse because it does not allow tidy information packages for public consumption.

The viability of a proposed solution may also have an impact upon a social problem's ability to compete for problem status in the public arenas. Wilmoth and Ball (1995, p. 319) suggest in their study of population pressure that when large scale programs of birth control came to be seen as viable solutions to the population problem, overpopulation was better able to compete in the public arenas. They note "Following Blumer, we argue that a *social problem* is a collective definition of a social phenomenon as bad. Merely identifying badness, however, does not make a social problem worthy of public attention: In order to compete for attention in the various public arenas, a plan of action is needed" (Wilmoth and Ball 1995, p. 1995).

In this analysis articles and wire reports advocating or discussing the viability of a solution to the global warming problem (see Figures 5 and 6) make up only a small portion of the total number of articles. In both the *Science* and *UPI* arenas the number of articles peaked in 1988 and declined rather sharply afterward. Further, these solutions were of three general types. First, most proposed solutions to the global warming problem were partial; that is, they targeted only one narrow component of the overall problem. Such partial solutions include planting forests to reduce current carbon dioxide levels, calling for voluntary industry reductions in greenhouse emissions, or promoting a so-called "carbon tax" on fossil fuels. Second, some solutions were largely experimental and were aimed at reducing or curbing the impact of current levels of greenhouse gases. Such solutions included the "Geritol fix," a process by which iron oxide is spread over the surface of the ocean thus promoting algae growth and carbon dioxide uptake, and the positioning of satellite mirrors in orbit around the earth thus reducing solar energy reaching the surface (Busch 1994, p. 1089). Third, some proposed solutions were opportunistic; that is, some industries foresaw a profit in dealing with the greenhouse effect. The nuclear power industry, for example, sought to capitalize on fears of global warming by promoting the building of reactors as a desirable alternative to the burning of fossil fuels.

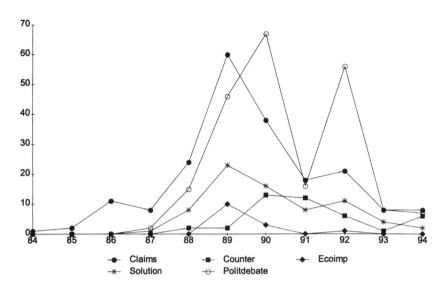

Figure 5. Annual Number of United Press International (UPI) Wire Reports on Global Warming by Category 1984-1994.

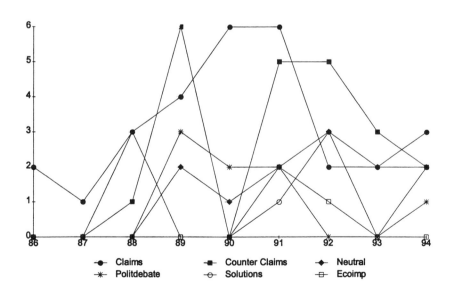

Figure 6. Annual Number of Articles on Global Warming in Science by Category, 1986-1994.

This analysis suggests that none of these proposed solutions galvanized public support or attention in the way that Wilmoth and Ball (1995) have suggested is necessary in order for a social problem to compete for attention in the various public arenas of discourse. In addition, many of these solutions (such as proposed carbon taxes and regulations to reduce other greenhouse gases) have the potential for rather negative economic impacts, a fact that also appears to have limited the ability of global warming to compete in the public arenas of discourse.

The economic cost of addressing global warming first came to public attention in 1989 (see Figure 5), and while only a small part of the total debate, it seems to have had significant impact upon the ability of global warming to compete in the public arenas of discourse. Indeed, articles and wire reports suggest that concerns over this cost were introduced into the public arenas at the apex of coverage for global warming in 1989 and 1990, specifically in regard to the Bush Administration's stated desire to avoid economically painful remediation efforts while taking a wait and see approach. This U.S. policy eventually led to a refusal to sign a global climate change treaty produced at the 1992 Earth Summit in Rio. While it is impossible to show a direct causal connection, it is likely that concern with the cost of addressing global warming may have had a significant impact upon the status of global warming as a social problem. Jamieson (1992, p. 141) states

> However, in my view, the most important force driving the backlash is not concern about the weakness of the science but the realization that slowing global warming or responding to its effects may involve large economic costs and redistributions, as well as radical revisions in lifestyle.

It may have been the record heat in 1988 and 1989 that allowed global warming to rise to an apex in the public arenas, but a lack of record heat alone did not cause its decline. Rather, its decline appears to be closely related to the perceived cost of doing anything about it together with a great deal of political controversy.

Political realities also seem to have played an important role in the status of global warming as a social problem. Prior to 1989, many articles and wire reports served to document calls for political action, global conferences, and other political measures to address what was perceived as a significant problem. Articles and wire reports with a political theme, then, reached a peak in 1989 and 1990. A resurgence of articles with a political theme also occurred in *UPI* wires in 1992. This, of course, coincides with a presidential election year and the Rio Earth Summit. A similar resurgence of interest was not found in *Science*. This was probably due to the fact that the journal has less to do with "political matters" and more to do with "scientific matters." It is interesting to note that this resurgence of political interest in 1992 was not matched by a resurgence of interest in any other coded category, and that following 1992 all coded categories fell to at or below 1986 levels.

Most interesting of all is the ratio of counter claims activity to claims activity during the period studied. If claims had experienced a honeymoon period relatively free of counter claims between 1984 and 1987, it appears that the honeymoon was definitely over by 1991. Counter claims articles in *Science* (see Figure 6) after 1991 rose dramatically and in 1992 and 1993 outstripped claims articles significantly. *UPI* wire reports show a similar pattern reaching a near parity with claims articles in 1993 and 1994 (see Figure 5). Counter claim activity was most pronounced in *Science* between 1991 and 1994 and involved the investigation of rival explanations for global warming that were originally offered in prior years.

CONCLUSIONS

This paper has attempted to discuss the development of global warming as a social problem by investigating the competitive factors that either helped or hindered its competition in the limited capacity of the public arenas of discourse. Based on the public arenas model of social problems which is itself derived from constructionist theory, six competitive factors were identified: the dramatic potential of global warming as a social problem, real world events, the complexity of the issue, the viability of a proposed solution, the economic impact of remediation, and existing political realities.

These competitive factors appear to have led to a distinct developmental trajectory. First, global warming became a newly identified social problem for which existing conceptual categories did not exist prior to 1984. Second, during this original period of incipiency scientific claims-makers made claims about global warming in the absence of organized counter claims. Third, these original claims were formulated into packages for public consumption often in terms of previously identified social problems such as ozone depletion, nuclear winter, and the asteroid theory of dinosaur extinction. Fourth, after the honeymoon period, counter claim packages arose concurrently with concern over the economic cost or remediation, existing political realities, and a general decline in coverage of global warming.

The intent of this paper was not to draw causal connections between the identified competitive factors and the developmental trajectory of global warming as a social problem. Rather, these findings should be taken as suggestive of possible relationships in need of further investigation. Such an investigation might profitably explore additional public arenas or perhaps the relationship of global warming to other competitors (other social problems). If we are to understand global warming as a competitive social problem, its success or failure is also intimately linked to how well other social problems are able to compete in the limited space provided by the public arenas of discourse at any given time.

REFERENCES

Anderson, C. 1993. "Tales of the Coming Mega-Greenhouse." *Science* 261: 553.

Bird, E.A.R. 1987. "The Social Construction of Nature: Theoretical Approaches to the History of Environmental Problems." *Environmental Review* 11: 255-264.

Busch, L. 1994. "Iron Fertilization: A Tonic, but No Cure for the Greenhouse." *Science* 263: 1089.

Douglas, M., and A. Wildavsky. 1982. *Risk and Culture: The Selection of Technological and Environmental Dangers.* Berkeley: University of California Press.

Downs, A. 1972. "Up and Down with Ecology—The 'Issue-Attention Cycle'." *Public Interest* 28: 38-50.

Dunlap, R.E. 1992. "Trends in Public Opinion Toward Environmental Issues: 1965-1990." Pp. 89-116 in *American Environmentalism: The U.S. Movement, 1970-1990,* edited by R.E. Dunlap and A.G. Mertig. New York: Taylor and Francis.

Flavin, C. 1996. "Facing Up to the Risks of Climate Change." Pp. 21-39 in *State of the World, 1996,* edited by L.R. Brown et al. New York: W.W. Norton.

Hansen, A. 1991. "The Media and the Social Construction of the Environment." *Media, Culture and Society* 13: 443-458.

Hilgartner, S., and C. Bosk. 1988. "The Rise and Fall of Social Problems: A Public Arenas Model." *American Journal of Sociology* 94: 53-78.

Jamieson, D. 1992. "Ethics, Public Policy, and Global Warming." *Science, Technology, and Human Values* 17: 139-153.

Kempton, W. 1991. "Public Understanding of Global Warming." *Society and Natural Resources* 4: 331-345.

Kerr, R. 1995. "Scientists See Greenhouse, Semiofficially." *Science* 269: 1667.

―――――. 1989. "Greenhouse Models vs. Reality." *Science* 244: 1042.

Kolberg, R. 1988. "Solar Maximum; Scientists Brace for Barrage of Solar Activity." *United Press International*, August 20.

Mazur, A., and J. Lee. 1993. "Sounding the Global Alarm: Environmental Issues in the US National News." *Social Studies of Science* 23: 681-720.

Newman, B. 1989. "Administration Altered NASA Scientists Testimony." *United Press International*, May 8.

Price, M. 1991. "Societal Aspects of Climate Change." *Society and Natural Resources* 4: 315-317.

Sagan, C., P. Ehrlich, D. Kennedy, and W. Roberts. 1984. *The Cold and the Dark: The World After Nuclear War*. New York: W.W. Morton.

Schutz, A. 1962. "Common-Sense and Scientific Interpretation." Pp. 3-47 in *The Problem of Social Reality: Collected Papers Volume One*. Boston: Martinus Nijhoff.

Schutz, A., and T. Luckmann. 1973. *The Structures of the Life World*. Evanston, IL: Northwestern University Press.

Spector, M., and J. Kitsuse. 1977. *Constructing Social Problems*. New York: Cummings.

Speed, B. 1991. "Reality Exists O.K.? An Argument Against Constructivism and Social Constructionism." *Journal of Family Therapy* 13: 395-409.

Taylor, P.J., and F.H. Buttel. 1992. "How Do We Know We Have Global Environmental Problems?: Science and the Globalization of Environmental Discourse." *Geoforum* 23: 405-416.

Thomason, B.C. 1982. *Making Sense of Reification: Alfred Schutz and Constructionist Theory*. London: Humanities Press.

Ungar, S. 1992. "The Rise and [Relative] Decline of Global Warming as a Social Problem." *The Sociological Quarterly* 33: 483-501.

Weber, R.P. 1990. *Basic Content Analysis*. Beverly Hills, CA: Sage.

Weiner, J. 1990. *The Next One Hundred Years: Shaping the Future of Our Living Earth*. New York: Bantam.

Wilmoth, J.R., and P. Ball. 1995. "Arguments and Action in the Life of a Social Problem: A Case Study of 'Overpopulation,' 1946-1990." *Social Problems* 42: 318-340.

INDEX

Research in Community Sociology

Edited by **Dan A. Chekki,** *Department of Sociology, University of Winnipeg*

Volume 6, New Communities in a Changing World
1996, 315 pp. $73.25
ISBN 0-7623-0040-X

CONTENTS: PART I. INTRODUCTION. The Social Landscape of New Communities in North America, *Dan A. Chekki.* PART II. THEORETICAL PERSPECTIVES. Using Classical Theorists to Reconceptualize Community Dynamics, *Jonathan H. Turner and Norman A. Dolch.* PART III. NEW IMMIGRANT COMMUNITIES. New Immigrant Communities in the United States and the Ideology of Exclusion, *Carol Schmid.* Blurring Borders: Constructing Transnational Community in the Process of Mexico-U.S. Migration, *Luin Goldring.* New Immigrant Communities in a Suburban Region, *Mark Baldassare.* The Attainment of Neighborhood Qualities among British, Chinese, and Black Immigrants in Toronto and Vancouver, *Eric Fong and Milena Guila.* PART IV. THE AIDS COMMUNITY. The Uncertainty, Diversity, and Change: The Aids Community in New York City, *Susan M. Chambré.* PART V. COMMUNITY IN CYBERSPACE. Lawyers on Line: Professional Identity and Boundary Maintenance in Cyberspace, *Debra J. Schleef.* PART VI. ENCLOSED COMMUNITY LIFE. Enclosure, Community, and Public Life, *Dennis R. Judd.* PART VII. COMMUNES—UTOPIAN COMMUNITIES. The Contemporary Communal Movement, *William L. Smith.* PART VIII. COMMUNITY DYNAMICS IN A NEW MILIEU. A New Community of Old Members: Old Order Mennonites in Upstate New York, *Daniel B. Lee.* Cultural Dynamics and Futuristic Scenarios of the Virasáiva Community in North America, *Dan A. Chekki.*

Also Available:
Volumes 1-5 (1990-1995) $73.25 each

JAI PRESS INC.
55 Old Post Road No. 2 - P.O. Box 1678
Greenwich, Connecticut 06836-1678
Tel: (203) 661- 7602   Fax: (203) 661-0792

Research in Community and Mental Health

Edited by **Joseph Morrissey,** *Sheps Center for Health Services Research, University of North Carolina at Chapel Hill*

Volume 8, 1995, 233 pp. $73.25
ISBN 1-55938-139-6

CONTENTS: PART I. ASSESSING THEORETICAL POSITIONS. Emotional Overinvolvement: A Review and Examination of Its Role in Expressed Emotion, *Dolores E. Kreisman and Richard Blumenthal.* Societal Reaction to Mental Disorder: A Test of Theoretical Propositions, *James R. Greenley and Runar Vilhjalmsson.* PART II. CAREGIVING FOR THE SERIOUSLY MENTALLY ILL. Child Care as a Neglected Dimension of Family Burden Research, *Gail Gamache, Richard C. Tessler, and Joanne Nicholson.* Factors Associated with Grief and Depressive Symptoms in Caregivers of People with Serious Mental Illness, *Elmer L. Struening, Ann Stueve, Phyllis Vine, Dolores E. Kreisman, Bruce G. Link, and Daniel B. Herman.* Dealing with Daughters' Difficulties: Caregiving Burden Experienced by Parents of Female Offspring with Severe Mental Illness, *Susan A. Pickett, Judith A. Cook, and Mardi L. Solomon.* Ethnic Differences in the Interpretation of Mental Illness: Perspectives of Caregivers, *Glen Milstein, Peter J. Guarnaccia, and Elizabeth Midlarsky.* PART III. RESOURCES SUPPORTING FAMILY MEMBERS OR THEIR ILL RELATIVES. The Provision of Mental Health Services to Families of Persons with Severe Mental Illness, *Jan Steven Greenberg, James R. Greenley, and Hea Won Kim.* Family and Social Network Supports for the Seriously Mentally Ill: Patient Perceptions, *Allan V. Horwitz and Susan C. Reinhard.* Roles and Resources: The Effects of Family Structure and Employment on Women's Psychosocial Resources and Psychological Distress, *William R. Avison.*

Also Available:
Volumes 1-7 (1979-1992) $73.25 each

JAI PRESS INC.
55 Old Post Road No. 2 - P.O. Box 1678
Greenwich, Connecticut 06836-1678
Tel: (203) 661- 7602   Fax: (203) 661-0792

J
A
I

P
R
E
S
S